Mastering PowerShell Scripting
From Basics to Expert Proficiency

Contents

1 Introduction to PowerShell **11**

1.1 What is PowerShell? 11

1.2 History and Evolution of PowerShell 14

1.3 Why Use PowerShell? 16

1.4 PowerShell Editions and Versions 18

1.5 PowerShell vs. Command Prompt 20

1.6 Understanding the Shell Interface 22

1.7 Introduction to PowerShell ISE and VS Code 25

1.8 Basic Syntax and Commands 28

1.9 PowerShell Community and Resources 30

1.10 First Steps: Running Your First PowerShell Command . 32

2 Setting Up Your PowerShell Environment **37**

2.1 Installing PowerShell on Windows 37

2.2 Installing PowerShell on macOS 40

2.3 Installing PowerShell on Linux 42

2.4 Updating PowerShell 45

2.5 Setting Up PowerShell ISE 48

2.6 Setting Up Visual Studio Code for PowerShell 51

2.7 Configuring Execution Policies 54

2.8 Customizing Your PowerShell Profile 56

2.9 Useful PowerShell Modules and How to Install Them . . 58
2.10 Navigating the PowerShell Help System 61

3 Basic Concepts and Commands 65
3.1 Understanding Cmdlets 65
3.2 Using Aliases 68
3.3 Basic Navigation: Working with the File System 70
3.4 Understanding and Using Parameters 73
3.5 Pipeline Concepts 76
3.6 Filtering and Sorting Data 78
3.7 Formatting Output 80
3.8 Basic String Manipulations 82
3.9 Wildcards and Regular Expressions 85
3.10 Introduction to PowerShell Providers 88

4 Working with Variables and Data Types 93
4.1 Introduction to Variables 93
4.2 Variable Types and Their Usage 95
4.3 Creating and Initializing Variables 97
4.4 Understanding PowerShell Data Types 100
4.5 Type Conversion and Casting 102
4.6 Using Arrays and Hash Tables 105
4.7 Scoping Rules and Best Practices 107
4.8 PowerShell Automatic Variables 109
4.9 Working with Null and Empty Values 112
4.10 Persistent Storage and Retrieving Data 114

5 Control Flow: Loops and Conditional Statements 119
5.1 Introduction to Control Flow 119
5.2 Conditional Statements: if, else, and elseif 121
5.3 Using the switch Statement 124

5.4 Looping with the for Statement 127
5.5 Using the foreach Statement 130
5.6 While Loops: while and do-while 132
5.7 Breaking Out of Loops 134
5.8 Understanding Continue Statement 136
5.9 Using Break and Continue in Nested Loops 138
5.10 Practical Examples of Control Flow 140

6 Functions and Scripts **145**

6.1 Introduction to Functions 145
6.2 Creating and Running Basic Functions 147
6.3 Using Parameters in Functions 150
6.4 Understanding Parameter Sets 153
6.5 Returning Values from Functions 156
6.6 Scope and Lifetime of Function Variables 158
6.7 Introduction to Scripts 161
6.8 Writing and Running PowerShell Scripts 164
6.9 Script Parameters and Arguments 167
6.10 Signing Scripts and Execution Policies 169

7 Working with Objects and the Pipeline **173**

7.1 Understanding Objects in PowerShell 173
7.2 Properties and Methods of Objects 176
7.3 Introduction to the Pipeline 179
7.4 Passing Objects Through the Pipeline 182
7.5 Filtering Objects in the Pipeline 184
7.6 Sorting and Selecting Objects 186
7.7 Using the ForEach-Object Cmdlet 188
7.8 Group-Object and Measure-Object Cmdlets 190
7.9 Exporting and Importing Objects 192

7.10 Advanced Pipeline Techniques 195

8 Error Handling and Debugging **199**

8.1 Introduction to Error Handling 199
8.2 Types of Errors: Terminating and Non-Terminating . . . 201
8.3 Using Try, Catch, and Finally 203
8.4 Working with Error Variables 205
8.5 Throwing Exceptions 207
8.6 Using the ErrorAction Parameter 210
8.7 Writing Robust Scripts with Error Handling 212
8.8 Introduction to Debugging 214
8.9 Using Breakpoints and the Debugger 216
8.10 Common Debugging Techniques 219

9 File Operations and Manipulation **223**

9.1 Introduction to File Operations 223
9.2 Reading from Files 226
9.3 Writing to Files 229
9.4 Copying, Moving, and Deleting Files 231
9.5 Working with File Paths 233
9.6 Creating and Managing Directories 235
9.7 Handling File Permissions 237
9.8 Using Get-Content and Set-Content 239
9.9 Using Import-Csv and Export-Csv 241
9.10 Handling Binary Files 244

10 Advanced Scripting Techniques **247**

10.1 Introduction to Advanced Scripting 247
10.2 Creating and Using Modules 249
10.3 Building Custom Cmdlets 252
10.4 Advanced Parameter Features 255

10.5 Working with JSON and XML 257
10.6 Leveraging PowerShell Remoting 260
10.7 Using Background Jobs 262
10.8 Handling Asynchronous Operations 265
10.9 Profile Scripting 268
10.10Best Practices and Script Optimization 270

Introduction

PowerShell is a task automation and configuration management framework from Microsoft, consisting of a command-line shell and associated scripting language built on the .NET framework. PowerShell was introduced to provide a robust, scalable, and object-oriented platform for automation and administrative tasks, suitable for both IT professionals and developers.

Understanding the fundamentals of PowerShell requires a look at its historical context. PowerShell was first released in 2006 as part of the Windows Management Framework, aimed at enhancing the capabilities provided by traditional command-line interfaces (CLI) like Command Prompt. Over the years, PowerShell has evolved into a versatile tool that goes beyond the constraints of managing Windows operating systems, supporting cross-platform functionalities on macOS and Linux through PowerShell Core.

One of the compelling reasons for adopting PowerShell is its ability to automate complex administrative tasks, supplying IT professionals with a powerful scripting language paired with a sophisticated command-line interface. This combination streamlines repetitive tasks, supports configuration management, and significantly reduces overhead in system administration. Additionally, PowerShell's integration with the .NET framework offers advanced capabilities, such as interacting with common language runtime (CLR) objects, that extend beyond the reach of traditional CLIs.

PowerShell is categorized into different editions and versions that continue to evolve. Windows PowerShell is the edition built on the .NET Framework, primarily used for automation on Windows machines. PowerShell Core, now simply referred to as PowerShell, runs on .NET Core, a cross-platform runtime, thereby enabling its use on a wider range of operating system environments, including macOS and various Linux distributions.

In contrast to traditional command-line interfaces like Command Prompt, PowerShell provides a more potent and versatile environment, equipped with a rich set of cmdlets (pronounced "command-lets"). Cmdlets are specialized .NET classes that implement particular operations, enabling users to manage system resources, execute processes, and configure environments efficiently. PowerShell's pipeline capability allows for the seamless flow of objects between cmdlets, facilitating complex data processing tasks.

The user interface of PowerShell is another distinguishing aspect. While it offers a familiar console-based interface, it also includes the Integrated Scripting Environment (ISE), providing a more interactive and user-friendly development space. For those using Visual Studio Code, PowerShell extensions are available to enhance scripting, debugging, and automation tasks within a widely-used text editor.

Basic syntax and command conventions in PowerShell are designed to be intuitive, yet powerful. Commands follow a Verb-Noun format, like 'Get-Process' or 'Set-ItemProperty', making them descriptive and easier to remember. PowerShell's consistent syntax and command structure significantly reduce the learning curve, allowing users to grasp fundamental concepts rapidly and apply them effectively.

The PowerShell community and available resources offer a wealth of knowledge and assistance. From forums and online repositories to official documentation and tutorial sites, an extensive support network is in place to help users at all levels, from novices to advanced practitioners.

To get started, consider running your first PowerShell command. Open a PowerShell console or ISE session, and try a simple cmdlet such as 'Get-Help', followed by the name of any other cmdlet. This will provide detailed information about its usage and parameters, demonstrating PowerShell's built-in help system.

In summary, this introductory chapter has outlined the core principles and contextual background of PowerShell, laying a foundation upon which further detailed and technical discussions will build. As we progress through the chapters, readers will gain both theoretical knowledge and practical skills, enabling them to leverage PowerShell's full potential for automation, configuration management, and beyond.

Chapter 1

Introduction to PowerShell

PowerShell, a versatile task automation and configuration management framework from Microsoft, integrates a command-line shell with a powerful scripting language. Originating to enhance the traditional command-line interfaces, PowerShell has evolved to support cross-platform functionalities. It automates complex administrative tasks, utilizes cmdlets for efficient system management, and provides a rich user experience through both the console and Integrated Scripting Environment (ISE). This chapter presents the essentials of PowerShell, preparing readers for deeper exploration in subsequent chapters.

1.1 What is PowerShell?

PowerShell is a cross-platform (Windows, macOS, and Linux) task automation and configuration management framework consisting of a command-line shell (referred to as the PowerShell console) and an associated scripting language built on the .NET framework and .NET Core. It was initially developed to address the limitations of traditional command-line interfaces (CLIs) and shell scripting languages by providing a more robust and automated solution to system administration tasks.

The PowerShell framework consists of the following key components:

- **Command-line Shell**: This is the interface where users can issue commands directly to the operating system. The PowerShell shell provides advanced features and capabilities that enhance user experiences and productivity beyond traditional CLIs.
- **Scripting Language**: PowerShell includes a powerful scripting language that supports complex logic, string manipulation, arithmetic operations, and more, allowing users to automate repetitive tasks efficiently.
- **Cmdlets**: Pronounced command-lets, these are specialized .NET classes that perform a specific function. Cmdlets are the building blocks of PowerShell's functionality, each designed to handle a particular task, such as file manipulation, system processes, or network configuration.
- **Providers**: This feature enables access to different data stores, such as the file system, registry, and certificate store, in a consistent manner.
- **Pipeline**: PowerShell uses pipelines to pass the output of one cmdlet directly as input to another, facilitating complex task automation through a series of simple, executable steps.

Example:

To illustrate how a basic cmdlet works in PowerShell, consider the cmdlet Get-ChildItem, which lists items (files and directories) in a directory.

```
Get-ChildItem -Path C:\\ExampleDirectory
```

The above command retrieves a list of items within C: ExampleDirectory.

The output might look something like this:

```
    Directory: C:\ExampleDirectory

Mode                LastWriteTime         Length Name
----                -------------         ------ ----
d-----        12/12/2022  11:55 AM                SubDirectory1
d-----        12/12/2022  11:55 AM                SubDirectory2
-a----         6/11/2022   8:45 PM           1234 File1.txt
-a----         6/11/2022   8:45 PM           5678 File2.txt
```

The versatility of PowerShell stems from several key features:

- **Object-Based Output**: Unlike traditional text-based command shells, PowerShell outputs objects instead of plain text. This object-oriented approach allows for more complex data manipulations. When a cmdlet produces output, it generates objects that contain properties and methods, which can be further processed or manipulated in the pipeline.
- **Consistency**: Cmdlets follow a consistent naming pattern of Verb-Noun. For example, Get-Item, Set-Item, and Remove-Item are cmdlets that perform operations on filesystem objects. This predictable naming convention helps users understand and remember cmdlets more easily.
- **Extensibility**: Users can write their own cmdlets, providers, and scripts to extend PowerShell's functionality. This extensibility makes PowerShell a flexible tool that can adapt to a wide range of administrative tasks.
- **Integrated Scripting Environment (ISE)**: PowerShell ISE provides a graphical interface for writing, testing, and debugging scripts. It includes features such as syntax highlighting, tab completion, and context-sensitive help, which can enhance productivity and reduce the learning curve for new users.

The effectiveness of PowerShell in automation and configuration management is amplified by its versatility across various platforms and its support for a wide range of technologies and protocols. Users can interact with cloud services, databases, REST APIs, and more through a comprehensive set of built-in cmdlets and custom modules available in repositories such as the PowerShell Gallery.

The following example demonstrates the power of the pipeline in PowerShell. We will fetch all files in a directory, filter them for a specific extension, and sort them by their last write time:

```
Get-ChildItem -Path C:\\ExampleDirectory\\*.txt |
Where-Object {\$\_.LastWriteTime -gt (Get-Date).AddDays(-30)} |
Sort-Object -Property LastWriteTime
```

This command retrieves all .txt files in C:
ExampleDirectory, filters out files not modified in the last 30 days, and sorts the results by their last modification time. The use of pipeline operators (|) allows these operations to be chained together efficiently.

Understanding what PowerShell is and how it functions lays the foundation for delving deeper into its capabilities. By leveraging its object-based approach, consistent cmdlets, and extensible design, users can automate complex tasks with ease and precision.

1.2 History and Evolution of PowerShell

PowerShell, developed by Microsoft, originated as a comprehensive task automation and configuration management framework. The inception of PowerShell marked a significant milestone in the history of command-line interfaces, drawing on the need to streamline system management tasks for administrators and developers alike. Initially codenamed "Monad," PowerShell was first released in November 2006 as part of the Windows PowerShell 1.0 package within Windows Server 2008.

PowerShell's design was driven by several key principles. It sought to overcome the limitations of traditional command-line interfaces (CLIs) by offering a more powerful, object-oriented approach to scripting. Unlike other CLIs that primarily dealt with text streams, PowerShell natively handled data as .NET objects, facilitating more complex manipulations and integrations.

Beginning with PowerShell 1.0, the primary focus was to provide a suite of built-in commands known as cmdlets (pronounced "command-lets"). These cmdlets were designed to perform common administrative tasks, ranging from managing file systems to handling network configurations. Each cmdlet followed the "Verb-Noun" naming convention, making them intuitive and self-descriptive. For example, Get-Process retrieves process information, whereas Set-Item modifies the properties of an item.

PowerShell 2.0 introduced major advancements in August 2009, coinciding with the release of Windows 7 and Windows Server 2008 R2. Key features included the introduction of the Integrated Scripting Environment (ISE), remoting capabilities, advanced functions, and enhancements to the cmdlet library. The ISE provided a GUI-based interface to create, debug, and execute PowerShell scripts, significantly easing the development experience. The remoting capability allowed administrators to execute commands on remote systems, fostering more flexible and scalable administrative operations.

Subsequent releases saw continued refinement and expansion of PowerShell's capabilities. PowerShell 3.0, bundled with Windows 8 and Windows Server 2012, delivered enhancements such as workflows for long-running tasks, robust job scheduling, and additional cmdlets.

With the unveiling of PowerShell 5.0 alongside Windows 10, Microsoft introduced critical updates including classes and enumerations to support object-oriented programming, enhancements to the Desired State Configuration (DSC), a new module for package management, and the PowerShell Gallery for sharing scripts and modules.

A key revolution in PowerShell's evolution was the release of PowerShell Core, announced in 2016 as part of the .NET Core initiative. Unlike its predecessors tied to the Windows NT kernel, PowerShell Core was built on .NET Core, rendering it cross-platform and capable of running on Linux, macOS, and Windows. PowerShell Core marked a pivotal transition towards a more inclusive and versatile automation tool, addressing the growing need for cross-platform administration in modern DevOps environments.

The subsequent versions, PowerShell 6.0 and PowerShell 7.0, further solidified this cross-platform journey. PowerShell 7, based on .NET 5, ensured even greater compatibility and performance improvements. One of the distinguishing features of PowerShell 7 is the pipeline parallelization with the ForEach-Object -Parallel parameter, which significantly improved the execution efficiency of scripts dealing with large data sets or complex processing tasks.

In summary, the evolution of PowerShell has been characterized by a consistent drive towards more powerful, flexible, and cross-platform solutions for system administration. Its transition from a Windows-only utility to a comprehensive and universal automation platform underscores its sustained relevance and adaptability in the face of evolving technological landscapes. PowerShell's continuous incorporation of community feedback and contributions ensures that it remains an indispensable tool for administrators and developers worldwide.

Let us observe a simple example of a cmdlet that reveals its powerful native parsing capability:

```
Get-Service | Where-Object {$_.Status -eq 'Running'}
```

The command above retrieves all services currently running on the system by piping the output of Get-Service into Where-Object, which filters the result set based on the Status property being equal to 'Running'.

The output might look like this:

```
Status   Name           DisplayName
------   ----           -----------
Running  EventLog        Windows Event Log
Running  PlugPlay        Plug and Play
Running  Power           Power
Running  Spooler         Print Spooler
```

PowerShell's paradigm of using objects over text offers clear advantages for both scripting and automation. This inherent capability facilitates more streamlined and reliable system management practices across diverse environments, showcasing why PowerShell persists as a crucial tool in any IT professional's toolkit.

1.3 Why Use PowerShell?

PowerShell stands out as a significant tool for orchestrating administrative tasks across diverse systems, offering numerous advantages that make it a preferred choice among IT professionals. This section delves into the key reasons for adopting PowerShell in various environments, highlighting its strengths in automation, versatility, consistency, and extensibility.

Automation: PowerShell excels in automating repetitive and complex tasks, which reduces the manual effort required for routine system administration activities. Automating tasks not only increases efficiency but also minimizes errors associated with manual interventions. A simple example involves the automation of user account creation in Active Directory:

```
# Automate user creation in Active Directory
Import-Module ActiveDirectory
New-ADUser -Name "John Doe" -SamAccountName "jdoe" -Path "OU=Users,DC=
    Company,DC=Com" -Enabled $true
```

Versatility: PowerShell's versatility extends to managing a wide range of systems including Windows, Linux, and macOS. Its cross-platform capabilities ensure that administrators can use a single toolset across different environments. This versatility is further enhanced by PowerShell Core, which is the open-source, cross-platform version of PowerShell, built on .NET Core.

Consistency: A hallmark of PowerShell is its consistent syntax and ubiquitous cmdlets, which provide a standardized way to perform various operations. The use of cmdlets, consistent noun-verb naming conventions, and object-oriented pipeline ensures that learning one part of PowerShell simplifies understanding other aspects. For instance, searching for processes can be performed uniformly across platforms:

```
# List all running processes
Get-Process
```

Extensibility: PowerShell is designed to be extensible, allowing users to create custom cmdlets and modules. This feature lets IT professionals extend functionality to meet specific needs. For instance, custom modules can be created to automate organization-specific processes, resulting in highly tailored solutions.

```
# Example of a custom function
function Get-CustomGreeting {
    param (
        [string]$Name
    )
    "Hello, $Name! Welcome to the PowerShell scripting guide."
}
# Execute the custom function
Get-CustomGreeting -Name "New User"
```

Interoperability: PowerShell facilitates seamless interaction with other Microsoft services, such as Azure, Microsoft 365, and Exchange Server, and supports integration with other management frameworks and APIs. This interoperability ensures that PowerShell can serve as a central scripting language for various IT management tasks.

Rich Object-Based Pipeline: PowerShell's object-based pipeline passes objects, not just text, between cmdlets, offering a more powerful and flexible approach to data manipulation. Each object in the pipeline retains its properties and methods, making it easier to process and manipulate data.

```
# Example displaying the richness of the pipeline
Get-Process | Where-Object {$_.CPU -gt 100} | Select-Object -Property ProcessName,
    CPU
```

Enhanced Security: PowerShell provides robust security features such as script signing, constrained language modes, and Just Enough Administration (JEA). These features help in enforcing security policies and minimizing the risk of executing unauthorized scripts.

```
# Example of enforcing security via script signing
Set-ExecutionPolicy -ExecutionPolicy RemoteSigned
```

Community and Ecosystem: A thriving community and rich ecosystem support PowerShell, where users can find numerous resources such as modules, scripts, forums, and documentation. The PowerShell Gallery, for instance, offers thousands of community-contributed modules and cmdlets.

The integration of these elements makes PowerShell an indispensable tool for modern IT automation and administration tasks. Its combination of automation capabilities, cross-platform versatility, consistent syntax, extensibility, interoperability, rich object-based pipeline, enhanced security, and robust community support all contribute to its extensive adoption and success in diverse IT environments.

1.4 PowerShell Editions and Versions

PowerShell has undergone significant transformations and enhancements since its inception, evolving through various editions and versions to accommodate different operating environments and user needs. This section delves into the distinctions between PowerShell editions and their versions, elucidating the specific contexts in which each is deployed.

As of this writing, PowerShell has two primary editions: Windows PowerShell and PowerShell (formerly known as PowerShell Core).

Windows PowerShell is the edition of PowerShell built on the .NET Framework, specifically targeting the Windows operating system. It started from PowerShell version 1.0 and has continued to evolve, incorporating more cmdlets, features, and capabilities with each release. The latest significant version within this edition is Windows PowerShell 5.1. This edition is particularly well-suited for managing Windows-based environments and integrates seamlessly with various Microsoft products such as Active Directory, Exchange, and SharePoint.

PowerShell (PowerShell Core) is the edition of PowerShell built on .NET Core, enabling it to be multi-platform. This edition supports Windows, macOS, Linux, and other operating systems. With PowerShell Core starting from version 6.0, it represents Microsoft's shift toward cross-platform automation. The latest version, as of this writing, is PowerShell 7.x, referred to simply as "PowerShell" to avoid confusion with Windows PowerShell.

The distinctions between these editions are more than just name and version. They embody different underpinnings due to the frameworks they rely on, affecting their compatibility and performance characteristics.

- **Windows PowerShell (Up to version 5.1)**
- Based on the .NET Framework.
- Available solely on Windows operating systems.
- Strong integration with Windows-specific technologies.
- Uses Windows-specific modules and functionality.
- **PowerShell (Starting with version 6.0)**
- Based on .NET Core, aiming at cross-platform capability.
- Supported on Windows, macOS, Linux, and other operating systems.
- Open source, with active community contributions.
- Continuous updates with new features, bug fixes, and performance improvements.

The transition from Windows PowerShell to PowerShell involves several design and operational considerations. Although PowerShell 7.0 is the successor to Windows PowerShell 5.1, it introduces new paradigms reflective of its broader scope and base on .NET Core. For instance, PowerShell 7.0 brought improvements such as pipeline parallelization via ForEach-Object -Parallel, new operators like the ternary operator (?:) and the pipeline chain operators (|| and &&), alongside enhanced and consistent error handling.

Here is a basic PowerShell script that demonstrates checking the version of PowerShell running on your system:

```
# This script checks the version of the running PowerShell
$PSVersionTable.PSVersion
```

Executing this script will output:

```
Major  Minor  Build  Revision
-----  -----  -----  --------
7      0      3      0
```

This output indicates that PowerShell 7.0.3 is the installed version. The PSVersionTable is a fundamental variable in PowerShell that provides detailed information about the version and the underlying runtime.

The divergence in versions affects script compatibility as well. Scripts written for Windows PowerShell might not run seamlessly in PowerShell 7.0 or higher due to changes in cmdlets, modules, and the underlying .NET Core. Users must validate and, where necessary, modify their scripts for compatibility across different versions.

Given the complexity and breadth of different environments, Microsoft provides guidelines and tools to facilitate the transition and compatibility checking. The use of the Compatibility module in PowerShell 7.0 aids in loading Windows PowerShell modules into PowerShell Core to ensure that cross-edition compatibility is achieved.

Overall, understanding the editions and versions of PowerShell is crucial for optimizing its use across different platforms and environments. PowerShell continues to evolve, providing greater capabilities and broader support, making it an indispensable tool for automation and configuration management.

1.5 PowerShell vs. Command Prompt

When comparing PowerShell with the traditional Command Prompt (cmd.exe), it is important to delineate their origins, capabilities, and the distinguishing features that set them apart. While both serve as command-line interfaces for Windows operating systems, they cater to different needs and use cases.

Command Prompt, also known as cmd.exe, is a legacy shell that dates back to the early days of DOS and Windows. It is primarily used for executing batch scripts, running simple commands, and performing file and directory manipulation tasks. Command Prompt operates on a text-based input/output model, where commands and their outputs are plain text. For instance, a basic directory listing command in Command Prompt is:

```
dir
```

This command lists all files and directories in the current directory. The output is purely textual:

```
 Volume in drive C has no label.
 Volume Serial Number is XXXX-XXXX

 Directory of C:\Users\Username

01/01/2023  02:30 PM    <DIR>          .
01/01/2023  02:30 PM    <DIR>          ..
01/01/2023  02:30 PM    <DIR>          Documents
01/01/2023  02:30 PM    <DIR>          Downloads
               4 File(s)              0 bytes
              12 Dir(s)  100,000,000,000 bytes free
```

In contrast, PowerShell is a more modern and advanced framework for managing and automating administrative tasks. It was designed with the intent to overcome the limitations of Command Prompt and other shells by introducing a robust scripting language and an extensive library of built-in commands known as cmdlets. One of the most significant differences is that PowerShell operates on an object-based model rather than a text-based model, which allows for more complex data manipulation and interaction.

For example, to list files in a directory using PowerShell, you use the Get-ChildItem cmdlet:

```
Get-ChildItem
```

This cmdlet retrieves objects representing the items in the specified location. The output is a series of objects that can be further manipulated, filtered, or processed:

```
    Directory: C:\Users\Username

Mode                 LastWriteTime         Length Name
----                 -------------         ------ ----
d-----        01/01/2023  02:30 PM                Documents
d-----        01/01/2023  02:30 PM                Downloads
```

These objects are not merely text strings but structured data that retain metadata, such as file size, type, and timestamps, which can be accessed and manipulated programmatically. This object-oriented nature of PowerShell enhances its proficiency in handling various administrative tasks.

Furthermore, PowerShell introduces advanced features such as Pipelines, Variables, and powerful Scripting Capabilities. The pipeline concept in PowerShell allows you to pass objects from one cmdlet to another, enabling intricate data processing workflows. For example, to list all text files and sort them by size, you can chain cmdlets together using the pipeline operator |:

```
Get-ChildItem -Filter *.txt | Sort-Object Length
```

Command Prompt lacks such advanced piping capabilities, making PowerShell a more suitable choice for complex administrative scripts. Additionally, PowerShell provides built-in support for Conditionals, Loops, and Error Handling constructs akin to those found in fully-fledged programming languages, which are limited in Command Prompt batch scripts.

Another crucial aspect is PowerShell's cross-platform capabilities. While Command Prompt remains confined to Windows environments, PowerShell Core (the open-source version of PowerShell) extends its reach to Linux and macOS systems, fostering a more consistent management and automation experience across diverse operating systems.

Moreover, PowerShell integrates seamlessly with modern development tools and frameworks, including .NET, Azure, and Docker, and can interface with REST APIs, providing a comprehensive environment for developers and system administrators alike.

In summary, while Command Prompt and PowerShell both serve to enhance command-line interactions, PowerShell distinctly outperforms with its advanced features, object-oriented approach, and cross-platform support, making it an indispensable tool for modern IT and development environments.

1.6 Understanding the Shell Interface

PowerShell's shell interface is designed to streamline task automation and configuration management for both novice and advanced users. The interface supports a text-based input method that allows users to interact with the system on a granular level.

The shell interface primarily interacts with cmdlets, scripts, executables, and .NET classes in the system. The command line interface (CLI) provides an immediate response to user commands, enabling real-time feedback and debugging.

Command Prompt vs. PowerShell Interface

While the Command Prompt interface traces its roots back to MS-DOS and provides a basic, non-graphical user interface (GUI) for executing commands, the PowerShell interface enhances and extends this functionality. PowerShell integrates deeply with the Windows operating system through cmdlets and offers advanced capabilities such as object-oriented scripting, which is not available in the Command Prompt.

Components of the PowerShell Interface

1. Prompt: This is the line where users input commands. By default, it displays the current working directory. 2. Cmdlets: PowerShell uses cmdlets (short for command-lets) to perform specific operations. Each cmdlet follows a verb-noun naming pattern, e.g., Get-ChildItem, making the function of the command clear. 3. Pipeline: This feature allows chaining commands together so the output of one cmdlet can be used as input to another. 4. Output: The results of the commands are displayed directly in the shell interface, allowing for immediate inspection.

```
Get-Process | Select-Object ProcessName, CPU
```

```
ProcessName   CPU
-----------   ---
explorer      1.25
powershell    0.15
```

The above example demonstrates a pipeline where Get-Process retrieves the list of current processes, and Select-Object filters the output to display only the ProcessName and CPU usage.

Common PowerShell Prompts and Input Handling

In PowerShell, different prompts serve various purposes, delineating the mode of operation:

- PS C: - Standard prompt indicating a ready state for input.
- » - Secondary prompt indicating an incomplete command spanning multiple lines.
- PS [File]:> - Indicates that commands are being executed from a file path.

PowerShell supports input commands, variables, and scripts:

```
$greeting = "Hello, PowerShell"
Write-Output $greeting
```

```
Hello, PowerShell
```

Here, the variable $greeting stores a string, which is output using Write-Output. Variables in PowerShell are prefixed with $, enhancing readability and organization within scripts.

Tab Completion in PowerShell

PowerShell's tab completion feature significantly enhances user efficiency by auto-completing commands and paths. Pressing the Tab key cycles through possible completions:

```
Get-Process -Name exp
```

Pressing Tab after typing exp completes it to explorer, assuming no other processes start with those letters. This feature ensures accuracy and speed in command line input.

Understanding the Concept of Aliases in PowerShell

Aliases are shorthand references to cmdlets. For instance, ls, commonly used in Unix-like systems, is an alias for Get-ChildItem in PowerShell. Use the Get-Alias cmdlet to view or create aliases:

```
Get-Alias -Name ls
```

```
CommandType    Name                              Definition
-----------    ----                              ----------
Alias          ls                                Get-ChildItem
```

Using Help System in PowerShell

The Get-Help cmdlet provides detailed documentation for all PowerShell commands. Using it effectively can significantly reduce the learning curve:

```
Get-Help Get-Process
```

This command retrieves information about the Get-Process cmdlet, including its syntax, parameters, and examples.

Customization of the PowerShell Interface

Customization in PowerShell can be achieved through profiles, which are special script files loaded at the start of each session. Users can define their environment settings, load modules, and configure preferences:

```
if (!(Test-Path -Path $PROFILE)) {
    New-Item -ItemType File -Path $PROFILE -Force
}
notepad $PROFILE
```

This script checks if the profile path exists, creates it if it does not, and opens it in Notepad for editing. Customization within the profile could include altering the prompt appearance, setting aliases, or defining functions.

Error Handling and Debugging

Error handling in PowerShell is implemented using try-catch blocks, which allow users to manage exceptions gracefully. The Write-Error cmdlet can generate custom error messages:

```
try {
   Get-Item "C:\NonExistentFile.txt"
} catch {
   Write-Error "The specified file does not exist."
}
```

```
Write-Error: The specified file does not exist.
```

This block attempts to retrieve a non-existent file and catches the resulting error, displaying a user-defined message. This mechanism is fundamental for robust script development.

Understanding these elements of the PowerShell shell interface lays the groundwork for mastering more advanced scripting and automation tasks. Engaging deeply with the interface capabilities enables efficient system management and automation.

1.7 Introduction to PowerShell ISE and VS Code

PowerShell Integrated Scripting Environment (ISE) and Visual Studio Code (VS Code) are two primary tools for developing and executing PowerShell scripts. Understanding both environments is crucial for efficient scripting and automation.

PowerShell ISE: PowerShell ISE is a host application for Windows PowerShell. It provides a rich graphical interface for executing and debugging PowerShell scripts. It includes features such as syntax coloring, tab completion, and the capability to execute commands directly in the script editor. Below is an example of a simple PowerShell script written and executed in PowerShell ISE:

```
# This script prints "Hello, World!" to the console
Write-Output "Hello, World!"
```

When executed in PowerShell ISE, the output will be:

```
Hello, World!
```

Visual Studio Code (VS Code): VS Code, a free and open-source code editor developed by Microsoft, extends its functionality to support

PowerShell through an extension. It provides an extensive range of features such as IntelliSense, debugging, and integrated terminal. To set up VS Code for PowerShell, follow these steps:

Algorithm 1: Setting up VS Code for PowerShell

Data: Install VS Code and PowerShell extension
Result: VS Code ready for PowerShell scripting

- Download and install Visual Studio Code from https://code.visualstudio.com/.
- Launch VS Code and navigate to the Extensions view by clicking the Extensions icon in the Activity Bar on the side of the window.
- Search for "PowerShell" in the Extensions view search bar and select ms-vscode.PowerShell.
- Click the Install button for the PowerShell extension.
- Once installed, select the PowerShell environment in the integrated terminal by clicking the terminal drop-down and choosing PowerShell.

Here is an identical script written in VS Code:

```
# This script prints "Hello, World!" to the console
Write-Output "Hello, World!"
```

Running this script in the integrated terminal of VS Code will yield:

```
Hello, World!
```

Feature Comparison: While PowerShell ISE is designed specifically for use with PowerShell, VS Code is a more versatile code editor suitable for multiple programming languages and environments. Here is a detailed comparison of noteworthy features:

- **IntelliSense and Snippets:**
- PowerShell ISE: Provides context-aware IntelliSense and predefined snippets for faster coding.
- VS Code: Offers IntelliSense with more advanced features, such as documentation on hover and customizable snippets.
- **Debugging:**

- PowerShell ISE: Supports breakpoints, variable watching, call stack inspection, and step-through debugging.
- VS Code: Includes robust debugging tools such as breakpoint configurations, watches, and inline variable evaluation.
- **Customizability:**
- PowerShell ISE: Limited to PowerShell-specific features and customizability.
- VS Code: Highly extensible with numerous extensions available in the marketplace—offering themes, key bindings, and settings customization.
- **Cross-platform Support:**
- PowerShell ISE: Available exclusively on Windows.
- VS Code: Cross-platform support, it runs on Windows, macOS, and Linux.

Practical Application: Both PowerShell ISE and VS Code can be used depending on the specific requirements of your development environment. For instance, if you are working exclusively on Windows and prefer a lightweight setup focused on PowerShell, PowerShell ISE is suitable. Alternatively, for a more integrated development experience with access to several languages and features, VS Code is advantageous.

The choice between PowerShell ISE and VS Code ultimately hinges on specific needs and preferences, whether it be simplicity and focus with ISE or extensibility and cross-platform availability with VS Code.

1.8 Basic Syntax and Commands

Understanding the fundamental syntax and basic commands of PowerShell is crucial for leveraging its extensive capabilities. The structure and command set are designed to be intuitive for those familiar with both traditional command-line interfaces and object-oriented programming.

PowerShell commands, also known as cmdlets, follow a verb-noun naming convention, which clearly describes the action and the target of the command. For example, Get-Process retrieves a list of active processes. Cmdlets are always written in PascalCase.

Variables: Variables in PowerShell are denoted with a $ prefix and can store data of various types including strings, integers, and objects. The following example demonstrates how to declare and use variables:

```
$greeting = "Hello, World"
$number = 42
$process = Get-Process

Write-Output $greeting # Outputs: Hello, World
Write-Output $number # Outputs: 42
Write-Output $process # Outputs a list of active processes
```

Operators: PowerShell supports a variety of operators, categorized as arithmetic, comparison, logical, and assignment operators, among others. Below are examples of some commonly used operators:

```
# Arithmetic Operators
$a = 10
$b = 4
$addition = $a + $b # 14
$subtraction = $a - $b # 6
$multiplication = $a * $b # 40
$division = $a / $b # 2.5

# Comparison Operators
$equal = $a -eq 10 # True
$notEqual = $b -ne 5 # True
$greaterThan = $a -gt 5 # True
$lessThan = $b -lt 10 # True

# Logical Operators
$and = ($a -gt 5) -and ($b -lt 10) # True
$or = ($a -lt 5) -or ($b -eq 4) # True

# Assignment Operators
$c = $a # Assignment
$c += $b # $c = $c + $b # 14
$c -= $b # $c = $c - $b # 10
$c *= $b # $c = $c * $b # 40
$c /= $b # $c = $c / $b # 10
```

Pipeline: One of PowerShell's powerful features is the pipeline (|), which allows the output of one cmdlet to be used as the input for another. This capability streams objects, not just text, enhancing functionality significantly. Example:

```
Get-Process | Sort-Object -Property CPU -Descending
```

This command retrieves the list of processes and sorts them based on their CPU usage in descending order.

Loops and Conditionals: PowerShell includes traditional control flow constructs such as if, else, for, foreach, while, and do-while. Examples include:

```
# If-Else Example
if ($a -gt $b) {
    Write-Output "$a is greater than $b"
} elseif ($a -eq $b) {
    Write-Output "$a is equal to $b"
} else {
    Write-Output "$a is less than $b"
}

# For Loop Example
for ($i = 0; $i -lt 5; $i++) {
    Write-Output "Iteration $i"
}

# While Loop Example
while ($a -gt $b) {
    Write-Output "$a is greater than $b"
    $a--
}
```

Functions: PowerShell allows the creation of functions using the function keyword. Functions can be simple or complex and support parameters to pass data into them:

```
function Get-Square {
    param (
        [int]$number
    )
    return $number * $number
}

$squaredValue = Get-Square -number 4
Write-Output $squaredValue # Outputs: 16
```

Comments: Comments are essential for documenting scripts and can be either single-line or multi-line:

```
# This is a single-line comment

<#
    This is a multi-line comment.
    It spans multiple lines.
#>
```

Modules: Modules are packages that contain cmdlets, functions, variables, and other tools built for specific purposes. They can be imported into a session using Import-Module:

```
Import-Module Az # Imports the Azure PowerShell module
```

To view all available modules, you can use:

```
Get-Module -ListAvailable
```

Finally, remember that PowerShell cmdlets and their usage should be tested and executed in a safe environment before applying them in production systems to prevent unintended consequences.

1.9 PowerShell Community and Resources

The PowerShell community is a dynamic and resource-rich ecosystem, providing a wealth of information, tools, and support for both novice and experienced users. Engaging with this community can significantly enhance understanding and proficiency in PowerShell.

Online Forums and Discussion Groups: The PowerShell community thrives on numerous online platforms where users can ask questions, share scripts, and provide solutions. Major forums include:

- **Microsoft Tech Community (PowerShell):** An official platform where users can interact directly with Microsoft engineers and other experienced users.
- **Stack Overflow:** A widely-used Q&A site where users can post issues and get responses from other developers and administrators.
- **Reddit (r/PowerShell):** A vibrant community where users share tips, scripts, and discuss various PowerShell-related topics.

Blogs and Websites: Numerous blogs and websites provide detailed articles, tutorials, and insights into PowerShell scripting and usage:

- **PowerShell.org:** A community-driven site featuring extensive resources, including articles, forums, and events.
- **Scripting Guys:** Managed by Microsoft, it offers numerous scripts and how-to articles.
- **Learn Microsoft PowerShell:** A comprehensive source of guides and tutorials to help deepen understanding of PowerShell functionalities.

Video Tutorials and Webinars: Visual learning through video tutorials and webinars can be more engaging and effective for some learners. Key providers include:

- **Microsoft Channel 9:** A platform for video content by Microsoft, including PowerShell tutorials and presentations by experts.
- **YouTube Channels:** Channels such as "Adam the Automator" and "TechThoughts" frequently publish high-quality PowerShell tutorials.

Books and Publications: For those preferring traditional reading material, many books delve deeply into PowerShell. Recommended titles include:

- **Learning PowerShell in a Month of Lunches by Don Jones and Jeffrey Hicks:** A practical guide that gradually builds proficiency.
- **PowerShell in Depth by Don Jones, Jeffrey Hicks, and Richard Siddaway:** A comprehensive resource covering advanced topics.

Conferences and User Groups: Participating in conferences and user group meetings can provide networking opportunities and exposure to advanced techniques:

- **PowerShell Conference Europe (PSConfEU):** An annual event featuring sessions by PowerShell experts.
- **PowerShell User Groups:** Local and virtual user groups gather regularly for discussions and presentations on PowerShell.

GitHub Repositories: Open-source repositories on platforms like GitHub are invaluable for learning and collaboration:

- **PowerShell Team's Repository:** The official repository maintained by the PowerShell Team at Microsoft, it includes source code, issues, and discussions.
- **Awesome PowerShell:** A curated list of PowerShell resources, including modules, scripts, and frameworks.

Social Media: Platforms like Twitter and LinkedIn are useful for staying up-to-date with the latest PowerShell news and updates:

- **Twitter:** Follow handles such as @PowerShellOrg and @MSPowerShell for updates and interaction.
- **LinkedIn:** Groups such as "PowerShell Professionals" provide forums for discussion and networking.

Documentation: Utilizing official and community-generated documentation can clarify concepts and provide accurate information:

- **Microsoft Docs:** The official documentation for PowerShell, highly detailed and regularly updated.
- **GitHub Wiki:** Often used by projects hosted on GitHub to provide user and developer guides.

Staying informed and involved with these resources can significantly expedite the learning curve and develop a more in-depth understanding of PowerShell.

1.10 First Steps: Running Your First PowerShell Command

The process of running your first PowerShell command is a fundamental step towards mastering scripting and automation. PowerShell commands, also known as cmdlets, are the building blocks for complex scripts and automation tasks. This section will guide you through executing your first PowerShell command, understanding its components, and interpreting the output.

To open the PowerShell interface, you can follow these steps:

- Press Win+R to open the Run dialog box.
- Type powershell and press Enter.

Once PowerShell is open, you will see a prompt that typically looks like this:

```
PS C:\Users\YourUsername>
```

The PS prefix indicates that you are in the PowerShell environment, followed by the current directory path. You are now ready to run your first command.

Example of Basic Command

A basic command you can run in PowerShell is Get-Process. This cmdlet retrieves a list of all processes currently running on your system. Type the following command and press Enter:

```
Get-Process
```

The output should be similar to the following:

```
Handles  NPM(K)    PM(K)      WS(K)     CPU(s)     Id  SI ProcessName
-------  ------    -----      -----     ------     --  -- -----------
    357      27    10952      23400       0.14    452   1 conhost
    268      16     4844       1232       0.03   2032   1 chrome
    ...
```

Here, the output includes several columns such as Handles, NPM(K), PM(K), WS(K), CPU(s), Id, SI, and ProcessName. Each row corresponds to a running process.

Understanding the Components

- Handles: Number of handles that the process has opened.
- NPM(K): Non-paged memory the process is using.
- PM(K): Paged memory the process is using.
- WS(K): Working set memory the process is using.
- CPU(s): Processor time being used by the process.
- Id: Process identifier.
- SI: Session identifier.
- ProcessName: Name of the process.

PowerShell cmdlets follow a Verb-Noun naming convention. For example, in Get-Process, Get is the verb that denotes the action to retrieve information, and Process is the noun indicating what information to retrieve.

Running a Command with Parameters

Cmdlets can be customized using parameters. For instance, to get processes with more than a certain amount of memory usage, use the -WorkingSet parameter. Type the following command:

```
Get-Process | Where-Object { \$_.WorkingSet -gt 50MB }
```

In this command:

- | (Pipeline operator): Passes the output of Get-Process to Where-Object.
- Where-Object: Filters objects passed from the previous command.
- $_.WorkingSet -gt 50MB: Specifies the condition that the process working set should be greater than 50MB.

Saving and Exporting Output

To save the output of a cmdlet to a file, you can use the Export-Csv cmdlet. For example:

```
Get-Process | Export-Csv -Path "C:\Users\YourUsername\Documents\processes.csv" -
    NoTypeInformation
```

This command exports the list of processes to a CSV file named processes.csv located in the Documents directory. The parameter -NoTypeInformation prevents the inclusion of type information in the CSV file.

Executing Scripts

You can also save a sequence of commands in a script file with a .ps1 extension. For instance, create a file named GetProcesses.ps1 with the following content:

```
Get-Process
```

To run the script, type the following command in the PowerShell prompt:

```
.\GetProcesses.ps1
```

The .
denotes the current directory.

Error Handling

When running commands, errors might occur. PowerShell provides error handling mechanisms to manage such scenarios. For example, use the try-catch block to handle errors gracefully:

```
try {
    Get-Process -Name "NonExistentProcess"
} catch {
    Write-Host "An error occurred: \$_."
}
```

In this snippet:

- try: Defines the block of code to attempt execution.
- catch: Specifies actions to take if an error occurs.
- Write-Host: Outputs a message to the console.

Starting with these basics will set a strong foundation for more complex scripting and automation tasks in PowerShell. Understanding how to run commands, interpret results, and handle common tasks equips you with the necessary skills to explore more advanced features and functionalities.

Chapter 2

Setting Up Your PowerShell Environment

This chapter details the installation and configuration of PowerShell across various operating systems including Windows, macOS, and Linux. It covers updating PowerShell, setting up Integrated Scripting Environment (ISE), and configuring Visual Studio Code for enhanced PowerShell scripting. Additionally, it includes guidelines for configuring execution policies, customizing PowerShell profiles, installing useful modules, and effectively navigating the PowerShell help system to ensure a robust and productive working environment.

2.1 Installing PowerShell on Windows

PowerShell is a versatile scripting and automation tool that has become an essential part of the Windows ecosystem. This section outlines the steps required to install PowerShell on Windows.

Step 1: Verify Pre-installation Requirements

Ensure that your system meets the necessary prerequisites:

- Windows 7 SP1, Windows 8.1, Windows 10, or Windows Server 2008 R2 SP1 and later versions.
- Update to the latest service pack to guarantee compatibility and

security.

- .NET Framework 4.7.2 or later.

Step 2: Download PowerShell

PowerShell 7, the latest version, is a cross-platform version of PowerShell that runs on Windows, macOS, and Linux. Visit the official PowerShell GitHub page to download the latest version. Direct link for your convenience:

```
https://github.com/PowerShell/PowerShell/releases/latest
```

Navigate to the "Assets" section of the release page to find the Windows installer packages. Select the appropriate installer, which is typically labeled PowerShell-7.x.y-win-x64.msi or PowerShell-7.x.y-win-x86.msi according to your system's architecture.

Step 3: Installing PowerShell Using the MSI Package

Once the MSI package is downloaded, follow these steps for installation:

- **Double-click the MSI file** to start the installation process. This action invokes the Windows Installer.
- **Accept the License Agreement**. Review the terms and conditions, then click "Next" to continue.
- **Select Installation Folder**. The default installation directory is:

  ```
  %ProgramFiles%\PowerShell
  ```

  Using the default path is recommended unless a different path is necessary for your configuration.
- **Configure Optional Features**:
  - **Enable PowerShell Remoting**: Allows remote management and automation.
  - **Add to PATH Environment Variable**: This ensures that PowerShell can be called from any command prompt or script without needing to specify the full path.
- **Click 'Install'**: Initiate the installation. Administrative privileges are required, as the installer will request elevated permissions.

- **Complete the Installation**: Once installation completes, click "Finish" to exit the setup wizard.

Step 4: Verification of Installation

To confirm successful installation, open a new Command Prompt or PowerShell session and run:

```
pwsh
```

The above command should start PowerShell 7, indicated by a version banner displaying the installed version. Additionally, verify the installation directory:

```
PS> $PSVersionTable.PSVersion
```

The output should display:

```
Major  Minor  Patch  Pre-lease  Build  DateTime
-----  -----  -----  ---------  -----  --------
7      x      y
```

where x and y represent the specific installed version.

Step 5: Ensuring Up-to-date .NET Runtime

PowerShell 7 relies on the .NET Core runtime. To ensure that you have the latest runtime, visit:

```
https://dotnet.microsoft.com/download/dotnet-core
```

Download and install the latest version of the .NET Core Runtime. This ensures compatibility and optimal performance of your PowerShell installation.

Step 6: Configuring Execution Policies

Execution policies define the conditions under which PowerShell loads configuration files and runs scripts. To set the execution policy, open PowerShell with administrative privileges and run:

```
Set-ExecutionPolicy -ExecutionPolicy RemoteSigned -Scope LocalMachine
```

This command sets the policy to RemoteSigned, allowing scripts created locally to run but requiring those from the internet to be signed by a trusted publisher. Verify your current execution policy with:

```
Get-ExecutionPolicy -List
```

Step 7: Setting Up Profiles and Modules

Creating a profile script customizes your PowerShell environment according to preference. To create or modify a profile, open PowerShell and execute:

```
if (!(Test-Path -Path $PROFILE)) {
    New-Item -Type File -Path $PROFILE -Force
}
notepad $PROFILE
```

This opens the profile in Notepad for editing. Common customizations include setting aliases, importing modules, and configuring the prompt. To install useful modules like PSReadLine for better command-line editing, run:

```
Install-Module PSReadLine -Scope CurrentUser -Force -SkipPublisherCheck
```

Confirm the installation by checking the module list:

```
Get-InstalledModule
```

Thoroughly inspect the output to ensure all necessary modules are installed.

By following these detailed steps, you ensure a robust and well-configured PowerShell environment, ready for advanced scripting and automation tasks.

2.2 Installing PowerShell on macOS

To install PowerShell on macOS, we start by ensuring that the system meets the minimum requirements. PowerShell Core requires macOS 10.12 (Sierra) or higher. It is also advisable to have a stable internet connection and administrative privileges.

Step 1: Install Homebrew

Homebrew is a package manager for macOS that simplifies the installation of software. Open the Terminal application and install Homebrew by running the following command:

```
/bin/bash -c "$(curl -fsSL https://raw.githubusercontent.com/Homebrew/install/
    HEAD/install.sh)"
```

After running the command, follow the on-screen instructions to complete the Homebrew installation. Verify that Homebrew is installed correctly by executing:

```
brew --version
```

```
Homebrew 3.x.x
```

Step 2: Install PowerShell

With Homebrew installed, proceed to install PowerShell by entering the following command in the Terminal:

```
brew install --cask powershell
```

This command downloads and installs the latest version of PowerShell using the Homebrew Cask extension. After installation, verify that PowerShell can be launched by typing:

```
pwsh
```

Upon successful installation, you should see the PowerShell prompt (PS >). To confirm the installed version, use the command:

```
$PSVersionTable.PSVersion
```

```
Major  Minor  Patch  PreReleaseLabel BuildLabel
-----  -----  -----  --------------- ----------
7      x      x
```

Step 3: Adding PowerShell to Shell Profile

To ensure that PowerShell is available whenever you open a new terminal window, it is beneficial to add PowerShell to your shell profile. For example, if you are using zsh (the default on macOS Catalina and later), add the following line to your .zshrc file:

```
echo 'export PATH="/usr/local/microsoft/powershell/7:$PATH"' >> ~/.zshrc
```

If you are using bash (the default on older versions of macOS), add the line to your .bash_profile or .bashrc file:

```
echo 'export PATH="/usr/local/microsoft/powershell/7:$PATH"' >> ~/.bash_profile
```

After modifying your profile, apply the changes by running:

```
source ~/.zshrc
```

or

```
source ~/.bash_profile
```

You should now be able to start PowerShell by simply typing pwsh from the terminal.

Step 4: Updating PowerShell

To keep PowerShell up to date, use Homebrew's upgrade feature. Regularly updating ensures that you have the latest features and security patches. Run the following command to upgrade PowerShell:

```
brew update
brew upgrade powershell --cask
```

This sequence first updates Homebrew itself and then upgrades the PowerShell installation to the latest version.

Step 5: Uninstalling PowerShell

If you need to remove PowerShell from your macOS system, you can do so easily with Homebrew. Open the Terminal and execute the following command:

```
brew uninstall --cask powershell
```

This command will remove PowerShell from your system.

By following these steps, PowerShell can be efficiently installed and managed on macOS, leveraging the simplicity and reliability of Homebrew. This enhances the ability to perform administrative tasks, automate scripts, and utilize PowerShell's powerful features on a macOS platform.

2.3 Installing PowerShell on Linux

PowerShell, initially a Windows-exclusive command-line interface and scripting language, has evolved into a cross-platform tool. This section details the steps required for installing PowerShell on various Linux distributions. The process leverages package management systems, ensuring a seamless and efficient installation.

Installing PowerShell on Ubuntu

Ubuntu users can install PowerShell through the Advanced Packaging Tool (APT). The steps are straightforward and require administrative privileges. Execute the following commands in your terminal:

```
# Update the list of packages
sudo apt-get update

# Install pre-requisite packages
sudo apt-get install -y wget apt-transport-https software-properties-common

# Import the Microsoft GPG key
wget -q https://packages.microsoft.com/keys/microsoft.asc -O- | sudo apt-key add -

# Register the Microsoft Ubuntu repository
sudo add-apt-repository "deb [arch=amd64] https://packages.microsoft.com/repos/
    microsoft-ubuntu-focal-prod focal main"

# Update the package list
sudo apt-get update

# Install PowerShell
sudo apt-get install -y powershell

# Verify installation
pwsh --version
```

Upon successful execution, PowerShell is installed and can be executed by typing pwsh in the terminal.

Installing PowerShell on CentOS/RHEL

For CentOS and Red Hat Enterprise Linux (RHEL) users, the installation can be performed using the YUM package manager. Follow the steps below:

```
# Register the Microsoft RedHat repository
sudo rpm -Uvh https://packages.microsoft.com/config/rhel/7/packages-microsoft-prod.
    rpm

# Install PowerShell
sudo yum install -y powershell

# Verify installation
pwsh --version
```

After running these commands, PowerShell will be available as pwsh.

Installing PowerShell on Fedora

Fedora users can utilize the DNF package management tool to install PowerShell. Follow these commands:

```
# Register the Microsoft Fedora repository
sudo rpm -Uvh https://packages.microsoft.com/config/fedora/30/packages-microsoft-
    prod.rpm

# Install PowerShell
```

```
sudo dnf install -y powershell

# Verify installation
pwsh --version
```

Executing the above commands will ensure that PowerShell is correctly installed on your Fedora system, accessible via pwsh.

Installing PowerShell on openSUSE

For openSUSE distributions, the Zypper package manager is used to install PowerShell. Proceed with the following commands:

```
# Register the Microsoft openSUSE repository
sudo rpm --import https://packages.microsoft.com/keys/microsoft.asc
sudo sh -c 'echo -e "[code]\nname=Microsoft openSUSE 15-Prod\nbaseurl=https://
    packages.microsoft.com/yumrepos/microsoft-sles-15-prod\nenabled=1\ngpgcheck
    =1\ngpgkey=https://packages.microsoft.com/keys/microsoft.asc" > /etc/zypp/
    repos.d/microsoft.repo'

# Install PowerShell
sudo zypper install -y powershell

# Verify installation
pwsh --version
```

As with the other distributions, PowerShell can be accessed by executing pwsh in the terminal.

Installing PowerShell from a Binary Archive

For distributions not directly supported via package management repositories, PowerShell can be installed from a binary archive. The steps are as follows:

```
# Download the PowerShell binary archive
wget https://github.com/PowerShell/PowerShell/releases/download/v7.1.3/powershell
    -7.1.3-linux-x64.tar.gz

# Create a target folder for the installation
mkdir ~/powershell

# Extract the file to the target folder
tar -xvf powershell-7.1.3-linux-x64.tar.gz -C ~/powershell

# Add PowerShell to the PATH
export PATH=$PATH:~/powershell

# Verify installation
pwsh --version
```

The binary distribution method ensures that PowerShell can be installed on most Linux distributions, provided the necessary dependencies are met.

Verifying Installation

To confirm a successful installation, execute:

```
pwsh -Command \$(\$PSVersionTable.PSVersion)
```

In the terminal, you should see output similar to:

```
Major  Minor  Patch  Pre-release Label
-----  -----  -----  -----------------
7      1      3
```

This verifies that PowerShell has been correctly installed and is functioning as expected. Hence, your Linux environment is now equipped with PowerShell, ready to run scripts and commands across different operating systems uniformly.

2.4 Updating PowerShell

Keeping your PowerShell up-to-date is essential for leveraging new features, performance improvements, and security patches. This section covers how to update PowerShell across different operating systems: Windows, macOS, and Linux. It also highlights the importance of determining the current installed version before proceeding with an update.

Determining the Current PowerShell Version

Before updating, it's crucial to know the current version of PowerShell installed on your system. You can determine this by executing the $PSVersionTable automatic variable. Here's how to do it:

```
$PSVersionTable.PSVersion
```

The output will display the version information in a System.Version object format.

```
Major  Minor  Build  Revision
-----  -----  -----  --------
6      2      3      0
```

Note the Major and Minor version numbers as these will help in determining the necessary update steps.

Updating PowerShell on Windows

On Windows, the update process can vary depending on whether you are using Windows PowerShell or PowerShell Core.

- Windows PowerShell: This version comes pre-installed with Windows and is updated via the Windows Update system. Ensure your Windows OS is up-to-date to get the latest version of Windows PowerShell.
- PowerShell Core: This can be updated using the MSI package. Follow these steps:
    1. Visit the [PowerShell GitHub releases page](https://github.com/PowerShell/PowerShell/releases).
    2. Download the latest MSI package that matches your system architecture.
    3. Run the installer and follow the on-screen instructions.
    4. Verify the update by rerunning $PSVersionTable.PSVersion.

Updating PowerShell on macOS

PowerShell on macOS is typically installed and updated using a package manager like Homebrew. Follow these steps to update:

```
brew update
brew upgrade --cask powershell
```

These commands update Homebrew itself and then the PowerShell package. Verify the installation by checking the version:

```
pwsh -v
```

PowerShell 7.2.0

Updating PowerShell on Linux

PowerShell updates on Linux systems can be managed using the package manager specific to the distribution. The steps provided cover common distributions.

Ubuntu/Debian:

```
sudo apt-get update
sudo apt-get upgrade powershell
```

CentOS/RHEL:

```
sudo yum update powershell
```

Fedora:

```
sudo dnf update powershell
```

After updating, verify the current version to ensure the update has been successfully applied.

```
pwsh -v
```

PowerShell 7.2.0

Checking for Pre-release Versions

You may wish to use a pre-release (preview) version of PowerShell to experiment with upcoming features. This can be done by downloading the appropriate package from the [PowerShell GitHub releases page](https://github.com/PowerShell/PowerShell/releases) and following the usual installation procedure for your operating system.

Automating PowerShell Updates

For environments where PowerShell is deployed to multiple systems, automating the update process can save time and ensure consistency. Windows environments can leverage Group Policy or WSUS (Windows Server Update Services) to manage updates, while macOS and Linux environments can use shell scripts.

Below is a sample PowerShell script that checks for the latest version and updates if necessary on Windows:

```
$currentVersion = $PSVersionTable.PSVersion
$latestVersion = (Invoke-RestMethod -Uri 'https://api.github.com/repos/PowerShell/
    PowerShell/releases/latest').tag_name

if ($currentVersion -ne $latestVersion) {
    Write-Host "Updating to PowerShell $latestVersion"
    $installer = "https://github.com/PowerShell/PowerShell/releases/download/
        $latestVersion/powershell-$latestVersion-win-x64.msi"
    Invoke-WebRequest -Uri $installer -OutFile "$env:temp\powershell-latest.msi"
    Start-Process msiexec.exe -ArgumentList "/i $env:temp\powershell-latest.msi /quiet
        " -Wait
    Remove-Item "$env:temp\powershell-latest.msi"
} else {
    Write-Host "PowerShell is up to date."
}
```

This script checks the PowerShell GitHub API for the latest release and compares it with the installed version. If an update is required, it downloads and installs the latest MSI package.

Keeping PowerShell up to date ensures access to the latest features, improved performance, and security enhancements. By integrating update checks into routine maintenance processes, system administrators can ensure a robust and secure scripting environment.

2.5 Setting Up PowerShell ISE

The PowerShell Integrated Scripting Environment (ISE) is an essential component for anyone aiming to proficiently script using PowerShell. PowerShell ISE provides a comprehensive environment for writing, testing, and debugging PowerShell scripts. By default, PowerShell ISE is included with Windows, but in certain scenarios, additional steps might be necessary to ensure its optimal configuration and usage. This section elucidates these processes to ensure your ISE is set up for maximum productivity.

Launching PowerShell ISE To initiate the PowerShell ISE, follow these steps:

- Press Win + R to open the Run dialog.
- Type powershell_ise.exe and press Enter.
- Alternatively, you can search for powershell ise in the Start menu and select the corresponding application.

Navigating the ISE Interface The ISE interface comprises several key components:

- The Script Pane: This is where you write and edit scripts.
- The Console Pane: This is where you execute commands, akin to the standard PowerShell console.
- The Command Add-on Pane: This optional pane helps with command discovery and can be toggled with Ctrl + D.

Customizing the ISE Environment Customizing the ISE allows you to tailor it to your scripting requirements. The customization options include altering the color scheme, font size, and layout.

```
# Changing the color scheme to 'Monokai'
$psISE.Options.ColorScheme = 'Monokai'

# Changing the font size
$psISE.Options.FontSize = 14
```

Using Profiles in PowerShell ISE Profiles in PowerShell ISE help automate the customization and setup processes each time the ISE is launched. To create or edit a profile, execute the following command:

```
# Ensuring the profile exists
if(-not (Test-Path -Path $profile)){
    New-Item -ItemType File -Path $profile -Force
}

# Opening the profile for editing
notepad $profile
```

In the profile file, you can define functions, aliases, and other preferences that should be loaded with your ISE.

Leveraging Add-ons and Snippets PowerShell ISE supports the use of add-ons and snippets to enhance scripting efficiency.

- Add-ons: The ISE add-ons can be used to extend its functionality. You can import add-ons using modules that define the add-on scripts.

  ```
  Import-Module -Name MyCustomAddOn
  ```

- Snippets: Snippets are predefined code blocks that can be quickly inserted into the script pane. To create a snippet, follow these steps:

  ```
  $snip = @'
  <CodeSnippet Format="1.0.0">
      <Header>
          <Title>MySnippet</Title>
          <Description>
          Custom code snippet example
          </Description>
          <Shortcut>custom</Shortcut>
      </Header>
      <Snippet>
          <Code Language="Powershell">
              <![CDATA[
              # Your code here
              ]]>
          </Code>
      </Snippet>
  ```

```
</CodeSnippet>
'@

$snip | Out-File -FilePath "$env:USERPROFILE\Documents\
    WindowsPowerShell\Snippets\MySnippet.snippet"
```

Debugging in PowerShell ISE ISE offers robust debugging features that facilitate the identification and resolution of errors in your scripts. Key features include breakpoints, stepping through code, and variable inspection.

- To set a breakpoint, click the left margin next to the line number or use the Set-PSBreakpoint cmdlet.

```
Set-PSBreakpoint -Script MyScript.ps1 -Line 10
```

- To step through code, use the F11 key to step into functions and scripts, and F10 to step over them.
- Variable inspection can be performed using the debugging pane or cmdlets like Get-Variable.

Command IntelliSense and Syntax Highlighting PowerShell ISE enhances scripting productivity by providing command IntelliSense and syntax highlighting. These features help reduce errors and improve code readability.

- **Command IntelliSense**: As you type, PowerShell ISE suggests cmdlets, parameters, and parameter values. Use Tab to auto-complete.
- **Syntax Highlighting**: Automatic color coding helps differentiate between command types, variables, and strings.

Saving and Running Scripts Scripts can be saved and executed directly from PowerShell ISE.

```
# To save a script
# Navigate to File > Save or press Ctrl+S

# To run a script
# Press F5 or click on the 'Run Script' button in the toolbar
```

Careful configuration and utilization of PowerShell ISE can significantly streamline scripting workflows, offering a powerful, user-friendly platform for developing PowerShell scripts. Employing the ISE features efficiently ensures a robust and productive scripting environment.

2.6 Setting Up Visual Studio Code for PowerShell

Setting up Visual Studio Code (VS Code) for PowerShell scripting requires a series of installations and configurations to ensure an optimized environment for writing and debugging scripts. VS Code is a highly extensible source-code editor that supports various programming languages, including PowerShell. Follow these instructions to prepare your VS Code environment for PowerShell.

- **Install Visual Studio Code**
  - **Windows:** Download the VS Code installer for Windows from the official website https://code.visualstudio.com/. Run the downloaded executable file and follow the installation steps.

```
# Example Visual Studio Code installation for Windows
VSCodeSetup-x64-<version>.exe
```

  - **macOS:** Download the VS Code package for macOS from the official website https://code.visualstudio.com/. Open the downloaded .dmg file and drag the Visual Studio Code.app to the Applications folder.

```
# Example Visual Studio Code installation on macOS
code-<version>.dmg
```

  - **Linux:** For Debian-based distributions, download and install the .deb package:

```
# Installation on Debian-based Linux
sudo apt install ./<package>.deb
```

    For Red Hat-based distributions, download and install the .rpm package:

```
# Installation on Red Hat-based Linux
sudo rpm -ivh <package>.rpm
```

- **Install PowerShell Extension for Visual Studio Code** Install the PowerShell extension to enable editing, running, and debugging PowerShell scripts within VS Code.

  - Open Visual Studio Code.
  - Navigate to the Extensions view by clicking on the Extensions icon in the Activity Bar on the side of the window, or by pressing Ctrl+Shift+X (Windows/Linux) or Cmd+Shift+X (macOS).
  - Enter *PowerShell* in the search bar and select *PowerShell* by Microsoft from the search results.
  - Click the *Install* button.

  The following is an example of searching and installing the PowerShell extension using the command palette:

```
# Command to open the command palette and install PowerShell extension
Ctrl+P (Windows/Linux) or Cmd+P (macOS)
ext install ms-vscode.PowerShell
```

- **Configure PowerShell as the Default Terminal**

  To configure PowerShell as the default integrated terminal:

  - Open VS Code settings via File > Preferences > Settings (Ctrl+, on Windows/Linux, Cmd+, on macOS).
  - Search for Terminal Integrated Shell.
  - In the settings, choose the appropriate shell path.
  - For Windows, set pwsh.exe as the default:

```
"terminal.integrated.shell.windows": "C:\\Program Files\\
    PowerShell\\<version>\\pwsh.exe"
```

  - For macOS, the path is typically:

```
"terminal.integrated.shell.osx": "/usr/local/bin/pwsh"
```

  - For Linux distributions, the path is commonly:

```
"terminal.integrated.shell.linux": "/usr/bin/pwsh"
```

- **Set Up Debugging for PowerShell**

  The PowerShell extension adds debugging support for PowerShell scripts. Configure debugging with the following steps:

- Open the Debug view by clicking the Debug icon in the Activity Bar on the side of the window or using Ctrl+Shift+D (Windows/Linux) or Cmd+Shift+D (macOS).
- Click on create a launch.json file link, then select *PowerShell*, which will create a launch.json file with default PowerShell configurations.
- The generated launch.json might look like the following:

```
{
    "version": "0.2.0",
    "configurations": [
        {
            "type": "PowerShell",
            "request": "launch",
            "name": "PowerShell Launch Script",
            "script": "${workspaceFolder}/<script>.ps1",
            "args": []
        }
    ]
}
```

- **Customize Settings for Enhanced Productivity**

  Modify the VS Code settings to enhance productivity when working with PowerShell scripts:

  - Navigate to File > Preferences > Settings (Ctrl+, on Windows/Linux, Cmd+, on macOS).
  - Use the search bar to find and tweak settings like powershell.codeFormatting.preset to apply desired formatting conventions:

```
"powershell.codeFormatting.preset": "OTBS"
```

  - Adjust the powershell.integratedConsole.showOnStartup setting to control the console's startup behavior:

```
"powershell.integratedConsole.showOnStartup": false
```

- **Leverage IntelliSense and Snippets**

  With the PowerShell extension, leverage IntelliSense and snippets to improve coding efficiency:

  - *IntelliSense* provides code completions for cmdlets, functions, and variables as you type.
  - *Snippets* are predefined code templates that insert commonly-used PowerShell constructs.

- Use IntelliSense by typing a cmdlet and pressing TAB to autocomplete:

```
# Example of using IntelliSense
Get-Process | Sort-Object -Property CPU
```

- Use snippets by typing a keyword and pressing TAB twice:

```
# Sample usage of PowerShell snippet
# Type "for" and press TAB twice
for ($i = 0; $i -lt 10; $i++) {
    <script here>
}
```

2.7 Configuring Execution Policies

Understanding and configuring execution policies in PowerShell is fundamental to ensuring that scripts run under the appropriate security context on your system. Execution policies are essentially the settings that determine which PowerShell scripts, if any, are allowed to run on a machine. These policies are not designed to be a security system to prevent the execution of untrusted scripts. Rather, they serve to help prevent the inadvertent execution of potentially harmful scripts by enforcing a level of script verification.

Execution policies can be set in several scopes, such as the local machine, the current user, and the current process. The most commonly used execution policies include:

- Restricted: Does not allow any scripts to run.
- AllSigned: Requires that all scripts and configuration files be signed by a trusted publisher.
- RemoteSigned: Requires that all scripts and configuration files downloaded from the internet be signed by a trusted publisher.
- Unrestricted: Allows all scripts and configuration files to run. Warns the user before running scripts and configuration files downloaded from the internet.
- Bypass: Nothing is blocked and no warnings or prompts are given.
- Undefined: Removes the execution policy from the current scope, reverting to the default policy, which is Restricted in most environments.

To check the current execution policy, the Get-ExecutionPolicy cmdlet is used. This cmdlet can display the execution policy for different scopes depending on the parameters provided.

```
Get-ExecutionPolicy
Get-ExecutionPolicy -List
Get-ExecutionPolicy -Scope CurrentUser
Get-ExecutionPolicy -Scope LocalMachine
```

The output will be as follows:

```
Restricted
MachinePolicy: Undefined
UserPolicy: Undefined
Process: Undefined
CurrentUser: Undefined
LocalMachine: Restricted
```

To change the execution policy, administrators can use the Set-ExecutionPolicy cmdlet. It is recommended to run this cmdlet with Administrator privileges to ensure that changes are applied properly:

```
Set-ExecutionPolicy -ExecutionPolicy RemoteSigned -Scope CurrentUser
```

The -Scope parameter specifies the scope for which the policy is being set. If it is omitted, the policy is set for the LocalMachine scope by default.

The following example sets the execution policy to RemoteSigned for the current user scope:

```
Set-ExecutionPolicy -ExecutionPolicy RemoteSigned -Scope CurrentUser
```

If you want to ensure that a script can run regardless of the system's assigned execution policy, you can temporarily change the execution policy for the duration of that script's execution. This is achieved by using the -ExecutionPolicy parameter in the powershell.exe command:

```
powershell.exe -ExecutionPolicy Bypass -File .\example.ps1
```

To force the policy change without confirming it interactively, you can append the -Force parameter:

```
Set-ExecutionPolicy -ExecutionPolicy Unrestricted -Force
```

Handling execution policies securely is crucial. Often, an environment may require custom scripts that are not signed. For these scenarios, setting the execution policy to RemoteSigned allows for a balance between security and flexibility since it permits the execution of unsigned scripts as long as they originate from the local machine.

It's equally vital to understand the implications of each setting in order to implement them responsibly. Systems and scripts that are not vetted and signed may introduce risks if allowed to run unchecked. Careful and prudent configuration of execution policies can mitigate such risks, providing a secure yet functional scripting environment for administrators and users alike.

Within enterprise settings, it is common practice to enforce execution policies through Group Policies applied to user and machine scopes. This ensures compliance with corporate security policies and reduces the likelihood of inadvertent script execution.

The following example demonstrates how to enforce an AllSigned execution policy at the local machine scope:

```
Set-ExecutionPolicy -ExecutionPolicy AllSigned -Scope LocalMachine
```

Execution policies can be overridden by using the -Scope parameter to specify a more restrictive policy within a more specific scope, such as the current user or process. This flexibility allows administrators to tailor execution policies precisely according to security requirements and operational needs.

By properly configuring execution policies, we can create a secure baseline for script execution, aid in script validation, and reduce the risk posed by potentially harmful scripts.

2.8 Customizing Your PowerShell Profile

PowerShell profiles enable users to personalize their shell environment for enhanced productivity and convenience. A PowerShell profile is essentially a script that runs every time PowerShell starts. This allows users to customize their command prompt, automatically load modules, set aliases, define functions, and configure environment variables.

PowerShell provides several profile locations to allow for varying levels of customization. These profiles are stored in different paths corresponding to the scope of their execution. The following list itemizes the various profiles:

- All Users, All Hosts: $PROFILE.AllUsersAllHosts
- All Users, Current Host: $PROFILE.AllUsersCurrentHost

- Current User, All Hosts: $PROFILE.CurrentUserAllHosts
- Current User, Current Host: $PROFILE.CurrentUserCurrentHost

The $PROFILE variable contains the fully qualified path to these profile scripts. The most commonly modified profile is the one specific to the current user and the current host, which can be accessed via $PROFILE or $PROFILE.CurrentUserCurrentHost.

To determine if a profile file exists, you can check the value of the relevant $PROFILE variable:

```
Test-Path $PROFILE
```

If the file does not exist, you should create it. Creating the profile for the current user and current host involves using the following command, which creates the necessary directory path if it does not already exist:

```
if (!(Test-Path -Path $PROFILE)) {
    New-Item -Type File -Path $PROFILE -Force
}
```

Once the profile file is ready, it can be edited using any text editor. For instance, to edit the profile using Visual Studio Code, you can invoke the following command:

```
code $PROFILE
```

Inside the profile, you can place any valid PowerShell commands. Common customizations include setting aliases, creating functions, and loading modules:

```
# Setting an alias
Set-Alias ll Get-ChildItem

# Defining a function
function Show-SystemInfo {
    Get-ComputerInfo | Select-Object CsName, WindowsVersion, CsPhysicalMemory
}

# Loading a module
Import-Module Az
```

These customizations are executed every time a new PowerShell session is started, providing a streamlined and personalized environment.

Lastly, it's essential to understand the security implications of modifying PowerShell profiles. Because profiles can execute any arbitrary script, it is imperative to secure profile scripts with appropriate file permissions to prevent unauthorized tampering. Ensuring the script's integrity helps maintain the intended configuration and user environment.

To verify the effective execution policy and make sure that the profile can run without issues, you can execute the following command:

```
Get-ExecutionPolicy
```

If necessary, the execution policy can be modified using:

```
Set-ExecutionPolicy -ExecutionPolicy RemoteSigned -Scope CurrentUser
```

Customizing your PowerShell profile significantly enhances the productivity and efficiency of your PowerShell environment by automating routine tasks and setting up your preferred configurations.

2.9 Useful PowerShell Modules and How to Install Them

PowerShell modules are packages of cmdlets, functions, workflows, variables, and aliases that enable administrators to manage complex tasks efficiently and effectively. Installing and leveraging these modules can significantly enhance your PowerShell scripting capabilities. Below, we will discuss several essential PowerShell modules and provide step-by-step instructions on how to install them.

Installing PowerShell Modules from the PowerShell Gallery

The PowerShell Gallery is a central repository for PowerShell content such as modules, scripts, and DSC resources. The easiest way to install modules from the PowerShell Gallery is by using the Install-Module cmdlet. Before installing any module, it is recommended to update the PowerShellGet module to ensure you have the latest version.

```
# Update PowerShellGet module
Install-Module -Name PowerShellGet -Force -AllowClobber

# Verify the installation
Get-Module -Name PowerShellGet -ListAvailable
```

Essential PowerShell Modules

- PSReadLine - Enhances the command-line editing experience with features such as syntax highlighting, multiline editing, and history search.

- Pester - A testing framework for PowerShell scripts and modules, enabling unit and integration testing.
- Az - A module designed for managing Azure resources.
- ActiveDirectory - Provides cmdlets for managing Active Directory.
- SqlServer - Contains cmdlets for managing SQL Server.

Installing the PSReadLine Module

The PSReadLine module improves command-line editing in PowerShell and offers features like syntax coloring, command-line completion, and better history management.

```
# Install the PSReadLine module
Install-Module -Name PSReadLine -Scope CurrentUser

# Import the module to start using it
Import-Module -Name PSReadLine

# Verify the installation
Get-Module -Name PSReadLine -ListAvailable
```

Installing the Pester Module

The Pester module is essential for conducting unit tests in PowerShell. It ensures that your scripts and modules work as expected by providing a framework for writing and running tests.

```
# Install the Pester module
Install-Module -Name Pester -Scope CurrentUser

# Verify the installation
Get-Module -Name Pester -ListAvailable
```

Installing the Az Module

The Az module is a comprehensive module for managing Azure resources. Frequent updates ensure that it supports the latest Azure features and services.

```
# Install the Az module
Install-Module -Name Az -Scope CurrentUser

# Verify the installation
Get-Module -Name Az -ListAvailable

# Import the module
Import-Module -Name Az
```

Installing the ActiveDirectory Module

The ActiveDirectory module allows administrators to manage Active Directory components such as users, groups, and computers.

```
# Install the RSAT tools if not already installed (Windows 10)
Add-WindowsCapability -Online -Name Rsat.ActiveDirectory.DS-LDS.Tools

# Import the ActiveDirectory module
Import-Module -Name ActiveDirectory

# Verify the installation
Get-Module -Name ActiveDirectory -ListAvailable
```

Installing the SqlServer Module

The SqlServer module provides cmdlets for managing SQL Server instances, databases, and other related objects.

```
# Install the SqlServer module
Install-Module -Name SqlServer -Scope CurrentUser

# Verify the installation
Get-Module -Name SqlServer -ListAvailable

# Import the module
Import-Module -Name SqlServer
```

Handling Module Conflicts and Dependencies

When installing multiple modules that may have conflicting cmdlets or functions, use the -AllowClobber parameter to overwrite the existing cmdlets. This ensures that you are using the specific cmdlet from the module you intend to use.

```
# Example of using -AllowClobber
Install-Module -Name ModuleName -Scope CurrentUser -AllowClobber
```

Updating Installed Modules

Keep all your modules up-to-date to benefit from the latest features and bug fixes. Use the Update-Module cmdlet to update modules installed from the PowerShell Gallery.

```
# Update all installed modules
Update-Module

# Update a specific module
Update-Module -Name ModuleName
```

Uninstalling Modules

If you need to remove a module that is no longer required, use the Uninstall-Module cmdlet.

```
# Uninstall a specific module
```

```
Uninstall-Module -Name ModuleName -AllVersions
```

Understanding these concepts and commands will significantly enhance your ability to manage your PowerShell environment. Mastering how to install, update, and manage PowerShell modules allows for a more streamlined and efficient administration of resources.

2.10 Navigating the PowerShell Help System

The PowerShell Help system is a comprehensive resource for understanding cmdlets, functions, workflows, aliases, providers, and scripts. It is designed to offer detailed documentation about each component within PowerShell. Users can efficiently navigate and utilize this system to enhance their scripting and command-line proficiency.

The primary cmdlet to access the help system is Get-Help. This cmdlet provides syntax details, parameter descriptions, usage examples, and more. The following example demonstrates its basic usage:

```
Get-Help Get-Process
```

The command Get-Help Get-Process retrieves detailed information about the Get-Process cmdlet.

To access more detailed help documentation, including examples, use the -Full parameter:

```
Get-Help Get-Process -Full
```

This command expands the basic help to include complete parameter definitions, detailed descriptions, and additional examples. For users who require only examples without full documentation, the -Examples parameter focuses solely on practical usage scenarios:

```
Get-Help Get-Process -Examples
```

To explore the syntax in greater depth, particularly useful for understanding the correct structure of cmdlets and parameters, use the -Syntax parameter:

```
Get-Help Get-Process -Syntax
```

To access online help with updated, comprehensive information, including intricate details that may not be available offline, the -Online parameter redirects users to Microsoft's official documentation:

```
Get-Help Get-Process -Online
```

The Update-Help cmdlet is crucial for maintaining up-to-date help files. This cmdlet downloads the newest help documentations from the internet. It is recommended to execute this periodically:

```
Update-Help
```

If an elevated permissions environment is required, open PowerShell as an administrator to execute Update-Help without encountering access issues.

For localized help information, you can specify the culture using the -UICulture parameter with Get-Help:

```
Get-Help Get-Process -UICulture en-US
```

Additionally, Get-Help accommodates wildcard characters to search for cmdlets or topics matching a pattern:

```
Get-Help *Process*
```

This retrieves all help topics related to the keyword Process.

Get-Command is another valuable cmdlet, complementing Get-Help, by discovering cmdlets, functions, workflows, aliases, and more:

```
Get-Command -Name Get-Process
```

To explore commands provided by specific modules, use the -Module parameter:

```
Get-Command -Module Microsoft.PowerShell.Management
```

The Help function is a user-friendly alias for Get-Help. It can be used interchangeably to retrieve help content:

```
Help Get-Process
```

For deeper insight into parameter sets, utilize the Get-Help cmdlet By typing either Ctrl and \ keys after parameter name while using Get-Help:

```
Get-Help New-Item -Parameter Ctrl\ \
```

Get-Help not only supports cmdlets but also provides invaluable insights into scripts, workflows, and providers. To harness its potential fully:

- Regularly update help files with Update-Help.
- Leverage the -Online parameter for the latest documentation.
- Utilize -Examples to understand practical applications of cmdlets.

Continuously engaging with the PowerShell Help system augments one's scripting capabilities, ensuring proficient command-line and scripting environments.

Chapter 3

Basic Concepts and Commands

This chapter introduces essential PowerShell concepts, including cmdlets, aliases, and basic navigation of the file system. It explores the use of parameters, the principles of the pipeline, and techniques for filtering and sorting data. Key topics such as output formatting, string manipulations, and the application of wildcards and regular expressions are discussed. Additionally, an overview of PowerShell providers is provided, equipping readers with foundational knowledge needed for effective script writing and command execution.

3.1 Understanding Cmdlets

Cmdlets, short for Command-lets, are the fundamental building blocks of PowerShell. They are specialized .NET classes which implement specific operations, comparable to functions in other scripting languages. The naming convention of cmdlets follows the verb-noun format, which enhances readability and predictability. For instance, Get-Content denotes a cmdlet that retrieves content, making it evident what action the cmdlet performs.

To discover cmdlets available in your PowerShell environment, you can use the Get-Command cmdlet. Below is an example demonstrating how to list cmdlets:

```
Get-Command
```

The above command retrieves all commands available in the session. To refine the search to cmdlets, you can specify the -CommandType parameter.

```
Get-Command -CommandType Cmdlet
```

Executing this command will list only cmdlets. The output will resemble:

```
CommandType     Name
-----------     ----
Cmdlet          Add-Content
Cmdlet          Get-Content
Cmdlet          Set-Content
...
```

Each cmdlet is designed to accomplish a specific task. Understanding the parameters available to cmdlets is essential for utilizing them effectively. For instance, the Get-Content cmdlet can retrieve the content of a specified file. Its basic usage is outlined below:

```
Get-Content -Path "C:\\example\\file.txt"
```

This command reads and displays the content of file.txt located in the C:
example directory. Parameters modify cmdlet behavior; for Get-Content, one can use -Encoding to specify file encoding:

```
Get-Content -Path "C:\\example\\file.txt" -Encoding UTF8
```

Cmdlets also support pipelining, which is a core feature in PowerShell allowing the output of one cmdlet to be used as input for another. For example, to get the content of all text files in a directory, you might use:

```
Get-ChildItem -Path "C:\\example" -Filter *.txt | Get-Content
```

Here, Get-ChildItem lists all .txt files within C:
example. This output is piped to Get-Content, which retrieves the content of each file.

Understanding the types of parameters is crucial for mastering cmdlet usage. Parameters can be mandatory or optional. Default values are used for optional parameters if they are not provided. Consider the Get-Process cmdlet:

```
Get-Process
```

This cmdlet retrieves all processes running on the system. You can refine the search by specifying the -Name parameter:

```
Get-Process -Name notepad
```

The above command will display processes named notepad.

Cmdlets can also use common parameters such as -Verbose, -Debug, -ErrorAction, and -WarningAction. These are standardized across all cmdlets and offer additional control over command execution. For instance,

```
Get-Content -Path "C:\\example\\file.txt" -Verbose
```

The -Verbose parameter provides more detailed output about what the cmdlet is doing during its execution. This can be particularly useful for debugging scripts or understanding command behavior.

Another important cmdlet is Get-Help, utilized to obtain detailed information about other cmdlets. For example, to learn more about the Get-Content cmdlet, execute:

```
Get-Help Get-Content
```

This displays a comprehensive help file for the Get-Content cmdlet, detailing its syntax, parameters, and examples.

Cmdlets can be extended by installing modules, which are collections of related cmdlets. To list available modules, use:

```
Get-Module -ListAvailable
```

For example, to use the Azure module to manage Azure resources, first ensure the module is installed, and then use cmdlets from that module:

```
Install-Module -Name Az
Import-Module -Name Az
Get-AzSubscription
```

Cmdlet development allows for extending PowerShell functionalities by creating custom cmdlets. Defined using C#, custom cmdlets compile to .NET assemblies. Below is a simplified example of a C# cmdlet class:

```
// Define the cmdlet class
[Cmdlet(VerbsCommon.Get, "CustomData")]
public class GetCustomDataCommand : Cmdlet
{
    [Parameter(Mandatory = true)]
    public string Input { get; set; }

    protected override void ProcessRecord()
```

```
    {
        WriteObject($"Input received: {Input}");
    }
}
```

Once compiled and loaded into PowerShell, this cmdlet can be executed like any built-in cmdlet:

```
Get-CustomData -Input "SampleInput"
```

Understanding how to utilize cmdlets effectively is paramount to leveraging the full power of PowerShell. This foundational knowledge is essential for building more complex scripts and automating tasks efficiently. Consequently, mastering the use of cmdlets forms a robust basis upon which advanced PowerShell functionalities can be explored.

3.2 Using Aliases

In PowerShell, an alias is an alternate name or shortcut for a cmdlet, function, script, executable file, or any other command element. Aliases provide a convenient way to simplify command input, reduce typing, and enhance readability. Although they are particularly useful for saving time in interactive sessions, they should be used judiciously in scripts to maintain clarity and ensure portability.

To create a PowerShell alias, the New-Alias cmdlet is employed. The syntax for New-Alias is straightforward:

```
New-Alias [-Name] <String> [-Value] <String> [-Description <String>] [-Option <
    ScopedItemOptions>]
```

Consider an example where we create an alias named ls for the Get-ChildItem cmdlet. This will allow us to list directory contents using the ls alias, which is shorter and reminiscent of UNIX-style commands:

```
New-Alias -Name ls -Value Get-ChildItem
```

Executing the following:

```
ls
```

will yield the same output as:

```
Get-ChildItem
```

```
    Directory: C:\Users\YourUserName


Mode                LastWriteTime         Length Name
----                -------------         ------ ----
d----        12/20/2022  10:23 AM                Documents
d----        11/15/2022  11:14 AM                Downloads
-a---         9/14/2022   8:35 PM           1024 notes.txt
```

To view all the aliases currently defined in your PowerShell session, use the Get-Alias cmdlet. This command lists all aliases along with the cmdlet names they reference:

```
Get-Alias
```

The output will look similar to the following:

```
CommandType     Name                                               Version    Source
-----------     ----                                               -------    ------
Alias           % -> ForEach-Object
Alias           ? -> Where-Object
Alias           cd -> Set-Location
Alias           cls -> Clear-Host
Alias           copy -> Copy-Item
Alias           cp -> Copy-Item
Alias           del -> Remove-Item
Alias           dir -> Get-ChildItem
Alias           ls -> Get-ChildItem
Alias           mv -> Move-Item
Alias           rm -> Remove-Item
```

For a more specific inquiry, you can use the Get-Alias cmdlet followed by the alias name:

```
Get-Alias ls
```

which results in:

```
Get-Alias ls

CommandType     Name                                               Version    Source
-----------     ----                                               -------    ------
Alias           ls -> Get-ChildItem
```

PowerShell allows for the removal and modification of aliases using Remove-Item and Set-Alias respectively:

To remove an alias:

```
Remove-Item Alias:\ls
```

To modify an existing alias or create a new alias with similar functionality:

```
Set-Alias -Name gci -Value Get-ChildItem
```

Now, gci will act as an alias for Get-ChildItem:

```
gci
```

will produce:

```
Directory: C:\Users\YourUserName


Mode            LastWriteTime        Length Name
----            -------------        ------ ----
d----     12/20/2022  10:23 AM              Documents
d----     11/15/2022  11:14 AM              Downloads
-a---      9/14/2022   8:35 PM         1024 notes.txt
```

The Export-Alias and Import-Alias cmdlets assist in maintaining alias consistency across sessions. To export aliases to a file:

```
Export-Alias -Path "C:\aliases.ps1"
```

To import the aliases in a subsequent session:

```
Import-Alias -Path "C:\aliases.ps1"
```

While aliases are instrumental for interactive use, their use in scripts should be minimized to avoid potential confusion or conflicts, especially when scripts are shared or maintained by different individuals. Frequent use of descriptive names through explicit cmdlets instead of cryptic aliases is recommended for scripts to enhance readability and maintainability.

3.3 Basic Navigation: Working with the File System

Navigating the file system is one of the fundamental tasks in PowerShell that every user should understand. PowerShell has a well-defined set of cmdlets for this purpose, making file and directory management intuitive and powerful. This section will cover the essential commands needed to navigate and manage the file system effectively.

To begin with, it is important to understand the current working directory. The Get-Location cmdlet retrieves the path of the current directory:

```
PS C:\> Get-Location
Path
----
C:\Users\Username
```

To change the current directory, use the Set-Location cmdlet, or its alias, cd. For example:

```
PS C:\> Set-Location C:\Scripts
```

Alternatively, using the alias:

```
PS C:\> cd C:\Scripts
```

To confirm the change, execute Get-Location:

```
PS C:\Scripts> Get-Location
Path
----
C:\Scripts
```

Listing the contents of a directory is done with the Get-ChildItem cmdlet, commonly aliased as dir or ls:

```
PS C:\Scripts> Get-ChildItem
```

The output will display files and directories in the current location:

```
    Directory: C:\Scripts
Mode              LastWriteTime        Length Name
----              -------------        ------ ----
-a----       1/1/2023  12:00 PM           120 script1.ps1
-a----       1/1/2023  12:01 PM           130 script2.ps1
d-----       1/1/2023  12:02 PM               MyScripts
```

Creating new directories is achieved with the New-Item cmdlet, specifying the item type as a directory using the -ItemType parameter:

```
PS C:\Scripts> New-Item -Path C:\Scripts\NewFolder -ItemType Directory

    Directory: C:\Scripts

Mode LastWriteTime Length Name
---- ------------- ------- ----
d----- 1/1/2023 12:03 PM NewFolder
```

To create files, use New-Item with the -ItemType parameter set to File:

```
PS C:\Scripts> New-Item -Path C:\Scripts\NewFolder\file1.txt -ItemType File

    Directory: C:\Scripts\NewFolder

Mode LastWriteTime Length Name
---- ------------- ------ ----
-a---- 1/1/2023 12:04 PM 0 file1.txt
```

Renaming files and directories is straightforward with the Rename-Item cmdlet:

```
PS C:\Scripts\NewFolder> Rename-Item -Path .\file1.txt -NewName file2.txt

    Directory: C:\Scripts\NewFolder
```

```
Mode LastWriteTime Length Name
---- ------------- ------ ----
-a---- 1/1/2023 12:04 PM 0 file2.txt
```

To copy items from one location to another, use Copy-Item. Here is an example of copying file2.txt to a new location:

```
PS C:\Scripts\NewFolder> Copy-Item -Path .\file2.txt -Destination C:\Scripts
```

Followed by confirming the file exists in the destination:

```
PS C:\Scripts> Get-ChildItem -Path C:\Scripts

    Directory: C:\Scripts

Mode LastWriteTime Length Name
---- ------------- ------ ----
-a---- 1/1/2023 12:04 PM 0 file2.txt
```

Moving items within the file system is accomplished with the Move-Item cmdlet:

```
PS C:\Scripts> Move-Item -Path file2.txt -Destination C:\Scripts\NewFolder
```

Confirming the file has moved:

```
PS C:\Scripts\NewFolder> Get-ChildItem

    Directory: C:\Scripts\NewFolder

Mode LastWriteTime Length Name
---- ------------- ------ ----
-a---- 1/1/2023 12:04 PM 0 file2.txt
```

To delete items, the Remove-Item cmdlet is used:

```
PS C:\Scripts\NewFolder> Remove-Item -Path .\file2.txt
```

Rechecking directory contents:

```
PS C:\Scripts\NewFolder> Get-ChildItem
```

```
    Directory: C:\Scripts\NewFolder

<no output>
```

Managing the file system in PowerShell involves knowing these cmdlets. Integrating them with scripting techniques maximizes their potential. Users need to further explore parameters and switches such as -Recurse, -Force, and -Filter to handle more complex scenarios, providing the flexibility and control PowerShell is known for. Here is the corrected LaTeX text of the section:

3.4 Understanding and Using Parameters

Parameters in PowerShell are a fundamental concept that allows for the customization and control of cmdlets' behavior. By providing specific values to parameters, users can influence how a cmdlet executes, fine-tuning its output to meet specific requirements.

A parameter in PowerShell can be thought of as an argument that modifies the behavior of a cmdlet. Each cmdlet comes with a set of predefined parameters that can be used to alter its default action. For example, the Get-ChildItem cmdlet, used to list directory contents, can be customized using various parameters like -Path, -Recurse, and -Filter.

To view a cmdlet's available parameters, you can utilize the Get-Help cmdlet:

```
Get-Help Get-ChildItem -Detailed
```

This command will display detailed help information for the Get-ChildItem cmdlet, including a list of all available parameters and their descriptions.

Mandatory and Optional Parameters

Parameters can be mandatory or optional. Mandatory parameters must be provided by the user for the cmdlet to execute, whereas optional parameters can be omitted. If a mandatory parameter is not provided, PowerShell prompts the user to supply the required value.

Consider the Read-Host cmdlet, which prompts the user for input. Its -Prompt parameter is optional:

```
Read-Host -Prompt "Enter your name"
```

Without the -Prompt parameter, the cmdlet still executes but without a user-friendly message. However, a parameter like the -Path in Get-ChildItem may often be required if the current directory context is not set appropriately.

Parameter Types

Parameters can accept various types of inputs such as strings, integers, arrays, and more complex objects. The type of each parameter is defined in the cmdlet's documentation. For instance, the -Filter parameter in Get-ChildItem expects a string value:

```
Get-ChildItem -Path "C:\\Logs" -Filter "*.log"
```

Positional Parameters

Parameters can be positional or named. Positional parameters allow you to omit the parameter name when providing its value. Position determines which value maps to which parameter:

```
Get-ChildItem "C:\\Logs"
```

In this case, "C:
Logs" is the value for the first positional parameter, -Path, of the Get-ChildItem cmdlet. Named parameters increase clarity, making scripts easier to read and maintain.

Switch Parameters

Switch parameters are boolean in nature, indicating a true or false condition simply by their presence or absence. For example, -Recurse in Get-ChildItem signifies that the cmdlet should include all items in the specified directory and its subdirectories:

```
Get-ChildItem -Path "C:\\Logs" -Recurse
```

Parameter Sets

Parameter sets allow a cmdlet to act differently based on the combination of parameters used. This provides flexibility within a single cmdlet to support diverse scenarios. By defining parameter sets, the cmdlet can offer various functionalities based on the parameters provided by the user. For example, the New-Item cmdlet can create both files and directories, distinguished by its parameter sets -ItemType File and -ItemType Directory:

```
New-Item -Path "C:\\Logs\\NewFile.txt" -ItemType File
New-Item -Path "C:\\Logs\\NewFolder" -ItemType Directory
```

Using Default Values

Some parameters have default values if not specified explicitly. For instance, the Format-Table cmdlet has a default setting for the -AutoSize switch:

```
Get-Process | Format-Table -AutoSize
```

Here, -AutoSize optimizes the column width based on the data but can be omitted if the default behavior is acceptable.

Advanced Parameter Features

PowerShell supports several advanced parameter attributes, such as making a parameter mandatory, validating its input, and setting default values. These are declared within a function or script and defined using attributes like [Parameter(Mandatory=$true)], [ValidateRange(1,100)], or [DefaultValue("DefaultValueText")].

```
function Example-Function {
    param (
        [Parameter(Mandatory=$true)]
        [string]$Name,

        [ValidateRange(1,100)]
        [int]$Count,

        [string]$Description = "Default Description"
    )
    Write-Output "Name: $Name"
    Write-Output "Count: $Count"
    Write-Output "Description: $Description"
}
```

This example defines a function with three parameters: a mandatory Name, a Count with validation ensuring it falls between 1 and 100, and an optional Description with a default value.

Pipeline Input

Parameters also determine whether a cmdlet can accept pipeline input. This feature allows the output of one cmdlet to be passed as an input parameter to another cmdlet, streamlining complex operations. For instance, the Select-Object cmdlet can take pipeline input:

```
Get-Process | Select-Object -Property Name, CPU
```

In this example, the output of Get-Process is piped into Select-Object, which processes each item in the pipeline, selecting and displaying only the Name and CPU properties.

PowerShell's parameter mechanism is a robust tool enabling precision and control, facilitating the creation of versatile, user-friendly scripts. Understanding how to leverage parameters effectively is fundamental to mastering PowerShell scripting.

3.5 Pipeline Concepts

In PowerShell, the pipeline is a fundamental concept enabling the passage of objects from one command to another. This facilitates streamlined data processing and command chaining, enhancing script readability and efficiency. The pipeline operator, represented by |, is used to separate commands in a pipeline sequence. Understanding the pipeline's behavior and capabilities is crucial for leveraging PowerShell's full potential.

When a command produces output, the PowerShell pipeline takes that output and passes it as an input to the next command. Each command in the pipeline processes the input objects and then passes the output objects along to the subsequent command. This continues until the final command in the pipeline executes. Consider the following example:

```
Get-Process | Where-Object { $_.CPU -gt 1 } | Sort-Object -Property CPU
```

In this pipeline, Get-Process retrieves all running processes, Where-Object filters the processes to include only those using more than 1 CPU second, and Sort-Object sorts the filtered processes by the CPU property.

To further dissect how the pipeline works, it's important to understand the role of the $ and $_ variables. The $_ variable is an automatic variable in PowerShell representing the current object in the pipeline. This variable is typically utilized within script blocks to perform operations on each object in the pipeline.

Let us take a deeper look at each component of the pipeline:

- **Get-Process**: This cmdlet retrieves the list of processes currently running on the system. The output consists of process objects, each containing information like Process ID, CPU usage, memory usage, etc.

```
PS> Get-Process

Handles NPM(K) PM(K) WS(K) VM(M) CPU(s) Id ProcessName
------- ------ ----- ----- ----- -------- -- -----------
139 5 1916 6884 48 12.23 1234 chrome
```

- **Where-Object**: The Where-Object cmdlet filters the objects passed down the pipeline based on a given condition. In this example, it checks if the CPU property of each process is greater than 1. The condition is defined within a script block enclosed in braces { }. The $_ variable represents the current object being processed.

```
Get-Process | Where-Object { $_.CPU -gt 1 }
```

```
Handles  NPM(K)    PM(K)      WS(K) VM(M)   CPU(s)     Id  ProcessName
-------  ------    -----      ----- ----- --------  --  -----------
139      5         1916       6884   48      12.23   1234  chrome
```

- **Sort-Object**: The Sort-Object cmdlet sorts the objects passed through the pipeline based on specified properties. In this example, the filtered list of processes is sorted by the CPU property.

```
Get-Process | Where-Object { $_.CPU -gt 1 } | Sort-Object -Property CPU
```

```
Handles  NPM(K)    PM(K)      WS(K) VM(M)   CPU(s)     Id  ProcessName
-------  ------    -----      ----- ----- --------  --  -----------
179      4         2200       7520   45      15.56   2345  notepad
139      5         1916       6884   48      12.23   1234  chrome
```

The pipeline's versatility extends beyond basic cmdlet chaining. PowerShell's ability to handle complex data structures in the pipeline input and output offers sophisticated data manipulation and processing. For instance, input can be filtered, sorted, grouped, formatted, and exported with a cohesive pipeline. Consider the following example, which demonstrates more advanced pipeline usage:

```
Get-Process | Where-Object { $_.CPU -gt 1 } | Sort-Object -Property CPU |
    Select-Object -Property Id, ProcessName, CPU |
    Export-Csv -Path 'C:\Processes.csv' -NoTypeInformation
```

Here, the Select-Object cmdlet is used to refine the output to include only the Id, ProcessName, and CPU properties, and Export-Csv exports the refined data to a CSV file.

ForEach-Object, another pivotal cmdlet in pipeline operations, processes each object individually. It is invoked with the -Process parameter, followed by a script block that executes for each pipeline object. Here's an example:

```
Get-Process | ForEach-Object -Process { $_.ProcessName }
```

The script block accesses the ProcessName property for each process, outputting the process names.

The Group-Object cmdlet aggregates objects based on a specified property, returning grouped object collections. This is useful for statistical summaries within script processing:

```
Get-Process | Group-Object -Property Company
```

```
Count Name                    Group
----- ----                    -----
   13 Microsoft Corporation   {powershell, svchost, ...}
    5 Unknown                 {chrome, notepad, ...}
```

Understanding outputs' format is crucial. Filtered data from Select-Object often needs precise shape for consumption by other applications or further PowerShell cmdlets.

Moreover, pipeline input can handle error objects via ErrorAction parameters or structured error handling cmdlets like Try, Catch, and Finally blocks. Error-handling provides robustness in scripts, ensuring fault-tolerance during the pipeline execution when working with uncertain input data.

Understanding and harnessing the PowerShell pipeline allows for complex, modular, and efficient scripts that process data streams intuitively. This will fundamentally enhance your script development skills and provide the necessary tools for sophisticated command chaining and processing sequences.

3.6 Filtering and Sorting Data

PowerShell provides robust capabilities for filtering and sorting data, enabling users to manipulate and manage data sets effectively. Filtering and sorting are indispensable for data analysis, reporting, and system management tasks. This section explores the essential cmdlets used for these purposes, such as Where-Object, Sort-Object, and various techniques to refine the output further.

To begin with filtering, PowerShell's Where-Object cmdlet allows you to filter objects based on their properties. It uses a script block to define the condition that each object must meet to be included in the output.

```
# Example: Filtering processes based on CPU usage
Get-Process | Where-Object {$_.CPU -gt 100}
```

In this example, Get-Process retrieves a list of all running processes. The pipeline ('|') sends these objects to Where-Object, which filters them to include only those with a CPU usage greater than 100.

The Where-Object cmdlet can also be used with various comparison operators: - -eq for equality, - -ne for inequality, - -lt for less than, - -le for less than or equal to, - -gt for greater than, - -ge for greater than or equal to.

You can combine multiple conditions using logical operators like -and, -or, and -not:

```
# Example: Filtering processes based on CPU usage and memory
Get-Process | Where-Object {$_.CPU -gt 100 -and $_.WorkingSet -lt 500MB}
```

Here, the script block specifies that processes must have a CPU usage greater than 100 and a working set (memory) less than 500MB.

In addition to filtering, sorting data is a fundamental task in data management. The Sort-Object cmdlet sorts objects based on the specified properties.

```
# Example: Sorting processes by CPU usage
Get-Process | Sort-Object -Property CPU
```

The -Property parameter specifies which property to sort by. By default, Sort-Object sorts in ascending order. To sort in descending order, use the -Descending switch.

```
# Example: Sorting processes by CPU usage in descending order
Get-Process | Sort-Object -Property CPU -Descending
```

You can sort by multiple properties by specifying a comma-separated list:

```
# Example: Sorting processes by CPU usage, then by process name
Get-Process | Sort-Object -Property CPU, Name
```

This command sorts processes first by CPU usage and then, among processes with the same CPU usage, by process name.

Filtering and sorting can be combined to achieve complex data manipulation:

```
# Example: Filtering processes by CPU usage, then sorting by working set size
Get-Process | Where-Object {$_.CPU -gt 50} | Sort-Object -Property WorkingSet
```

In this example, processes are first filtered to include only those with a CPU usage greater than 50. The resulting set is then sorted by the working set size (memory).

For more advanced needs, custom script blocks can be used to define sorting criteria:

```
# Example: Custom sorting based on a calculated property
Get-Process | Sort-Object -Property @{Expression={$_.CPU + $_.WorkingSet};
    Ascending=$true}
```

Here, a calculated property is used, represented by a hashtable. The Expression key contains a script block that calculates the value to sort by (in this case, the sum of CPU usage and working set size), and Ascending determines the sort order.

When dealing with large data sets or requiring specific types of filtering, more advanced cmdlets and techniques like Select-Object and Group-Object can be used in combination with the aforementioned cmdlets to refine data further.

Understanding how to effectively filter and sort data in PowerShell extends your ability to manage and analyze data efficiently, providing a solid foundation for scripting and automation tasks.

3.7 Formatting Output

The ability to format output effectively is essential for creating readable and easily interpretable scripts. PowerShell provides several mechanisms for customizing the display of output, which includes formatting tables, customizing object properties, and generating custom views.

Using Format Cmdlets: PowerShell includes a suite of formatting cmdlets that allow you to control the output display. The primary cmdlets are Format-Table, Format-List, Format-Wide, and Format-Custom.

- Format-Table: Presents output in a tabular format.
- Format-List: Displays output as a list of properties.
- Format-Wide: Shows a single property of an object per line.
- Format-Custom: Offers advanced customization options.

Format-Table is commonly used when the data contains multiple properties, and you want to see them in columns. For example, to display services with their names and statuses, you can use:

```
Get-Service | Format-Table -Property Name, Status
```

This will produce an output similar to:

```
Name            Status
----            ------
AdobeARMservice  Stopped
AppHostSvc        Running
Appinfo          Stopped
```

The -AutoSize parameter of Format-Table can automatically adjust column widths to fit the data:

```
Get-Service | Format-Table -Property Name, Status -AutoSize
```

Format-List is useful when you need a detailed view of object properties. It displays each property on a new line:

```
Get-Process | Format-List -Property Name, ID, CPU
```

This will result in:

```
Name       : explorer
Id         : 4568
CPU        : 2.255

Name       : powershell
Id         : 1123
CPU        : 23.890
```

For summarizing large volumes of data, Format-Wide can be used. It displays one property per line across multiple columns:

```
Get-Process | Format-Wide -Property Name -Column 2
```

And the output is:

```
explorer            powershell
svchost             services
```

Format-Custom allows you to define your own view for objects. This level of customization is done through the creation of XML files, which specify how objects should be displayed. An example is creating a ps1xml file defining custom formatting for a bespoke type.

Creating Custom Column Headers: You may need to customize column headers for clarity. The Select-Object cmdlet can be used in conjunction with hash tables to rename properties:

```
Get-Process | Select-Object @{Name='ProcessName';Expression={$_.Name}}, @{
    Name='ProcessID';Expression={$_.ID}} | Format-Table
```

Resulting in:

```
ProcessName   ProcessID
-----------   ---------
explorer      4568
powershell    1123
```

Out-GridView: For more interactive data exploration, PowerShell provides Out-GridView. This cmdlet opens a new window to display formatted output in a GUI grid, facilitating filtering and sorting:

```
Get-Service | Out-GridView
```

Launching the above command produces an interactive window where the user can filter and sort the columns as needed.

Exporting Data: PowerShell also supports exporting formatted data into various formats. Common exporting cmdlets include Export-Csv, ConvertTo-Json, and Export-Clixml.

Exporting services to a CSV file:

```
Get-Service | Export-Csv -Path services.csv -NoTypeInformation
```

This command creates a CSV file with the services information. Using -NoTypeInformation omits the type information line at the top of the file, which is often unnecessary for CSV data.

Converting data to JSON:

```
Get-Service | ConvertTo-Json
```

This outputs the service information as a JSON string, facilitating interoperability with web services and applications that consume JSON data.

Pipeline Considerations: It's crucial to understand that format cmdlets consume the pipeline input and do not pass objects down the pipeline. Thus, formatting should typically be the last operation in a command sequence. For example, the following will not work as intended:

```
Get-Process | Format-Table Name | Export-Csv -Path processes.csv
```

Instead, structure the command so exporting happens before formatting:

```
Get-Process | Select-Object Name | Export-Csv -Path processes.csv
```

Effective output formatting enhances the readability and comprehension of data, making it easier to analyze and communicate findings.

3.8 Basic String Manipulations

PowerShell offers a plethora of tools for text and string manipulation, which is a critical aspect of many scripts. String operations play a vital role in data processing, scripting, and automation tasks, enabling users to handle text data effectively. Whether it is concatenation, insertion, extraction, or modification of strings, gaining proficiency in string manipulations is essential for any PowerShell user.

Concatenation

String concatenation involves combining two or more strings into one. In PowerShell, the concatenation operator is the plus sign (+). This operator allows the addition of one string to another, creating a new string.

```
$string1 = "Hello"
$string2 = "World"
$result = $string1 + " " + $string2
Write-Output $result
```

```
Hello World
```

In the above example, $string1 and $string2 are concatenated with a space in between to form the resultant string "Hello World".

Substrings

Extracting substrings from a given string can be performed using the Substring() method. This method requires the starting index and may optionally include the length of the substring to be extracted.

```
$originalString = "PowerShell Scripting"
$substring1 = $originalString.Substring(0, 10)
$substring2 = $originalString.Substring(11)
Write-Output $substring1
Write-Output $substring2
```

```
PowerShell
Scripting
```

In the example, the Substring() method extracts "PowerShell" starting from index 0 and "Scripting" starting from index 11, demonstrating how substrings can be obtained.

String Length

The length of a string can be determined using the Length property. This property returns the number of characters in the string, which can be essential for various string operations.

```
$string = "PowerShell"
$length = $string.Length
Write-Output $length
```

```
10
```

Here, the length of the string "PowerShell" is determined to be 10 characters.

String Replacement

Replacing substrings within a string is another fundamental operation. The Replace() method facilitates this by substituting all occurrences of a specified substring with another substring.

```
$originalString = "Hello PowerShell"
$replacedString = $originalString.Replace("PowerShell", "World")
Write-Output $replacedString
```

```
Hello World
```

In this case, the Replace() method replaces "PowerShell" with "World", resulting in the string "Hello World".

String Splitting

Splitting a string into an array of substrings based on a delimiter is achieved using the Split() method. This method is particularly useful when parsing structured string data.

```
$originalString = "apple,orange,banana"
$array = $originalString.Split(',')
foreach ($item in $array) {
    Write-Output $item
}
```

```
apple
orange
banana
```

Here, the Split(',') method divides the string into an array using the comma (,) as a delimiter, producing the array elements "apple", "orange", and "banana".

Trimming

Trimming involves removing whitespace or other specified characters from the beginning and/or end of a string. The Trim(), TrimStart(), and TrimEnd() methods provide this functionality.

```
$stringWithSpaces = " PowerShell "
$trimmedString = $stringWithSpaces.Trim()
Write-Output $trimmedString
$trimmedStart = $stringWithSpaces.TrimStart()
Write-Output $trimmedStart
$trimmedEnd = $stringWithSpaces.TrimEnd()
Write-Output $trimmedEnd
```

```
PowerShell
PowerShell
  PowerShell
```

This demonstrates trimming the string " PowerShell " with different methods, yielding varied results based on whether both sides, the start, or the end are trimmed.

Case Conversion

Changing the case of a string is facilitated through the ToUpper() and ToLower() methods. These methods convert all characters in the string to uppercase or lowercase, respectively.

```
$string = "PowerShell"
$upperString = $string.ToUpper()
$lowerString = $string.ToLower()
Write-Output $upperString
Write-Output $lowerString
```

```
POWERSHELL
powershell
```

In this example, the ToUpper() and ToLower() methods convert "PowerShell" to "POWERSHELL" and "powershell" respectively.

Command parameter expansion uses $() for inline command expressions, enabling dynamic string content generation based on command output.

```
$currentDate = $(Get-Date)
$greetingString = "Hello, today is $currentDate"
Write-Output $greetingString
```

```
Hello, today is 04/15/2023 13:45:30
```

This renders a string that includes the current date and time, demonstrating the integration of command output within a string. Proficiency in these fundamental string manipulations enhances the versatility and robustness of PowerShell scripts.

3.9 Wildcards and Regular Expressions

Wildcards and regular expressions are essential tools for pattern matching and string manipulation in PowerShell. They allow for sophisticated query construction and data filtering, enabling users to perform complex searches with minimal effort. Understanding the distinctions and proper applications of wildcards and regular expressions will enhance your scripting capabilities significantly.

PowerShell supports wildcards in various cmdlets such as Get-ChildItem, Remove-Item, and others that interact with the file system or collections of objects. Wildcards provide a simple but powerful mechanism for pattern matching.

- * (asterisk) - Represents zero or more characters.
- ? (question mark) - Represents exactly one character.
- [ ] (square brackets) - Specifies a range or set of characters.
- [!] - Specifies characters not to be matched.

For instance, the asterisk (*) can be used to match any combination of characters in a file or directory name:

```
Get-ChildItem -Path "C:\Users\*\Documents"
```

This command retrieves documents from all user folders under C:\Users. Similarly, the question mark (?) can be used to match any single character:

```
Get-ChildItem -Path "C:\Users\Public\Doc?.txt"
```

This command will match Doc1.txt, Doc2.txt, and so on.

Square brackets ([]) allow for more specific matches. For example:

```
Get-ChildItem -Path "C:\Users\Public\Doc[123].txt"
```

This matches Doc1.txt, Doc2.txt, and Doc3.txt but not Doc4.txt.

Regular expressions (*regex*) in PowerShell offer even more flexibility and power for pattern matching. They are used in various cmdlets and operators, especially in the -match operator, where they provide extensive string manipulation capabilities.

A regular expression is a sequence of characters that defines a search pattern. Basic elements of regular expressions include:

- . (dot) - Matches any single character except newline.
- * (asterisk) - Matches zero or more of the preceding element.
- + (plus) - Matches one or more of the preceding element.
- { } (curly braces) - Specifies exact number or range of occurrences.
- [] (square brackets) - Matches any one of the enclosed characters.

- (|) (pipe inside parentheses) - Acts as a logical OR.
- \ (backslash) - Escapes special characters.

Consider using regular expressions to find a sequence of files:

```
Get-ChildItem | Where-Object { $_.Name -match '^Report[0-9]{4}\.txt$' }
```

This command uses the regex {Report}[0-9]{4}txt$ to match filenames starting with "Report" followed by a four-digit number and ending with ".txt". Here:

- ^ asserts the position at the start of a string.
- Report matches the literal characters "Report".
- [0-9]{4} matches exactly four digits.
- \. escapes the dot (.) so it matches a literal period.
- $ asserts the position at the end of a string.

Another powerful feature of regex is the ability to perform substitutions and replacements. Using the -replace operator, you can modify text based on a pattern:

```
"User123_script.ps1" -replace 'User(\d+)_', 'Admin$1_'
```

This command transforms "User123_script.ps1" into "Admin123_-script.ps1" by capturing the numeric part using $1, which references the first captured group.

Regular expressions can be particularly useful for text extraction, validation, or complex replacements within scripts. Here is an example using a sample text to extract email addresses:

```
$text = "Contact us at support@example.com or sales@example.org"
$emailRegex = "\b[A-Za-z0-9._%+-]+@[A-Za-z0-9.-]+\.[A-Z|a-z]{2,}\b"
$matches = $text -match $emailRegex
if ($matches) {
    $text -split "\s" | ForEach-Object {
        if ($_ -match $emailRegex) {
            Write-Output $_
        }
    }
}
```

This script defines an email regex [A-Za-z0-9._% +-]+@[A-Za-z0-9.-]+[A-Z|a-z]{2,}, which checks the input text for valid email addresses and then outputs each match.

Both wildcards and regular expressions elevate the proficiency level of PowerShell scripting, equipping users with versatile tools for numerous use cases. Proficiency in these techniques is crucial for administering and automating tasks efficiently and accurately.

3.10 Introduction to PowerShell Providers

PowerShell providers enable users to access different types of data stores via a unified interface. They bridge PowerShell cmdlets and various storage systems, presenting data in a consistent, navigable format similar to a file system structure. This section elaborates on the fundamental concepts, usage, and key providers available in PowerShell.

PowerShell providers abstract the underlying data sources and allow them to be accessed and manipulated as if they were hierarchical file systems. The cmdlets provided by these providers facilitate tasks such as navigation, retrieval, and alteration of data across different data stores.

Accessing Providers

To view the list of available providers on your system, use the Get-PSProvider cmdlet. This will display all currently registered providers along with relevant details.

```
Get-PSProvider
```

```
Name          Capabilities                          Drives
----          ------------                          ------
Registry      ShouldProcess                         {HKLM, HKCU}
Alias         ShouldProcess                         {Alias}
Environment   ShouldProcess                         {Env}
FileSystem    Filter, ShouldProcess, Credentials    {C, D}
Function      ShouldProcess                         {Function}
Variable      ShouldProcess                         {Variable}
Certificate   ShouldProcess                         {Cert}
```

Get-PSProvider lists providers such as FileSystem, Registry, Alias, Environment, Function, Variable, and Certificate. Each provider exposes data through a series of drives, similarly to how file systems use drives like C: or D:.

Navigating Providers

The provider drives are mapped just as traditional file system drives would be. You can use standard filesystem navigation cmdlets (Set-Location, Get-ChildItem, Remove-Item) for interacting with these data stores.

For example, to navigate to the environment variables, use the Env: drive:

```
Set-Location Env:
```

To list all the environment variables:

```
Get-ChildItem
```

```
Name                    Value
----                    -----
ALLUSERSPROFILE         C:\ProgramData
APPDATA                 C:\Users\User\AppData\Roaming
CommonProgramFiles      C:\Program Files\Common Files
CommonProgramFiles(x86) C:\Program Files (x86)\Common Files
NUMBER_OF_PROCESSORS    4
OS                      Windows_NT
```

Examples of Using Key Providers

FileSystem Provider

The FileSystem provider allows access to the file system, presenting a view similar to Windows Explorer. Essential cmdlets for this provider include Get-Item, Get-ChildItem, Copy-Item, Move-Item, Remove-Item, and New-Item.

To copy a file from one location to another:

```
Copy-Item -Path C:\FolderA\File.txt -Destination C:\FolderB\File.txt
```

Registry Provider

Similar to the file system, the registry is accessible using the Registry provider. The provider exposes two primary drives: HKLM: for HKEY_LOCAL_MACHINE and HKCU: for HKEY_CURRENT_USER.

To navigate to the HKEY_CURRENT_USER\Software path:

```
Set-Location HKCU:\Software
```

To view the keys under this path:

```
Get-ChildItem
```

```
Hive: HKEY_CURRENT_USER\Software

Name                Property
----                --------
Adobe               {}
Apple Inc.          {}
Microsoft           {}
Mozilla             {}
Oracle              {}
```

Alias Provider

The Alias provider maps command shortcuts to their full cmdlet names, making interaction more intuitive. To list all aliases:

```
Get-ChildItem Alias:
```

```
CommandType     Name                    Definition
-----------     ----                    ----------
Alias           %                       ForEach-Object
Alias           ?                       Where-Object
Alias           cd                      Set-Location
Alias           cp                      Copy-Item
Alias           del                     Remove-Item
```

You can create a new alias using New-Item or Set-Alias:

```
Set-Alias -Name list -Value Get-ChildItem
```

Environment Provider

The Environment provider offers access to environment variables. To modify an environment variable:

```
$env:Path = "$env:Path;C:\NewPath"
```

Variable Provider

The Variable provider handles PowerShell variables. To explore variables currently defined:

```
Get-ChildItem Variable:
```

```
Name                Value
----                -----
$                   C:\
PSHome              C:\Windows\System32\WindowsPowerShell\v1.0
PWD                 C:\Users\User
```

Creating a new variable is straightforward:

```
New-Item Variable:\MyVariable -Value "Hello World"
```

Certificate Provider

The Certificate provider exposes digital certificates stored in the certificate store. Access the Cert: drive to navigate the certificate hierarchy.

To list all certificates in the current user's personal store:

```
Get-ChildItem Cert:\CurrentUser\My
```

```
    PSParentPath: Microsoft.PowerShell.Security\Certificate::CurrentUser\My

Thumbprint                Subject
----------                -------
A1B2C3D4E5F6                CN=example.com, OU=IT, O=Example Corp, L=City, S=State, C=US
7C8D9EA101112               CN=anotherexample.com, OU=Finance, O=Example Corp, L=City, S=State, C=US
```

Providers integrate seamlessly with cmdlets, allowing intuitive navigation and manipulation of a variety of data stores.

Chapter 4

Working with Variables and Data Types

This chapter provides an in-depth look at variables and data types in PowerShell. It covers the creation and initialization of variables, understanding of PowerShell's data types, type conversion, and casting. Key topics such as working with arrays and hash tables, scoping rules, automatic variables, and handling null and empty values are discussed. Additionally, methods for storing and retrieving data persistently are examined, giving readers comprehensive knowledge on efficiently managing data within PowerShell scripts.

4.1 Introduction to Variables

Variables in PowerShell are fundamental building blocks that allow scripters to store, retrieve, and manipulate data. A variable, in essence, is a named space in the memory that holds a value. This section elucidates the nature, declaration, and basic manipulation of variables in PowerShell to lay a solid foundation for subsequent discussions on variable types, scoping, and data handling.

In PowerShell, variable names are prefixed by a dollar sign ($), followed by an identifier that adheres to specific naming rules. These rules dictate that variable names can contain alphanumeric characters and underscores (_), but cannot start with a number. They are case-insensitive by default.

Variables in PowerShell do not require an explicit declaration of type. Instead, they are dynamically typed, meaning their type is inferred from the value they are assigned. Here is an example of simple variable assignment and usage:

```
$greeting = "Hello, World"
Write-Output $greeting
```

```
Hello, World
```

In this example, $greeting is a variable that holds a string value. The Write-Output cmdlet is used to display the value of the variable.

PowerShell variables can store different types of data: strings, integers, arrays, hash tables, and even complex objects. This dynamic typing allows flexibility but requires cautious handling to avoid unintended behavior due to implicit type conversions.

Implicit type conversion can be illustrated with the following example:

```
$num = 5 # Integer
$stringNum = "10" # String
$result = $num + $stringNum
Write-Output $result
```

```
15
```

Here, $result holds the value 15 because PowerShell implicitly converts the string "10" into an integer before performing the addition. This implicit conversion can lead to errors if not carefully managed, especially in scripts handling mixed data types.

Consider the reassignment of variables. It is straightforward and simply overwrites the existing value:

```
$message = "Initial Message"
$message = "Updated Message"
Write-Output $message
```

```
Updated Message
```

In the above example, $message first holds the value "Initial Message", which is then updated to "Updated Message".

For a better understanding of variable scopes, it is crucial to grasp the concept of variable lifetime and accessibility within different script blocks, functions, or modules. PowerShell supports different scopes: global, local, script, and private. Understanding these scopes is essential for structuring scripts correctly and avoiding variable conflicts.

Automatic variables in PowerShell are predefined variables that store state information and can be used for various purposes, such as accessing the current pipeline item or the last error message. Examples include $_, which refers to the current object in the pipeline, and $Error, which contains an array of error objects from the most recent command.

To summarize, this section has introduced the basic concept of variables in PowerShell, their naming conventions, dynamic typing, and simple manipulations. Understanding these foundations prepares readers to delve deeper into variable types, conversions, and advanced topics in PowerShell scripting.

4.2 Variable Types and Their Usage

PowerShell variables can hold various types of data, including numbers, strings, arrays, and more. Understanding these variable types and their usage is crucial for writing efficient and functional PowerShell scripts. This section explores the major variable types in PowerShell, provides examples of their usage, and discusses when and why to use each type.

PowerShell variables are dynamically typed, meaning that the type of the variable is determined at runtime based on the value assigned to it. This flexibility allows for straightforward variable manipulation but requires an understanding of how PowerShell interprets different data types.

String Variables

String variables hold textual data. A string is a sequence of characters, such as letters, digits, symbols, and whitespace. In PowerShell, strings can be defined using double quotes (") or single quotes ('. Double-quoted strings allow for variable interpolation and escape characters, while single-quoted strings treat characters literally.

```
$name = "John Doe"
$greeting = 'Hello, World!'

# Using double quotes for variable interpolation
$message = "Welcome, $name"
```

name, greeting, and message are string variables. The message variable demonstrates string interpolation.

Integer and Floating-Point Variables

PowerShell distinguishes between integers (whole numbers) and floating-point numbers (numbers with decimal points). These numerical types allow for arithmetic operations and mathematical calculations.

```
$intNumber = 42
$floatNumber = 3.14
```

intNumber is an integer, and floatNumber is a floating-point number. Arithmetic operations can be performed on these variables directly.

```
# Addition
$sum = $intNumber + $floatNumber

# Multiplication
$product = $intNumber * 2
```

Boolean Variables

Boolean variables can hold one of two values: $True or $False. These are used for logical operations and conditional expressions.

```
$isTrue = $True
$isFalse = $False

if ($isTrue) {
    Write-Output "Condition is true."
} else {
    Write-Output "Condition is false."
}
```

isTrue and isFalse are boolean variables that control the flow of logic in conditional statements.

Array Variables

Arrays store multiple values in a single variable. Each value (or element) in an array is indexed, allowing for sequential access.

```
$numbers = 1, 2, 3, 4, 5

# Accessing array elements
$firstNumber = $numbers[0]

# Modifying array elements
$numbers[1] = 10

# Adding elements to the array
$numbers += 6
```

numbers is an array variable. Arrays are particularly useful for storing collections of related elements.

Hash Table Variables

Hash tables, also known as dictionaries or associative arrays, store key-value pairs. Each entry in a hash table consists of a unique key and a value associated with that key. Hash tables are beneficial for managing data with named keys.

```
$person = @{
    Name = "John"
    Age = 30
    City = "New York"
}

# Accessing hash table elements
$name = $person["Name"]

# Adding a new key-value pair
$person["Country"] = "USA"
```

person is a hash table variable containing information about an individual. Hash tables allow easy access and modification of data using keys.

Variable types in PowerShell are versatile and provide the means to handle various kinds of data effectively. Using the correct variable type based on the context and requirements of your script is essential for optimal performance and readability. Understanding how to work with each type enhances your ability to write robust and efficient PowerShell scripts.

4.3 Creating and Initializing Variables

In PowerShell, variables are used to store data that can be retrieved, modified, and manipulated during script execution. A variable in PowerShell is denoted by a dollar sign ($) followed by the variable name. Variable names in PowerShell are not case-sensitive, meaning that $Var, $var, and $VAR refer to the same variable.

The process of creating and initializing variables in PowerShell is straightforward. The syntax to create a variable and assign it a value is:

```
$variableName = value
```

Here, $variableName is the name of the variable, and value is the data assigned to it. Variables in PowerShell do not require explicit declaration before initialization, allowing dynamic typing based on the assigned value.

Example: Basic Variable Initialization

```
$greeting = "Hello, World!"
$year = 2023
$pi = 3.14159
$isPowerShellFun = $true
```

In this example: - $greeting is assigned a string value "Hello, World!". - $year is assigned an integer value 2023. - $pi is assigned a floating-point number. - $isPowerShellFun is assigned a Boolean value $true.

Assigning Values to Multiple Variables

PowerShell allows multiple variables to be initialized at once by separating each assignment with a semicolon. This can be useful for organizing code and initializing related variables together:

```
$name = "Alice"; $age = 29; $occupation = "Engineer"
```

This initialization assigns "Alice" to $name, 29 to $age, and "Engineer" to $occupation.

Initializing Variables with Expressions

Variables can also be initialized using expressions, including arithmetic operations, function calls, and concatenations:

```
$sum = 5 + 3
$product = 7 * 6
$datetime = Get-Date
$fullName = $firstName + " " + $lastName
```

In this example: - $sum is initialized with the result of 5 + 3. - $product is initialized with the product of 7 and 6. - $datetime is initialized with the current date and time retrieved by the Get-Date cmdlet. - $fullName is the concatenated result of $firstName and $lastName with a space in between.

Array Initialization

Arrays in PowerShell are a collection of items stored in a single variable. To initialize an array, use the following syntax:

```
$array = @(item1, item2, item3)
```

Example:

```
$numbers = @(1, 2, 3, 4, 5)
$words = @("apple", "banana", "cherry")
```

This syntax initializes $numbers with an array of integers and $words with an array of strings.

Hash Table Initialization

Hash tables in PowerShell are collections of key-value pairs. To initialize a hash table:

```
$hashTable = @{key1 = value1; key2 = value2}
```

Example:

```
$person = @{
    Name = "Bob"
    Age = 30
    Occupation = "Developer"
}
```

This code creates a hash table stored in the variable $person with the specified keys and values.

Handling Null Values

To denote a variable with no value, use $null. This is particularly useful when initializing variables intended to be populated later in the script:

```
$emptyVar = $null
```

Assigning $null to a variable ensures that it exists and can be checked later for a value.

Updating Variable Values

Once a variable is initialized, its value can be updated simply by reassigning it:

```
$greeting = "Goodbye, World!"
$year = 2024
```

In this example, $greeting is updated to a new string, and $year to a new integer.

PowerShell's flexibility allows dynamic variable creation and initialization, promoting effortless data management throughout your scripting tasks.

4.4 Understanding PowerShell Data Types

PowerShell, an object-oriented scripting language, leverages the .NET type system, offering comprehensive support for diverse data types. Mastery of these data types is crucial for writing efficient and effective PowerShell scripts. This section delves into the fundamental data types supported by PowerShell and illustrates how they are leveraged within scripts.

PowerShell supports several primary data types:

- **Strings**
- **Integers**
- **Floating-point numbers**
- **Booleans**
- **Arrays**
- **Hash tables**
- **Custom objects**

Strings are sequences of characters and are defined using either single or double quotes. Single-quoted strings are literal and do not expand variables or expressions within them. Double-quoted strings allow for variable expansion and expression evaluation:

```
$singleQuoted = 'This is a literal $string.'
$doubleQuoted = "This is an expanded string with variable: $variable"
```

Outputting the `$singleQuoted` and `$doubleQuoted` variables illustrates this distinction:

```
This is a literal $string.
This is an expanded string with variable: <value of $variable>
```

Integers and **Floating-point numbers** are numerical data types where integers are whole numbers and floating-point numbers allow for decimal points. PowerShell implicitly determines the data type of numerical values based on the presence of a decimal point:

```
$integerValue = 42
$floatingPointValue = 42.0
```

To check the type of a variable, the `GetType()` method can be useful:

```
$integerValue.GetType()
$floatingPointValue.GetType()
```

```
IsPublic IsSerial Name  BaseType
-------- -------- ----  --------
True     True     Int32 System.ValueType
True     True     Double System.ValueType
```

Booleans are binary values representing $true or $false. They are primarily used for control flow and logical operations:

```
$isTrue = $true
$isFalse = $false

if ($isTrue -and -not $isFalse) {
    Write-Output "Condition is met."
}
```

Arrays are collections of values, allowing the storage of multiple items in a single variable. They are defined using the @() syntax:

```
$array = @(1, 2, 3, "four", 5.0)
```

To access array elements, index notation is used:

```
$firstElement = $array[0]
$secondElement = $array[1]
```

```
1
2
```

Hash tables store key-value pairs and are defined using the @{ key = value } syntax. They provide fast lookups based on keys:

```
$hashTable = @{
    "Name" = "John Doe"
    "Age" = 30
    "Occupation" = "Developer"
}
```

Accessing a hash table's value is performed using its key:

```
$name = $hashTable["Name"]
$age = $hashTable["Age"]
```

```
John Doe
30
```

Custom objects offer the ability to create complex data structures by defining properties, using New-Object or pscustomobject. This can be useful for storing related data logically encapsulated within an object:

```
$person = [PSCustomObject]@{
    FirstName = "Jane"
```

```
    LastName = "Doe"
    Age = 29
    Occupation = "Designer"
}
```

Accessing properties of custom objects uses a dot notation:

```
$firstName = $person.FirstName
$lastName = $person.LastName
```

```
Jane
Doe
```

Understanding how PowerShell operates with these data types can significantly enhance the capability of scripts. Correct application of data types allows for improved data handling, script performance, and readability, ultimately leading to more robust and maintainable code.

4.5 Type Conversion and Casting

Type conversion and casting are essential concepts in PowerShell, enabling scriptwriters to transform data from one type to another. These processes are crucial for data manipulation and ensure that scripts perform operations on compatible data types. Understanding the subtleties of type conversion and casting in PowerShell empowers scriptwriters to handle data effectively and avoid runtime errors.

PowerShell supports both implicit and explicit type conversion. Implicit conversion happens automatically when the context demands it, whereas explicit conversion requires the scriptwriter's intervention to guide PowerShell in interpreting a value as a different type.

Implicit Type Conversion

PowerShell exhibits flexibility by automatically converting types when required. This feature simplifies script writing but can sometimes lead to unexpected behavior if not carefully considered.

Consider the following example where PowerShell implicitly converts a string to an integer for arithmetic operations:

```
$a = "10"
$b = 5
$result = $a + $b
Write-Output $result
```

The output from the above script will be:

15

In this scenario, PowerShell recognizes that the operation involves an arithmetic addition and thus implicitly converts the value of $a from a string to an integer before performing the addition.

Explicit Type Conversion

Explicit type conversion, also known as casting, allows scriptwriters to specify the type to which they want to convert a value. This is done by enclosing the desired type in square brackets before the value.

Here is an example illustrating explicit conversion:

```
$a = "100.25"
$b = [int]$a
Write-Output $b
```

The output will be:

100

In this case, $a is explicitly cast to an integer using [int]. The fractional part of the original value is truncated in the process.

Several common type casting operators in PowerShell include:

- [string] - Converts the value to a string.
- [int] - Converts the value to an integer.
- [bool] - Converts the value to a boolean.
- [datetime] - Converts the value to a datetime type.
- [double] - Converts the value to a double-precision floating-point number.

Handling Conversion Errors

When performing explicit type conversion, it is essential to ensure that the source value is compatible with the target type. If not, PowerShell will throw a conversion error.

Consider the following code that attempts to cast a non-numeric string to an integer:

```
$a = "hello"
$b = [int]$a
Write-Output $b
```

Executing this script results in the following error:

```
Cannot convert value "hello" to type "System.Int32". Error: "Input string was not in a correct format."
At line:2 char:1
+ $b = [int]$a
+ ~~~~~~~~~~~~
    + CategoryInfo          : InvalidArgument: (:) [], RuntimeException
    + FullyQualifiedErrorId : InvalidCastFromStringToInteger
```

To prevent such errors, it is good practice to validate the input before conversion. PowerShell provides various methods to validate types peacefully.

```
$a = "hello"
try {
    $b = [int]$a
    Write-Output $b
} catch {
    Write-Output "Invalid conversion: $_"
}
```

The output will now be:

```
Invalid conversion: Cannot convert value "hello" to type "System.Int32". Error: "Input string was not in a correct format."
```

Using the try and catch blocks captures the error and allows for graceful handling. This prevents the script from terminating unexpectedly and enables the scriptwriter to manage conversion failures safely.

Conversion Methods

PowerShell also supplies a variety of methods for type conversion that can be more explicit or versatile than simple casting. For instance, [Convert] class methods can handle complex type conversions.

Consider converting a hexadecimal string to an integer using [Convert]::ToInt32 method:

```
$hexString = "FF"
$number = [Convert]::ToInt32($hexString, 16)
Write-Output $number
```

This script outputs:

```
255
```

The [Convert]::ToInt32 method precisely converts the hexadecimal string to its integer equivalent, accentuating PowerShell's extensive type conversion capabilities.

Understanding and utilizing type conversion and casting efficiently are crucial tools in the PowerShell scripting arsenal. PowerShell's blend of implicit and explicit conversions, coupled with advanced conversion methods, provides robust mechanisms to manage and manipulate diverse data types effectively.

4.6 Using Arrays and Hash Tables

In PowerShell, arrays and hash tables are two pivotal data structures that allow the storage and management of collections of items. Arrays store ordered collections of elements, while hash tables store key-value pairs. Understanding their creation, manipulation, and usage is crucial for efficient script writing.

Arrays
An array is an ordered collection of elements that can be of any data type. Arrays are flexible in PowerShell, enabling the storage of disparate data types within a single array. Arrays are created by enclosing the elements in a comma-separated list within parentheses or by using the array sub-expression operator '@()'.

```
# Creating an array using parentheses
$array1 = (1, 2, 3, 4)
# Creating an array using array sub-expression operator
$array2 = @("PowerShell", 42, $true, 3.14)
```

Accessing and manipulating elements in an array is straightforward. Arrays are zero-indexed, meaning the first element is at index '0'. Individual elements can be accessed using their index, enclosed in square brackets.

```
# Access first element
$firstElement = $array1[0] # Output: 1

# Access third element
$thirdElement = $array2[2] # Output: True
```

PowerShell arrays are dynamic, meaning they can be resized by adding or removing elements. Adding elements to an array can be achieved using the addition operator '+='.

```
# Adding an element
$array1 += 5 # Array becomes (1, 2, 3, 4, 5)
```

To remove an element from an array, the 'Where-Object' cmdlet can be utilized to filter out the elements that do not match the condition specified.

```
# Removing an element
$array1 = $array1 | Where-Object { $_ -ne 3 } # Array becomes (1, 2, 4, 5)
```

Iterating over the elements of an array is often necessary when performing actions on each element. This can be done using loops such as 'foreach' and 'for'.

```
# Using foreach loop
foreach ($element in $array1) {
  Write-Output $element
}

# Using for loop
for ($i = 0; $i -lt $array1.Count; $i++) {
  Write-Output $array1[$i]
}
```

Hash Tables

Hash tables in PowerShell, also known as associative arrays, store key-value pairs. They provide efficient retrieval of values when the key is known. Hash tables are created using the syntax '@' with keys and values defined within as pairs, separated by '='.

```
# Creating a hash table
$hashTable = @{
    Name = "PowerShell"
    Version = 7.1
    IsScriptingLanguage = $true
}
```

Accessing hash table values is done using the key enclosed in square brackets, or by using the dot notation. The hash table will return the corresponding value.

```
# Accessing by key
$name = $hashTable["Name"] # Output: "PowerShell"

# Accessing using dot notation
$version = $hashTable.Version # Output: 7.1
```

Adding or updating key-value pairs in a hash table is straightforward. Assign a value to a new or existing key.

```
# Adding new key-value pair
$hashTable["Author"] = "Unknown"

# Updating existing key-value pair
$hashTable["Version"] = 7.2
```

Removing key-value pairs is done using the ‘Remove()‘ method.

```
# Removing a key-value pair
$hashTable.Remove("Author")
```

Iterating over hash table entries can be performed using the ‘foreach‘ loop, where each entry is a ‘[DictionaryEntry]‘ object containing ‘Key‘ and ‘Value‘ properties.

```
foreach ($entry in $hashTable.GetEnumerator()) {
    Write-Output "Key: $($entry.Key), Value: $($entry.Value)"
}
```

Combining arrays and hash tables can leverage the strengths of both structures, enabling the creation of complex data storage solutions. Arrays can store multiple hash tables, and hash tables can contain arrays as values.

```
# Array of hash tables
$arrayOfHashTables = @(
    @{ ID = 1; Name = "First" },
    @{ ID = 2; Name = "Second" }
)

# Hash table containing an array
$hashTableWithArray = @{
    Items = @( "Item1", "Item2", "Item3" )
}
```

The above techniques enable efficient data management and provide powerful capabilities for handling complex data structures in PowerShell scripts.

4.7 Scoping Rules and Best Practices

In PowerShell, understanding variable scope is critical for writing reliable and maintainable scripts. Scoping determines the visibility and lifetime of variables, functions, aliases, and other entities in a script. The primary scopes in PowerShell are Global, Local, Script, and Private. Knowing how these scopes function helps in controlling access to variables and avoiding unintended side effects.

The Global scope encompasses the entire PowerShell session. Variables assigned in the global scope are accessible throughout the session, across all functions, scripts, and command executions. To explicitly declare a variable in the global scope from within a function or script, it is prefixed with $global:. Below is an example:

```
$global:VariableName = "This is a global variable"
```

The Local scope is the default scope for variables created within a function or script. These variables exist only within the context where they are created and are not accessible outside that context. For instance:

```
function TestLocalScope {
    $LocalVariable = "I am local"
    Write-Output $LocalVariable
}
TestLocalScope
# Trying to access $LocalVariable outside its scope will result in an error
# Write-Output $LocalVariable
```

The Script scope is used to declare variables that are accessible throughout a specific script. When a script defines variables with the script scope modifier ($script:), these variables persist for the life of the script but not beyond it.

```
$script:ScriptVar = "Visible throughout this script"
```

The Private scope restricts the variable's visibility to the entity where it is defined, preventing it from being accessed or modified outside its defining scope. This is particularly useful for protecting internal script components from external interactions. Here's an example:

```
function TestPrivateScope {
    $private:PrivateVar = "I am a private variable"
    Write-Output $PrivateVar
}
TestPrivateScope
# Outside the function, $PrivateVar is unavailable
# Write-Output $PrivateVar
```

When dealing with nested scopes, PowerShell follows a hierarchical approach. For example, within a function (local scope), one can access global variables unless they are shadowed by local variables of the same name. If variable names conflict across scopes, the innermost scope variable takes precedence.

PowerShell also provides a way to explicitly enforce the scope context by using scope modifiers. This is crucial when you want to update a global or script-level variable from inside a function or script. The following demonstrates assigning values to both a global and a script-level variable within a function:

```
function SetVariables {
    $global:GlobalVar = "Updated global variable"
    $script:ScriptVar = "Updated script variable"
}
```

```
SetVariables
Write-Output $GlobalVar
Write-Output $ScriptVar
```

Best practices for scoping in PowerShell recommend minimizing the use of global variables to reduce dependencies and potential conflicts. Use local variables by default and prefer script scope variables where necessary to maintain a clear boundary of where a variable is accessible. Encapsulating variables and limiting their exposure ensures modularity and eases debugging.

Structuring scripts with well-defined scoping rules aids in maintaining state consistency and functionality predictability. This encapsulation strategy mitigates risks associated with variable collision, enhances script readability, and supports code reuse. Adopting these conventions not only improves script reliability but also aids in maintaining clean and effective codebases.

The careful application of scoping rules ensures that variables, functions, and other constructs serve their intended purposes in a controlled environment, balancing accessibility with encapsulation. Through the disciplined use of these practices, one enhances the robustness and maintainability of PowerShell scripts.

4.8 PowerShell Automatic Variables

PowerShell automatic variables are preset variables that store information related to the PowerShell environment, the state of the system, or specific operations. These variables are intrinsic to PowerShell and are available without prior declaration or initialization. They are fundamental in scripting and automation tasks due to their role in conveying context-sensitive information. Below is a detailed explanation of some crucial automatic variables, their purposes, and how to effectively use them in scripting.

$_ (the pipeline object)

The $_ variable, often referred to as the pipeline object, holds the current object being processed in the pipeline. This variable is extensively utilized in pipeline operations and script blocks.

```
# Example of using the pipeline object
(Get-Process | Where-Object { $_.CPU -gt 100 })
```

In this script, $_ represents each process object passed along the pipeline. The script filters and returns processes where the CPU usage exceeds 100.

$Args

The $Args variable is an array that contains the arguments passed to a script, function, or script block. This variable is especially useful when dealing with user-defined functions or scripts requiring dynamic input.

```
# Example of using $Args in a function
function Display-Message {
    Write-Host "You passed the following arguments: $Args"
}

# Calling the function with arguments
Display-Message "Hello" "World" "123"
```

```
You passed the following arguments: Hello World 123
```

$Error

The $Error variable is an array that contains a record of the most recent PowerShell errors. Each error is stored as an element in the array, with the newest error at index 0.

```
# Example of generating and accessing errors
Get-Item nonexistentitem
Write-Host "Latest error: $($Error[0].Exception.Message)"
```

```
Get-Item : Cannot find path 'nonexistentitem' because it does not exist.
Latest error: Cannot find path 'nonexistentitem' because it does not exist.
```

$PSCmdlet

The $PSCmdlet variable provides access to the cmdlet or advanced function from which it is accessed. It is particularly beneficial for obtaining context within advanced functions, enabling the use of cmdlet methods and properties.

```
# Example of using $PSCmdlet in an advanced function
function Get-CmdletInfo {
    [CmdletBinding()]
    param ()
    Write-Host "Cmdlet Name: $($PSCmdlet.MyInvocation.InvocationName)"
}

# Calling the function
Get-CmdletInfo
```

```
Cmdlet Name: Get-CmdletInfo
```

$PSVersionTable

The $PSVersionTable variable stores a table of information about the PowerShell environment, including version numbers and platform specifics.

```
# Example of displaying PowerShell version information
$PSVersionTable
```

```
Name                         Value
----                         -----
PSVersion                    7.2.0
PSEdition                    Core
GitCommitId                  7.2.0
OS                           Microsoft Windows 10.0.19042
Platform                     Win32NT
PSCompatibleVersions         {1.0, 2.0, 3.0, 4.0...}
PSRemotingProtocolVersion    2.3
SerializationVersion         1.1.0.1
WSManStackVersion            3.0
```

$LastExitCode

The $LastExitCode variable holds the exit code of the last run Win32 executable. This is particularly valuable when working with native commands and scripts that require exit code verification for flow control.

```
# Example of checking the exit code of a cmd command
cmd /c "exit 1"
Write-Host "Last exit code: $LastExitCode"
```

```
Last exit code: 1
```

$PID

The $PID variable stores the process identifier (PID) of the active PowerShell session. This can be used in monitoring or managing the PowerShell process itself.

```
# Display the PID of the current PowerShell session
Write-Host "Current PowerShell PID: $PID"
```

```
Current PowerShell PID: 1234
```

$true, $false, and $null

$true and $false are Boolean constants representing logical truth and falsity, respectively. $null represents a null value or absence of data.

```
# Usage of $true, $false, and $null
if ($null -eq $null) { Write-Host "Null comparison is true" }
if ($true -and -not $false) { Write-Host "Boolean logic works" }
```

```
Null comparison is true
Boolean logic works
```

These automatic variables form the backbone of scripting in PowerShell by providing contextual and environmental data that allows scripts to be dynamic and responsive to system and user states. Understanding and utilizing these variables effectively can significantly enhance script functionality and robustness.

4.9 Working with Null and Empty Values

In PowerShell, null and empty values serve a crucial role in controlling flow and evaluating conditions within scripts. Understanding how to handle them effectively ensures robust and error-free scripts. This section delves into the nuances of null and empty values, outlining their detection and management.

A $null value in PowerShell signifies the absence of any object. It is comparable to the null reference in other programming languages like C# or Java. The $null can be assigned to any variable or used as a placeholder for uninitialized variables.

```
$variable = $null
```

Empty values, on the other hand, refer to instances where a variable contains a type-specific manifestation of 'nothing'. For strings, this can be an empty string (""), and for arrays, it would be an empty array (@()).

```
$stringVariable = ""
$arrayVariable = @()
```

Checking for Null and Empty Values

PowerShell provides several methods for checking null and empty values. An essential function for this is the use of the -eq and -ne operators, which are used to test for equality and inequality, respectively.

```
if ($variable -eq $null) {
    Write-Output "Variable is null"
}
```

When checking for empty values, different approaches are necessary depending on the data type. For strings, the -eq operator checks if the string is equal to an empty string.

```
if ($stringVariable -eq "") {
    Write-Output "String is empty"
}
```

For arrays, PowerShell's .Count property can be leveraged to ascertain whether the array contains elements.

```
if ($arrayVariable.Count -eq 0) {
    Write-Output "Array is empty"
}
```

Managing Null Values in Scripts

Handling null values requires careful consideration, particularly in functions and loops. Consider a scenario where a function returns *null*:

```
function Get-Value {
    return $null
}

$result = Get-Value
if ($result -eq $null) {
    Write-Output "Function returned null"
}
```

In loops, encountering a null value might necessitate breaking out to prevent errors.

```
$array = @($null, 1, 2, 3)
foreach ($item in $array) {
    if ($item -eq $null) {
        Write-Output "Null value encountered, exiting loop"
        break
    }
    Write-Output $item
}
```

Coalescing Null and Empty Values

PowerShell's ?, the conditional operator, provides a concise method for handling null and empty values by assigning default values.

```
$value = $null
$defaultValue = "Default"
$result = $value ? $value : $defaultValue
Write-Output $result # Outputs: Default
```

Similarly, for empty strings, one can use:

```
$stringValue = ""
$defaultString = "Default String"
$resultString = $stringValue ? $stringValue : $defaultString
Write-Output $resultString # Outputs: Default String
```

Handling Cmdlet Outputs with Null and Empty Values

Often cmdlets return null or empty objects when certain conditions are not met or data is not found. Robust error handling practices are necessary.

```
$process = Get-Process -Name "NonExistentProcess" -ErrorAction SilentlyContinue
if ($process -eq $null) {
    Write-Output "Process not found"
}

$files = Get-ChildItem -Path "C:\NonExistentPath" -ErrorAction SilentlyContinue
if ($files.Count -eq 0) {
    Write-Output "No files found"
}
```

Summary and Best Practices

When dealing with null and empty values in PowerShell, proper checks and default assignments prevent unexpected errors and enhance script reliability. Utilize -eq and .Count for effective checks, and consider default values to manage potential null returns from functions or cmdlets.

4.10 Persistent Storage and Retrieving Data

One of the crucial aspects of scripting in PowerShell is the ability to store data persistently and retrieve it when necessary. This allows scripts to maintain state across different executions and sessions. Persistent storage can be achieved using various methods such as file systems, databases, and other data storage services. This section delves into techniques for storing and retrieving data effectively using PowerShell.

Data can be stored in different formats such as plain text, JSON, XML, CSV, and databases. Each format has its own strengths and is best suited for certain kinds of data and operations.

Storing Data in Text Files

The simplest form of persistent storage is using plain text files. PowerShell provides cmdlets like Out-File, Set-Content, and Add-Content to write data to text files. The following example demonstrates how to store data in a text file:

```
# Define the data to store
$data = @"
This is line 1
This is line 2
This is line 3
"@

# Store data in a text file
$data | Out-File -FilePath "C:\Data\example.txt"
```

Out-File writes the output of the command to a specified file. The Set-

Content cmdlet can also be used for this purpose. It overwrites existing content if the file already exists:

```
# Overwrite existing file or create new file
Set-Content -Path "C:\Data\example.txt" -Value $data
```

To append data to an existing file, use the Add-Content cmdlet:

```
# Append data to the existing file
Add-Content -Path "C:\Data\example.txt" -Value "This is a new line"
```

To retrieve and read the data from the text file, the Get-Content cmdlet is used:

```
# Read data from the text file
$retrievedData = Get-Content -Path "C:\Data\example.txt"
$retrievedData
```

The output will display the content of the file line by line.

```
This is line 1
This is line 2
This is line 3
This is a new line
```

Storing Data in JSON Files

JSON (JavaScript Object Notation) is a lightweight data interchange format that is easy for humans to read and write, and easy for machines to parse and generate. PowerShell includes cmdlets for working with JSON data. To convert a PowerShell object to a JSON string, use the ConvertTo-Json cmdlet, and to store this in a file, combine it with Out-File:

```
# Define a PowerShell object
$data = @{
    Name = "John Doe"
    Age = 30
    City = "New York"
}

# Convert the object to a JSON string
$jsonData = $data | ConvertTo-Json

# Save JSON data to a file
$jsonData | Out-File -FilePath "C:\Data\example.json"
```

To retrieve and read data from a JSON file, use the Get-Content cmdlet combined with the ConvertFrom-Json cmdlet:

```
# Read JSON data from file
$jsonData = Get-Content -Path "C:\Data\example.json" -Raw

# Convert JSON string to PowerShell object
$data = $jsonData | ConvertFrom-Json
```

```
$data
```

The output will be a PowerShell object that represents the JSON structure.

Storing Data in XML Files

XML (eXtensible Markup Language) is another format for data storage, often used for configuration files. PowerShell provides cmdlets to convert to and from XML. To convert a PowerShell object to an XML string and save it to a file, use the Export-Clixml cmdlet:

```
# Define a PowerShell object
$data = @{
    Name = "Jane Doe"
    Age = 28
    City = "London"
}

# Save the object as XML
$data | Export-Clixml -Path "C:\Data\example.xml"
```

To read the XML file and convert it back to a PowerShell object, use the Import-Clixml cmdlet:

```
# Read object from XML file
$data = Import-Clixml -Path "C:\Data\example.xml"
$data
```

Storing Data in CSV Files

CSV (Comma-Separated Values) is a common format for tabular data. PowerShell provides cmdlets like Export-Csv and Import-Csv for working with CSV files. To store data in a CSV file, use:

```
# Define a collection of objects
$data = @(
    [PSCustomObject]@{Name="Alice"; Age=32; City="Paris"}
    [PSCustomObject]@{Name="Bob"; Age=45; City="Berlin"}
)

# Save the objects to a CSV file
$data | Export-Csv -Path "C:\Data\example.csv" -NoTypeInformation
```

To read data from a CSV file and convert it back to objects, use:

```
# Read objects from the CSV file
$data = Import-Csv -Path "C:\Data\example.csv"
$data
```

Using Databases for Persistent Storage

For more complex data storage requirements, relational databases like

SQL Server or NoSQL databases like MongoDB may be used. PowerShell can interact with these databases using various modules and cmdlets. The Invoke-Sqlcmd cmdlet from the SqlServer module can be used to interact with SQL Server:

```
# Define the connection string
$connectionString = "Server=localhost;Database=ExampleDB;Integrated Security=
    True;"

# Define the SQL query
$query = "SELECT * FROM Users;"

# Execute the query and retrieve data
$data = Invoke-Sqlcmd -ConnectionString $connectionString -Query $query
$data
```

These commands and the various data storage methods discussed allow PowerShell scripts to efficiently manage and retrieve persistent data. Understanding and implementing these techniques is vital for creating robust and maintainable scripts.

Chapter 5

Control Flow: Loops and Conditional Statements

This chapter explores control flow mechanisms in PowerShell, focusing on loops and conditional statements. It details the use of conditional constructs like 'if', 'else', and 'elseif', along with the 'switch' statement. Looping structures such as 'for', 'foreach', 'while', and 'do-while' are discussed, including techniques for breaking out of loops and using the 'continue' statement. Practical examples are provided to illustrate the application of these constructs in script development, ensuring readers can implement effective control flow in their PowerShell scripts.

5.1 Introduction to Control Flow

In PowerShell scripting, control flow mechanisms enable the execution of code in a structured and logical manner. Control flow structures dictate the order in which statements and instructions within scripts are executed, allowing for the implementation of conditions, loops, and branching paths that can adjust dynamically during runtime.

Control flow in PowerShell hinges on two main constructs: conditional statements and loop statements. Conditional statements, such as if, else, and elseif, as well as the switch statement, facilitate decision-making within scripts by allowing different code blocks to execute based on specific conditions. Loop statements, including for, foreach, while, and do-while, enable repetitive execution of code blocks, which is pivotal for tasks requiring iteration over collections of items or repeated operations until a certain condition is met.

Consider the following basic example of an if statement that evaluates whether a number stored in a variable is positive:

```
$number = 10

if ($number -gt 0) {
    Write-Host "The number is positive."
}
```

In this example, the Write-Host cmdlet will output The number is positive. only if the condition $number -gt 0 (where -gt stands for "greater than") evaluates to True. This introductory illustration highlights the core purpose of control flow: to direct script execution based on evaluative conditions.

Loop constructs are equally integral to PowerShell scripting, providing mechanisms for iteratively processing arrays, collections, or sets of data. Here's a simple for loop that outputs the numbers 1 to 5:

```
for ($i = 1; $i -le 5; $i++) {
    Write-Host $i
}
```

This for loop initializes a variable $i to 1, checks the condition $i -le 5 (where -le means "less than or equal to"), and increments $i after each iteration using $i++. As long as the condition $i -le 5 holds true, the loop executes the Write-Host command, thereby printing the value of $i.

PowerShell's control flow statements can be used in concert with each other to form complex, multifaceted scripts. Their correct application allows script developers to harness conditional logic and iterate over data efficiently.

```
$numbers = @(1, 2, 3, 4, 5)

foreach ($number in $numbers) {
    if ($number % 2 -eq 0) {
        Write-Host "$number is even."
    } else {
        Write-Host "$number is odd."
    }
}
```

In this example, a foreach loop iterates over an array $numbers. During each iteration, it checks if the current element ($number) is even or odd using the modulus operator (%) and prints an appropriate message. This combination of loop and conditional statements demonstrates the power and flexibility of control flow in PowerShell.

Moreover, understanding when and how to exit loops prematurely using the break statement, or to skip the current iteration and move to the next using the continue statement, is essential for efficient script execution. Consider:

```
$numbers = @(1, 2, 3, 4, 5)

foreach ($number in $numbers) {
    if ($number -eq 3) {
        break
    }
    Write-Host $number
}
```

Here, the script terminates the loop when $number equals 3, preventing further processing of the rest of the array. Conversely, using continue:

```
$numbers = @(1, 2, 3, 4, 5)

foreach ($number in $numbers) {
    if ($number -eq 3) {
        continue
    }
    Write-Host $number
}
```

This modified loop skips the iteration where $number equals 3, continuing with the next iteration. Understanding and utilizing these control flow tools effectively can significantly impact the efficiency and correctness of PowerShell scripts. Proper application of control flow ensures scripts not only run correctly but also handle various scenarios and edge cases gracefully.

5.2 Conditional Statements: if, else, and elseif

In PowerShell scripting, conditional statements are fundamental constructs that allow the execution of code segments based on specific conditions. The primary conditional statement used in PowerShell is the if statement, which can be extended with else and elseif clauses to handle multiple scenarios.

The basic syntax of an if statement in PowerShell is as follows:

```
if (<condition>) {
    <statements>
}
```

Here, <condition> is a Boolean expression that evaluates to either $true or $false. The <statements> block is executed only if the <condition> evaluates to $true. If the condition evaluates to $false, the PowerShell interpreter skips the <statements> block.

For scenarios where different actions are needed based on whether the condition evaluates to $true or $false, the else clause can be used in conjunction with the if statement. The syntax is shown below:

```
if (<condition>) {
    <statements_if_true>
} else {
    <statements_if_false>
}
```

In this case, if <condition> evaluates to $true, the <statements_if_true> block is executed. Otherwise, the <statements_if_false> block is executed.

To handle multiple conditions, the elseif clause is utilized. This allows for branching logic where different blocks of code are executed based on a series of conditions. The syntax for using elseif is as follows:

```
if (<condition1>) {
    <statements_if_condition1>
} elseif (<condition2>) {
    <statements_if_condition2>
} elseif (<condition3>) {
    <statements_if_condition3>
} else {
    <statements_if_all_conditions_false>
}
```

Here, <condition1>, <condition2>, and <condition3> are all Boolean expressions. The PowerShell interpreter evaluates these conditions in sequence. The first <condition> that evaluates to $true causes the corresponding block of statements to be executed, and all subsequent conditions are ignored. If none of the conditions evaluates to $true, the <statements_if_all_conditions_false> block, specified by the else clause, is executed.

Consider the following practical example that demonstrates the use of if, else, and elseif statements to classify numbers:

```
$number = Read-Host "Enter a number"
```

```
if ($number -lt 0) {
    Write-Output "The number is negative."
} elseif ($number -eq 0) {
    Write-Output "The number is zero."
} else {
    Write-Output "The number is positive."
}
```

In this script:

- The user is prompted to enter a number, which is assigned to the variable $number.
- The if statement checks if the number is less than 0 and outputs "The number is negative" if true.
- If the first condition is false, the elseif statement checks if the number is equal to 0 and outputs "The number is zero" if true.
- If both the if and elseif conditions are false, the else block executes, outputting "The number is positive."

PowerShell conditional statements can also handle complex conditions involving logical operators such as -and, -or, and -not. For example:

```
$age = Read-Host "Enter your age"

if ($age -ge 0 -and $age -le 12) {
    Write-Output "Child"
} elseif ($age -ge 13 -and $age -le 19) {
    Write-Output "Teenager"
} elseif ($age -ge 20 -and $age -le 64) {
    Write-Output "Adult"
} elseif ($age -ge 65) {
    Write-Output "Senior"
} else {
    Write-Output "Invalid age entered."
}
```

In this script:

- The user is prompted to enter their age, which is stored in the variable $age.
- The first if statement uses the -and operator to check if the age is between 0 and 12. If true, it outputs "Child."
- If the first condition is false, subsequent elseif statements evaluate other age ranges using the -and operator.

- If all previous conditions are false, the else block outputs "Invalid age entered."

Correct use of conditional statements enhances the logical flow of scripts, making them responsive to different input scenarios and providing appropriate feedback or actions based on evaluated conditions. Integrating logical operators further refines condition checking, allowing more precise and efficient code structures. The ability to handle multiple conditions robustly is an essential skill in mastering PowerShell scripting, enabling developers to create dynamic and flexible scripts.

5.3 Using the switch Statement

The switch statement in PowerShell provides a powerful mechanism for handling multiple conditions based on a single expression's value. Unlike the if-else chain which evaluates conditions sequentially, the switch statement evaluates the expression once and directs the control flow to the matching case block.

In its simplest form, the switch statement syntax is as follows:

```
switch (expression) {
    case1 {
        # code block for case1
    }
    case2 {
        # code block for case2
    }
    ...
    default {
        # default code block
    }
}
```

The expression is evaluated once, and its value is compared against each case in order. If a matching case is found, the corresponding block of code is executed. If no case matches, the default block, if present, is executed.

Consider a practical example where we classify a given value:

```
$number = 3

switch ($number) {
    1 { "The number is one" }
    2 { "The number is two" }
    3 { "The number is three" }
    default { "The number is not between one and three" }
}
```

```
The number is three
```

In this example, the switch statement evaluates the variable $number and matches it to the case 3, resulting in the output "The number is three".

PowerShell's switch statement supports several advanced features:

1. Pattern Matching: The switch statement can use regular expressions to match patterns. To enable pattern matching, the -regex option is used.

```
$text = "PowerShell"

switch -regex ($text) {
    '^Power' { "Starts with Power" }
    'Shell$' { "Ends with Shell" }
    '.' { "Contains at least one character" }
}
```

```
Starts with Power
Ends with Shell
Contains at least one character
```

In the above example, the input "PowerShell" is evaluated against multiple regular expression patterns. Since the text starts with "Power", ends with "Shell", and contains at least one character, all respective blocks execute.

2. Multiple Conditions: The same script block can be associated with multiple values by specifying all the values on separate lines before the script block.

```
$day = "Tuesday"

switch ($day) {
    "Saturday" { "Weekend" }
    "Sunday" { "Weekend" }
    "Monday" { "Weekday" }
    "Tuesday" { "Weekday" }
    "Wednesday" { "Weekday" }
    "Thursday" { "Weekday" }
    "Friday" { "Weekday" }
}
```

```
Weekday
```

"Tuesday" matches one of the cases which results in the output "Weekday".

3. Using Default Case: A default case can be included to cover scenarios when none of the specified cases match.

```
$color = "Yellow"
```

```
switch ($color) {
    "Red" { "Stop" }
    "Green" { "Go" }
    "Blue" { "Sky" }
    default { "Color not recognized" }
}
```

```
Color not recognized
```

Since "Yellow" does not match any of the defined cases, the default block executes.

4. Invoking Command: The switch statement can execute a command for each match. This feature is particularly useful in scenarios that require actions such as invoking functions.

```
function Process-Red { "Processing Red" }
function Process-Green { "Processing Green" }
function Process-Blue { "Processing Blue" }

$input = "Green"

switch ($input) {
    "Red" { Process-Red }
    "Green" { Process-Green }
    "Blue" { Process-Blue }
}
```

```
Processing Green
```

When the input matches "Green", the Process-Green function is invoked.

5. Execution Control: Just like loops, switch statements support break and continue to control the flow of execution. break exits the switch statement immediately, while continue goes to the next iteration if looping constructs are involved.

```
$values = 1..5

foreach ($value in $values) {
    switch ($value) {
        1 { "One"; continue }
        3 { "Three"; break }
        default { "Other: $value" }
    }
}
```

```
One
Other: 2
Three
```

In this case, continue ensures the loop proceeds to the next iteration skipping further evaluation, while break stops the entire switch from executing further cases.

Through these examples and additional features, it is evident that understanding the switch statement enhances scripting versatility and control. The ability to match exact values, use regular expressions, combine multiple conditions, and control execution provides a robust toolkit for conditional script execution. This knowledge builds upon the foundation of conditional statements, enabling more intricate and efficient control flow in PowerShell scripting.

5.4 Looping with the for Statement

The for statement in PowerShell is a fundamental control flow mechanism that allows for compact and versatile loops. The for loop is particularly useful when the number of iterations is known beforehand or can be determined by manipulating a counter variable. The syntax of a for loop in PowerShell includes three main components: initialization, condition, and iteration. The general form of the for loop can be expressed as follows:

```
for (initialization; condition; iteration)
{
    # Code to execute in the loop
}
```

Here is a detailed breakdown of the elements in the for loop syntax:

- **Initialization:** This part is executed once, before the loop starts. It typically initializes one or more loop control variables.
- **Condition:** This boolean expression is evaluated before each iteration of the loop. If the condition evaluates to true, the loop body is executed. If it evaluates to false, the loop terminates.
- **Iteration:** This part is executed after each iteration of the loop body. It typically updates the loop control variable(s).

Consider a basic example where we want to print numbers from 1 to 10:

```
for ($i = 1; $i -le 10; $i++)
{
    Write-Host $i
}
```

In this script:

- $i = 1 initializes the loop control variable $i.
- $i -le 10 is the condition that checks if $i is less than or equal to 10.
- $i++ increments $i by 1 after each iteration.

Every iteration prints the current value of $i to the host.

```
1
2
3
4
5
6
7
8
9
10
```

In more complex scenarios, multiple variables can be initialized, updated, or checked. For example, to iterate over numbers and simultaneously calculate their squares:

```
for ($i = 1; $i -le 10; $i++)
{
    $square = $i * $i
    Write-Host "Number: $i, Square: $square"
}
```

The output of this script will be:

```
Number: 1, Square: 1
Number: 2, Square: 4
Number: 3, Square: 9
Number: 4, Square: 16
Number: 5, Square: 25
Number: 6, Square: 36
Number: 7, Square: 49
Number: 8, Square: 64
Number: 9, Square: 81
Number: 10, Square: 100
```

It is essential to understand how to manage loop control variables to prevent infinite loops, which can cause scripts to hang or become unresponsive. Below is an example that incorrectly manages the loop control variable, leading to an infinite loop:

```
for ($i = 1; $i -le 5;) # iteration step is missing
{
    Write-Host $i
}
```

This script does not have an iteration step to update $i, causing it to print the number 1 indefinitely.

A practical application of the for loop can be found in scenarios requiring operations on arrays. Suppose we have an array of integers, and we want to print only the even numbers from the array:

```
$array = 1, 2, 3, 4, 5, 6, 7, 8, 9, 10
for ($i = 0; $i -lt $array.Length; $i++)
{
    if ($array[$i] % 2 -eq 0)
    {
        Write-Host $array[$i]
    }
}
```

The array $array has 10 elements. We loop through each element using $i as the index. The condition $array[$i] % 2 -eq 0 checks if the element is even before printing it.

```
2
4
6
8
10
```

Variables defined within the for loop scope can be used for more complex operations or transformations. Consider calculating the factorial of a number using the for loop:

```
$number = 5
$factorial = 1
for ($i = 1; $i -le $number; $i++)
{
    $factorial *= $i
}
Write-Host "Factorial of $number is $factorial"
```

```
Factorial of 5 is 120
```

In the loop:

- $i starts at 1 and increments up to $number.
- On each iteration, $factorial is multiplied by $i to compute the factorial.

To traverse multidimensional arrays or nested data structures, nested for loops are employed. Consider iterating through a 2D array (array of arrays):

```
$matrix = @(
    @(1, 2, 3),
    @(4, 5, 6),
    @(7, 8, 9)
)
```

```
for ($i = 0; $i -lt $matrix.Length; $i++)
{
    for ($j = 0; $j -lt $matrix[$i].Length; $j++)
    {
        Write-Host $matrix[$i][$j]
    }
}
```

The outer loop iterates over the rows, and the inner loop iterates over the columns.

Effective usage of the for statement in PowerShell provides a powerful tool for managing repetitive tasks and iterating over data structures, making it a cornerstone of procedural script development.

5.5 Using the foreach Statement

The foreach statement in PowerShell provides an efficient way to iterate through items in a collection, such as an array, hashtable, or any enumerable object. Unlike the traditional for loop where iteration is controlled through an explicit index, the foreach loop abstracts the iteration by directly providing access to each item in the collection, thereby simplifying the script and reducing the potential for errors associated with index management.

The general syntax for the foreach statement is as follows:

```
foreach ($element in $collection) {
    # body of the loop
    # code to process $element
}
```

In this context, $element represents the variable that holds the current item from $collection during each iteration of the loop. The body of the loop contains the script block that processes each item.

Consider a practical example where we wish to iterate through an array of computer names and perform a specific action on each. Here is a script that uses the foreach statement:

```
$computerNames = @('Server1', 'Server2', 'Server3')

foreach ($computer in $computerNames) {
    Write-Host "Checking status of $computer"
    # Implement logic to check the status
}
```

In this script, $computerNames is an array containing the names of servers. The foreach loop iterates through each server name, printing a message to the console.

The foreach statement can be particularly powerful when dealing with nested collections. Consider a scenario where each item in the collection is itself a collection: a hashtable containing various properties of servers. Below is an example demonstrating this:

```
$servers = @(
    @{ Name = 'Server1'; IP = '192.168.1.1'; Status = 'Online' },
    @{ Name = 'Server2'; IP = '192.168.1.2'; Status = 'Offline' },
    @{ Name = 'Server3'; IP = '192.168.1.3'; Status = 'Online' }
)

foreach ($server in $servers) {
    Write-Host "Name: $($server.Name), IP: $($server.IP), Status: $($server.Status)"
}
```

In the above script, $servers is an array of hashtables, where each hashtable represents a server with properties such as Name, IP, and Status. The foreach loop processes each server, printing its properties to the console.

When working with more complex objects, the foreach statement can be used to simplify the iteration. For example, if you are dealing with a collection of custom objects or objects retrieved from a cmdlet.

Suppose we have created a custom object to represent users:

```
$users = @(
    [PSCustomObject]@{ Name = 'Alice'; Age = 30; Role = 'Admin' },
    [PSCustomObject]@{ Name = 'Bob'; Age = 25; Role = 'User' },
    [PSCustomObject]@{ Name = 'Charlie'; Age = 28; Role = 'User' }
)

foreach ($user in $users) {
    Write-Host "User: $($user.Name), Age: $($user.Age), Role: $($user.Role)"
}
```

In this script, $users is an array of custom objects, each representing a user with properties like Name, Age, and Role. The foreach loop iterates through each user, printing the details to the console.

One important aspect of the foreach statement in PowerShell is that it allows for modifying collection items directly within the loop. This feature can be advantageous when you need to adjust properties of objects in a collection dynamically. Consider the following use case where we update a property of each object in the collection:

```
foreach ($user in $users) {
    if ($user.Role -eq 'User') {
        $user.Role = 'Guest'
    }
    Write-Host "Updated User: $($user.Name), Role: $($user.Role)"
}
```

Here, the script iterates through the $users collection and updates the Role property for users with the role 'User' to 'Guest'. The modified roles are then printed to the console.

The power and simplicity of the foreach statement make it a fundamental control flow construct in PowerShell scripting. It allows for clear and concise iteration over collections, enabling effective data processing and manipulation.

5.6 While Loops: while and do-while

The while and do-while loops are fundamental control flow tools in PowerShell, allowing for the repetition of a block of code as long as a specified condition is true. Understanding the subtle differences and appropriate use cases for these loops is essential for efficient script development.

The while Loop

The while loop in PowerShell repeatedly executes a block of code as long as a given condition evaluates to true. The general syntax is as follows:

```
while (<condition>) {
    <statements>
}
```

<condition> is a boolean expression that determines whether the loop continues to execute. The <statements> are executed repeatedly until the <condition> evaluates to false.

Consider the following example that counts from 1 to 5:

```
$count = 1
while ($count -le 5) {
    Write-Output $count
    $count++
}
```

This script initializes a variable $count to 1 and then uses a while loop to display the value of $count and increment it by 1 on each iteration. The loop continues until $count exceeds 5.

```
1
2
3
4
5
```

The do-while Loop

The do-while loop, unlike the while loop, executes the block of code at least once before evaluating the condition. The syntax is as follows:

```
do {
    <statements>
} while (<condition>)
```

Because the <statements> are executed before the condition is evaluated, it guarantees that the code block will run at least once. This characteristic differentiates the do-while loop from the while loop.

Consider the same counting example using a do-while loop:

```
$count = 1
do {
    Write-Output $count
    $count++
} while ($count -le 5)
```

The resulting output is identical to that of the while loop example:

```
1
2
3
4
5
```

Practical Considerations

Choosing between while and do-while depends on whether the code block needs to execute at least once. For example, when collecting user input that must be validated, a do-while loop ensures that the prompt is displayed before any validation logic is applied:

```
do {
    $input = Read-Host -Prompt "Enter a number between 1 and 10"
} while ([int]$input -lt 1 -or [int]$input -gt 10)
Write-Output "You entered a valid number: $input"
```

This script continuously prompts the user until they provide a valid number between 1 and 10. The condition is checked after each input.

Combining Logic with Loops

In more complex scenarios, the logic within the while or do-while loop may interact with other control flow constructs. Here is a script that processes input until the user decides to quit:

```
do {
    $input = Read-Host -Prompt "Enter a command (type 'exit' to quit)"
    switch ($input) {
        "sayhello" { Write-Output "Hello!" }
        "exit" { Write-Output "Goodbye!" }
        default { Write-Output "Unknown command" }
    }
} while ($input -ne "exit")
```

In this case, the loop continues to prompt for commands until the user types exit. Each input is processed using a switch statement, demonstrating how different control flow mechanisms can be combined effectively within a loop.

Resource Management

It is also crucial to consider resource management in loops. An improperly terminated or infinite loop may lead to resource exhaustion. Always ensure that the loop's condition will eventually fail or include a mechanism to break out of the loop under certain conditions to prevent script hang-ups:

```
$count = 1
while ($true) {
    Write-Output $count
    $count++
    if ($count -gt 100) { break }
}
```

Here, a while loop with a condition that always evaluates to true ($true) will run indefinitely unless a break condition is explicitly specified.

Understanding and utilizing while and do-while loops efficiently enhances the control flow within your PowerShell scripts, promoting robust and predictable automation.

5.7 Breaking Out of Loops

In PowerShell scripting, control flow within loops can be enriched by strategically breaking out of loops under certain conditions. This mechanism is primarily facilitated by the break statement. Integrating break into your scripts enables you to terminate loops prematurely, which can be essential in various scenarios, such as error handling or improving efficiency by exiting loops once the desired results are achieved.

The break statement halts the nearest enclosing loop immediately, regardless of the loop's condition. Consider the following example, which demonstrates a simple use of break within a foreach loop:

```
$numbers = 1..10
foreach ($num in $numbers) {
    if ($num -eq 5) {
        break
    }
    Write-Output "Processing number: $num"
}
```

In this example, the $numbers array contains integers from 1 to 10. The foreach loop iterates over each number in the array. When the condition $num -eq 5 is met, the break statement is executed, causing an immediate exit from the loop. The output of the code is as follows:

```
Processing number: 1
Processing number: 2
Processing number: 3
Processing number: 4
```

The loop stops processing numbers as soon as it encounters the number 5. Without the break statement, the loop would continue to iterate over the remaining numbers in the array.

Another common use case for the break statement is within a while loop. In scenarios where you need to exit the loop based on dynamic conditions evaluated during the execution, break becomes particularly useful. Below is an example illustrating this application:

```
$i = 0
while ($true) {
    $i++
    Write-Output "Iteration: $i"
    if ($i -ge 3) {
        break
    }
}
```

In this example, the while loop is configured with a condition $true, making it an infinite loop. The loop increments the variable $i on each iteration. When $i reaches or exceeds 3, the break statement is executed, terminating the loop. The output of the script is:

```
Iteration: 1
```

```
Iteration: 2
Iteration: 3
```

break can also be employed effectively in nested loops to control the flow of multi-level iterations. Consider a situation where we have a nested for loop, and we need to exit the inner loop based on a condition:

```
for ($outer = 1; $outer -le 3; $outer++) {
    for ($inner = 1; $inner -le 3; $inner++) {
        if ($inner -eq 2) {
            break
        }
        Write-Output "Outer: $outer, Inner: $inner"
    }
}
```

This script employs two for loops, where the outer loop iterates from 1 to 3 and the inner loop also iterates from 1 to 3. When the inner loop's variable $inner equals 2, the break statement is activated, terminating the inner loop while allowing the outer loop to continue. The output of this script is:

```
Outer: 1, Inner: 1
Outer: 2, Inner: 1
Outer: 3, Inner: 1
```

This output shows that each inner loop terminates as soon as the condition $inner -eq 2 is met, and the script then proceeds with the next iteration of the outer loop.

Understanding the implications of excessive use of break is important. While it provides a powerful way to manage loop control flow, overusing break can lead to complex and difficult-to-maintain code. Proper commenting and clear logic can help mitigate these issues.

In developing robust PowerShell scripts, practitioners should be mindful of ensuring that the logic governing the use of break is transparent and justified within the context of the script's objectives. This approach ensures that the use of the break statement enhances script clarity and maintains functional integrity.

5.8 Understanding Continue Statement

The continue statement in PowerShell is a control flow keyword that immediately moves the execution of script back to the start of the loop, skipping all subsequent commands in the current iteration. This control flow mechanism is particularly beneficial for controlling the finer detail of loop iterations, ensuring certain conditions or states can be bypassed without completely terminating the loop.

To illustrate, consider the operation of a foreach loop processing a collection of numbers. Suppose the script's aim is to display only even numbers from the collection. By using the continue statement, the script can efficiently skip over odd numbers and proceed directly to the next iteration.

```
$numbers = 1..10

foreach ($number in $numbers) {
    if ($number % 2 -ne 0) {
        continue
    }
    Write-Host "Even number: $number"
}
```

In this example, the conditional statement if ($number % 2 -ne 0) checks whether the number is odd. If the condition evaluates to true (i.e., the number is odd), the continue statement is executed, causing the loop to skip to the next iteration, omitting the Write-Host command for odd numbers. The output of executing this script will be:

```
Even number: 2
Even number: 4
Even number: 6
Even number: 8
Even number: 10
```

The continue statement is also useful within while and for loops. When utilized in these contexts, it performs similarly, bypassing the remaining code in the current iteration and returning control to the start of the loop.

Consider another example employing a for loop that iterates through a range of values, outputting those that are divisible by 3:

```
for ($i = 1; $i -le 15; $i++) {
    if ($i % 3 -ne 0) {
        continue
    }
    Write-Host "$i is divisible by 3"
}
```

Here, within the for loop, the condition if ($i % 3 -ne 0) checks for numbers not divisible by three. The continue statement causes the loop to skip any iteration where the number is not divisible by three, ensuring only the numbers 3, 6, 9, 12, and 15 are displayed:

```
3 is divisible by 3
```

```
6 is divisible by 3
9 is divisible by 3
12 is divisible by 3
15 is divisible by 3
```

It is also crucial to understand the interaction of the continue statement with nested loops. When continue is used in the inner loop of a nested structure, it affects only the innermost loop. For example, consider nested foreach loops designed to pair items from two different collections, but only displaying the pairs where the sum of the items is even:

```
$outer = 1..3
$inner = 4..6

foreach ($o in $outer) {
    foreach ($i in $inner) {
        if (($o + $i) % 2 -ne 0) {
            continue
        }
        Write-Host "Pair: $o, $i"
    }
}
```

In this nested loop, the continue statement skips to the next iteration of the inner loop whenever the sum of the items is odd. The output will be pairs whose sums are even:

```
Pair: 1, 5
Pair: 2, 4
Pair: 2, 6
Pair: 3, 5
```

Understanding the nuances of the continue statement allows for more refined control over looping constructs, aiding in the development of efficient and readable scripts. By strategically skipping over unnecessary iterations, scripts become both simpler and more effective. This utility showcases why continue is an indispensable part of a PowerShell scripter's toolkit.

5.9 Using Break and Continue in Nested Loops

In complex scripting scenarios, nested loops often become necessary to traverse multidimensional data structures or to perform repetitive tasks within sublists. It is crucial to understand how the break and continue statements work within these nested structures to control the flow of the script effectively.

Let us start by examining a nested loop scenario and incorporate the break statement. Consider the following PowerShell script which iterates through a 2D array to find a specific element, terminating both the inner and outer loops when the element is found:

```
$matrix = @(
    @(1, 2, 3),
    @(4, 5, 6),
    @(7, 8, 9)
)

$searchValue = 5
$found = $false

for ($i=0; $i -lt $matrix.Length; $i++) {
    for ($j=0; $j -lt $matrix[$i].Length; $j++) {
        if ($matrix[$i][$j] -eq $searchValue) {
            $found = $true
            Write-Output "Value $searchValue found at position ($i, $j)"
            break
        }
    }
    if ($found) {
        break
    }
}
```

Executing the script yields the following output:

```
Value 5 found at position (1, 1)
```

The script showcases the use of the break statement within both the inner and the outer loops. Once the searchValue is found, the inner loop breaks first. An additional check if ($found) ensures that the outer loop also exits immediately, preventing any further unnecessary iterations.

Next, we consider the continue statement within nested loops. The continue statement skips the remaining code in the current iteration and proceeds with the next iteration of the enclosing loop. In nested loops, the continue statement only affects the loop where it is invoked. Below is an example where we skip over even numbers in a 2D array:

```
for ($i=0; $i -lt $matrix.Length; $i++) {
    for ($j=0; $j -lt $matrix[$i].Length; $j++) {
        if ($matrix[$i][$j] % 2 -eq 0) {
            continue
        }
        Write-Output "Odd value: $($matrix[$i][$j]) at position ($i, $j)"
    }
}
```

Executing the script results in:

```
Odd value: 1 at position (0, 0)
```

```
Odd value: 3 at position (0, 2)
Odd value: 5 at position (1, 1)
Odd value: 7 at position (2, 0)
Odd value: 9 at position (2, 2)
```

In this example, whenever an even number is encountered, the continue statement causes the script to skip the current iteration of the inner loop and proceed to the next value, ensuring only odd numbers are processed and displayed.

When dealing with more complex nested loops, it is often useful to maintain precise control over which loop is affected by the break or continue statement. PowerShell does not provide labeled break or continue statements, meaning that the flow must be controlled through conditional checks and appropriate structuring of loops:

```
$exitFlag = $false

for ($i=0; $i -lt $matrix.Length; $i++) {
    if ($exitFlag) {
        break
    }
    for ($j=0; $j -lt $matrix[$i].Length; $j++) {
        if ($matrix[$i][$j] -gt 7) {
            $exitFlag = $true
            break
        }
        if ($matrix[$i][$j] % 2 -eq 0) {
            continue
        }
        Write-Output "Processed odd value: $($matrix[$i][$j])"
    }
}
```

In this code, break terminates the inner loop when the matrix value exceeds 7, and the outer loop is subsequently terminated due to the exitFlag. The continue statement skips processing for even numbers within the inner loop.

Understanding and employing break and continue statements proficiently is critical to managing nested loops and ensuring the script performs efficiently and correctly. Careful placement and checks using Boolean flags can provide fine-grained control over the script's execution flow without excessive complexity.

5.10 Practical Examples of Control Flow

In this section, we will delve into practical examples of control flow using PowerShell. The examples provided here will integrate various control flow constructs, demonstrating their application in real-world scenarios. These examples assume a grounding in the basic concepts discussed in the previous sections such as if, else, elseif, switch, for, foreach, while, do-while, break, and continue statements.

Example 1: Processing a List of Files

This example showcases a script that processes a list of files in a directory, checking for files with a specific extension and performing a clean-up operation.

```
# Get all files in the directory
$files = Get-ChildItem -Path "C:\ExampleDirectory"

foreach ($file in $files) {
    if ($file.Extension -eq ".log") {
        Write-Output "Deleting file: $($file.FullName)"
        Remove-Item -Path $file.FullName
    } elseif ($file.Extension -eq ".tmp") {
        Write-Output "Deleting temporary file: $($file.FullName)"
        Remove-Item -Path $file.FullName
    } else {
        Write-Output "Skipping file: $($file.FullName)"
    }
}
```

In this script, Get-ChildItem retrieves all items in the specified directory. The foreach loop iterates over each file, and the if-elseif-else construct checks the file extension. Log and temporary files are deleted, while other files are skipped.

Example 2: Parsing a Configuration File

Consider a scenario where you need to parse a configuration file and perform actions based on its contents. Assume the configuration file has key-value pairs.

```
# Read configuration file
$config = Get-Content -Path "C:\ExampleConfig.txt"

foreach ($line in $config) {
    $parts = $line -split "="
    $key = $parts[0].Trim()
    $value = $parts[1].Trim()

    switch ($key) {
        "LogLevel" {
            Write-Output "Setting log level to $value"
            # Code to set log level
            break
        }
        "MaxConnections" {
            Write-Output "Setting maximum connections to $value"
            # Code to set max connections
```

```
            break
        }
        "EnableFeatureX" {
            if ($value -eq "True") {
                Write-Output "Feature X is enabled"
                # Code to enable Feature X
            } else {
                Write-Output "Feature X is disabled"
                # Code to disable Feature X
            }
            break
        }
        default {
            Write-Output "Unknown configuration key: $key"
        }
    }
}
```

Here, Get-Content reads the configuration file into an array of strings, with each line representing a key-value pair. The foreach loop iterates through each line, splitting it into key and value, and the switch statement handles different configuration settings.

Example 3: Monitoring System Resource Usage

A more complex example involves monitoring CPU and memory usage, taking action if usage exceeds defined thresholds.

```
# Define thresholds
$cpuThreshold = 80
$memoryThreshold = 70

while ($true) {
    # Get CPU and memory usage
    $cpuUsage = (Get-WmiObject Win32_Processor | Measure-Object -Property
        LoadPercentage -Average).Average
    $memoryUsage = (Get-WmiObject Win32_OperatingSystem).
        TotalVisibleMemorySize - (Get-WmiObject Win32_OperatingSystem).
        FreePhysicalMemory

    $memoryUsagePercentage = ($memoryUsage / (Get-WmiObject
        Win32_OperatingSystem).TotalVisibleMemorySize) * 100

    if ($cpuUsage -gt $cpuThreshold) {
        Write-Output "High CPU usage detected: $cpuUsage%"
        # Code to handle high CPU usage
    }

    if ($memoryUsagePercentage -gt $memoryThreshold) {
        Write-Output "High memory usage detected: $memoryUsagePercentage%"
        # Code to handle high memory usage
    }

    Start-Sleep -Seconds 10
}
```

This script continuously monitors CPU and memory usage. The while loop runs indefinitely, retrieving system resource information using Get-WmiObject. If usage exceeds the thresholds, appropriate messages are displayed and actions can be taken. The loop pauses for 10 seconds using Start-Sleep before repeating.

Example 4: Recursive Directory Traversal

Recursively traversing directories can be useful for file management tasks. The following example demonstrates a recursive function to list all files in a directory and its subdirectories.

```
function Get-AllFiles {
    param (
        [string]$path
    )

    $items = Get-ChildItem -Path $path

    foreach ($item in $items) {
        if ($item.PSIsContainer) {
            # Recursively call the function for directories
            Get-AllFiles -path $item.FullName
        } else {
            Write-Output $item.FullName
        }
    }
}

# Initial call to the function
Get-AllFiles -path "C:\ExampleDirectory"
```

The Get-AllFiles function accepts a directory path as a parameter and lists all files within that directory, including its subdirectories. If an item is a directory (as determined by PSIsContainer), the function calls itself recursively. The initial call to Get-AllFiles starts the traversal.

These examples illustrate how control flow constructs can be applied to craft effective PowerShell scripts for a variety of tasks, from file management and configuration parsing to system monitoring and directory traversal. By further modifying and building upon these examples, you can address specific requirements and optimize script performance in complex scenarios.

Chapter 6

Functions and Scripts

This chapter introduces the concepts of functions and scripts in PowerShell. It covers creating and running basic functions, using parameters, and understanding parameter sets. The chapter also explains returning values from functions, scope and lifetime of function variables, and introduces scripting fundamentals. Writing, running, and passing arguments to PowerShell scripts are discussed, as well as signing scripts and configuring execution policies, providing a comprehensive guide for effective script and function development.

6.1 Introduction to Functions

Functions are essential constructs in PowerShell that allow developers to encapsulate a series of commands into a single callable unit. This encapsulation promotes code reuse, simplifies maintenance, and enhances the readability of scripts. In PowerShell, functions are defined using the `function` keyword followed by a name and a script block.

```
# Basic Function Syntax
function FunctionName {
    # Function code here
}
```

The name of a function should be descriptive and follow standard naming conventions to facilitate understanding and consistency. Within the braces, PowerShell code is written to perform specific tasks, operations, or calculations.

To provide a practical example, consider a function that calculates the square of a number:

```
function Get-Square {
    param ($number)
    return $number * $number
}
```

Here, the function Get-Square accepts a single parameter $number and returns its square. This basic example illustrates the convenience of encapsulating repetitive operations into functions. You can call the function as follows:

```
$square = Get-Square -number 5
Write-Output $square
```

The output will be:

```
25
```

Functions in PowerShell not only help in organizing code but also support parameters that enhance their versatility. Parameters act as inputs to functions, making them dynamic and adaptable to different contexts. By using parameters, functions avoid hardcoding values, thereby improving flexibility and reusability.

PowerShell supports a variety of parameter attributes and features, such as default values, mandatory parameters, and validation sets, which can be utilized to define robust and user-friendly functions. Here is an example demonstrating a function with a mandatory parameter:

```
function Get-Cube {
    [CmdletBinding()]
    param (
        [Parameter(Mandatory=$true)]
        [int]$number
    )
    return $number * $number * $number
}
```

In this example, the parameter $number is marked as mandatory, ensuring that the user must provide a value when calling the function. The CmdletBinding attribute is used to create a more cmdlet-like function, incorporating advanced features such as pipeline input and common parameters.

Calling this function without providing the required parameter will result in an error:

```
Get-Cube
```

The resulting error message:

```
Get-Cube : Cannot process command because of one or more missing mandatory parameters: number.
```

When the user provides a value for the $number parameter, the function computes and returns the cube of the input value. Functions can also include multiple parameters, each with its own set of attributes and validation logic, allowing for complex and nuanced operations.

The process for defining and invoking PowerShell functions remains consistent regardless of complexity. Developers can incrementally build upon basic functions, integrating error handling, logging, and other standardized practices, thereby creating modular and maintainable scripts.

Evaluating the scope and definition of functions in larger scripts is essential. Well-structured functions pave the way for testing individual components, ensuring each part functions correctly before incorporating them into broader workflows. Attention to encapsulating specific tasks within functions not only fosters clarity but also significantly reduces the chances of introducing errors during script development and expansion.

In summary, functions in PowerShell serve as a cornerstone of script development. Their ability to encapsulate and encapsulate logic, handle parameters dynamically, and promote reusability is crucial for both novice and advanced scripting tasks. Understanding the fundamentals of function creation and invocation provides a strong foundation for further exploring more complex scripting constructs in PowerShell. Functions, when used effectively, streamline processes and facilitate efficient script construction and execution.

6.2 Creating and Running Basic Functions

Creating basic functions in PowerShell is straightforward and involves defining the function using the function keyword followed by the function name, a set of parentheses, and a script block containing the function code. This process enhances code reusability and modularity, allowing users to encapsulate specific tasks within self-contained units.

The syntax to define a basic function is as follows:

```
function <FunctionName> {
```

```
    <code>
}
```

To solidify understanding, consider the creation of a simple function named Greet-User that outputs a greeting message.

```
function Greet-User {
    Write-Output "Hello, User!"
}
```

To run or invoke the Greet-User function, simply call the function by its name:

```
Greet-User
```

The output will be:

```
Hello, User!
```

PowerShell functions may also include parameters to accept input values, providing flexibility and enabling dynamic behavior. Parameters are specified within the parentheses following the function name. To add parameters, use the param keyword, followed by the parameter definitions in a script block.

An example of a function with parameters is as follows:

```
function Greet-Person {
    param (
        [string]$Name,
        [int]$Age
    )
    Write-Output "Hello, $Name! You are $Age years old."
}
```

This function can be invoked with arguments to output a personalized greeting:

```
Greet-Person -Name "Alice" -Age 30
```

The output will be:

```
Hello, Alice! You are 30 years old.
```

Functions may also contain positional parameters, allowing users to provide arguments without explicitly naming them. This is achieved by enclosing the parameter definitions within the param block and leveraging powers of position to reduce verbosity.

For instance, modifying Greet-Person to support positional parameters involves specifying the argument position within the parameter attributes:

```
function Greet-Person {
    param (
        [string][Position(0)]$Name,
        [int][Position(1)]$Age
    )
    Write-Output "Hello, $Name! You are $Age years old."
}
```

The function can then be called using positional arguments:

```
Greet-Person "Alice" 30
```

The output remains consistent while reducing input verbosity:

```
Hello, Alice! You are 30 years old.
```

Returning values from functions is essential for processing outputs mathematically or logically. A return statement explicitly returns a value from a function, although PowerShell also implicitly returns the output of the last statement executed.

Consider a simple example where a function calculates the square of a number:

```
function Get-Square {
    param (
        [int]$Number
    )
    return $Number * $Number
}
```

Invoking this function:

```
$result = Get-Square -Number 4
Write-Output $result
```

The output would be:

```
16
```

In implicit return scenarios, a function may omit the return keyword, relying on PowerShell's default behavior:

```
function Get-Square {
    param (
        [int]$Number
    )
    $Number * $Number
}
```

Called in the same manner:

```
$result = Get-Square -Number 4
```

```
Write-Output $result
```

The output remains:

```
16
```

Executing and running functions effectively requires understanding the scoping rules, which dictate variable visibility. Local scope confines variable visibility to the function, while global scope allows cross-function accessibility. Functions can explicitly declare scopes for variables using global:, script:, local:, and private: prefixes.

For a practical demonstration, consider this example of a global variable within a function:

```
$global:message = "Global message"

function Display-Message {
    $message = "Local message"
    Write-Output $message
}

Display-Message
Write-Output $global:message
```

Execution provides insight into scope considerations:

```
Local message
Global message
```

Following these foundational techniques, users can efficiently create and run PowerShell functions to bolster script effectiveness, leading to systematic task automation and enhanced code organization.

6.3 Using Parameters in Functions

In PowerShell, parameters allow functions to accept input, making them versatile and reusable. By defining parameters, we enhance the function's flexibility, enabling it to perform tasks based on the provided inputs. This section will delve into the syntax and practices for using parameters in PowerShell functions, ensuring that readers can efficiently create dynamic and adaptable scripts.

To define parameters in a function, we utilize the param keyword or the Param() block. These approaches enable you to specify one or more parameters, each potentially with default values, data types, validation rules, and more.

The basic syntax for defining parameters in a function is as follows:

```
function FunctionName {
    param (
        [DataType]$ParameterName1,
        [DataType]$ParameterName2 = DefaultValue
    )
    # Function code here
}
```

DataType specifies the type of data the parameter accepts (e.g., int, string, bool, etc.). Let's consider an example where we create a function that takes two parameters: a name and an age, and then prints out a greeting message:

```
function Greet-User {
    param (
        [string]$Name,
        [int]$Age
    )
    Write-Output "Hello, $Name. You are $Age years old."
}
```

To call this function and pass values to the parameters, you would use the following syntax:

```
Greet-User -Name "Alice" -Age 30
```

The output will be:

```
Hello, Alice. You are 30 years old.
```

Using Default Values

In some cases, it might be useful to provide default values for parameters. When a default value is specified, the function uses this value if the parameter is not supplied when the function is called. For example:

```
function Greet-User {
    param (
        [string]$Name = "User",
        [int]$Age = 18
    )
    Write-Output "Hello, $Name. You are $Age years old."
}
```

If the function is called without arguments:

```
Greet-User
```

The output will be:

```
Hello, User. You are 18 years old.
```

Mandatory Parameters

To enforce that a parameter must be provided by the caller, mark the parameter as mandatory. This is achieved using the [Parameter(Mandatory=$true)] attribute:

```
function Greet-User {
    param (
        [Parameter(Mandatory=$true)][string]$Name,
        [int]$Age
    )
    Write-Output "Hello, $Name. You are $Age years old."
}
```

Calling this function without the mandatory Name parameter will result in a prompt requesting the parameter value:

```
Greet-User -Age 30
```

The output will be:

```
cmdlet Greet-User at command pipeline position 1
Supply values for the following parameters:
Name:
```

Parameter Validation

PowerShell supports various validation attributes to ensure parameters meet certain criteria before executing the function. Examples include [ValidateRange()], [ValidateSet()], and [ValidatePattern()]. Below is an example using [ValidateRange()] to ensure the age falls within a certain range:

```
function Greet-User {
    param (
        [string]$Name,
        [ValidateRange(0, 120)][int]$Age
    )
    Write-Output "Hello, $Name. You are $Age years old."
}
```

Example with Multiple Validation Attributes

Let's create a function that validates a username (must be non-empty and a member of a specific set) and a password (must have a minimum length):

```
function Register-User {
    param (
        [ValidateNotNullOrEmpty()][ValidateSet("Alice", "Bob", "Charlie")][string]
            $Username,
        [ValidatePattern("^(?=.*[A-Za-z])(?=.*\d)[A-Za-z\d]{8,}$")][string]$Password
    )
    Write-Output "User $Username is successfully registered."
}
```

In this example, Username must be one of "Alice", "Bob", or "Charlie", and Password must be at least 8 characters long, containing both letters and digits.

Named vs. Positional Parameters

PowerShell functions can accept parameters by position as well as by name. If no Position attribute is specified, parameters are assumed to be named. To specify positional parameters, use the Position attribute:

```
function Add-Numbers {
    param (
        [Parameter(Position=0)][int]$a,
        [Parameter(Position=1)][int]$b
    )
    Write-Output ($a + $b)
}
```

You can call this function using either:

```
Add-Numbers -a 5 -b 10
```

or by relying on positions:

```
Add-Numbers 5 10
```

Both invocations return:

```
15
```

Integrating parameters effectively within PowerShell functions significantly enhances their utility and adaptability. By meticulously defining parameters, establishing default values, enforcing mandatory fields, and incorporating validation, functions become robust tools that cater to a wide array of scripting needs.

6.4 Understanding Parameter Sets

When working with functions in PowerShell, understanding and effectively utilizing parameter sets is crucial for creating robust and flexible functions. Parameter sets in PowerShell allow function designers to define multiple sets of parameters, each offering a different way to invoke the function. This capability is invaluable when a function needs to support multiple scenarios that should not be used simultaneously.

A parameter set is essentially a grouping of parameters that function together. Each parameter set defines a unique combination or subset of parameters that can be used to execute a command. PowerShell determines which parameter set is being used based on the unique parameter or combination of parameters supplied by the user. It ensures that only one parameter set is employed when a function is called, avoiding conflicts between parameters that should not coexist.

```
function Get-InventoryItem {
    [CmdletBinding(DefaultParameterSetName='ByName')]
    param (
        [Parameter(ParameterSetName='ByName', Mandatory=$true)]
        [string]$Name,

        [Parameter(ParameterSetName='ByID', Mandatory=$true)]
        [int]$ItemID,

        [Parameter(ParameterSetName='ByCategory', Mandatory=$true)]
        [string]$Category
    )

    switch ($PSCmdlet.ParameterSetName) {
        'ByName' { "Searching by Name: $Name" }
        'ByID' { "Searching by ID: $ItemID" }
        'ByCategory' { "Searching by Category: $Category" }
    }
}
```

In the example above, the Get-InventoryItem function is defined with three parameter sets: ByName, ByID, and ByCategory. Each parameter set has one mandatory parameter, ensuring that when the function is called, the user must provide a parameter that matches exactly one of these sets. The CmdletBinding attribute includes a DefaultParameterSetName, which specifies the default parameter set to use if the user does not explicitly specify a parameter that belongs to a particular set.

When the function is executed, PowerShell uses the $PSCmdlet.ParameterSetName variable to determine which parameter set is being used and performs the appropriate action. The switch statement in the function evaluates this variable and executes the corresponding block of code.

Consider the following example function calls to understand how different parameter sets can be invoked:

```
Get-InventoryItem -Name "Widget"
Get-InventoryItem -ItemID 123
Get-InventoryItem -Category "Tools"
```

These invocations correspond to the ByName, ByID, and ByCategory parameter sets, respectively.

```
Searching by Name: Widget
Searching by ID: 123
Searching by Category: Tools
```

It is essential to ensure that parameter sets are mutually exclusive and that no parameters are unintentionally shared among sets, as this can lead to ambiguity. Suppose parameters are shared across sets; these parameters should not be mandatory unless correctly prioritized through the design to avoid conflicts.

Here's an example extending the previous function to include optional parameters that are shared across parameter sets:

```
function Get-InventoryItem {
    [CmdletBinding(DefaultParameterSetName='ByName')]
    param (
        [Parameter(ParameterSetName='ByName', Mandatory=$true)]
        [string]$Name,

        [Parameter(ParameterSetName='ByID', Mandatory=$true)]
        [int]$ItemID,

        [Parameter(ParameterSetName='ByCategory', Mandatory=$true)]
        [string]$Category,

        [Parameter()]
        [switch]$Detailed
    )

    switch ($PSCmdlet.ParameterSetName) {
        'ByName' {
            if ($Detailed) {
                "Searching by Name with details: $Name"
            } else {
                "Searching by Name: $Name"
            }
        }
        'ByID' {
            if ($Detailed) {
                "Searching by ID with details: $ItemID"
            } else {
                "Searching by ID: $ItemID"
            }
        }
        'ByCategory' {
            if ($Detailed) {
                "Searching by Category with details: $Category"
            } else {
                "Searching by Category: $Category"
            }
        }
    }
}
```

In this modification, the $Detailed parameter is optional and shared across all parameter sets. It acts as a switch parameter to provide detailed output if specified. When passed, PowerShell evaluates the current parameter set and checks if the $Detailed switch is set, effectively refining the output based on the presence of this shared optional parameter.

```
Get-InventoryItem -Name "Widget" -Detailed
Get-InventoryItem -ItemID 123
Get-InventoryItem -Category "Tools" -Detailed
```

```
Searching by Name with details: Widget
Searching by ID: 123
Searching by Category with details: Tools
```

Understanding parameter sets enables the delivery of more versatile functions by clearly defining distinct pathways for parameter input. This ensures functions can handle multiple use cases seamlessly without parameter conflicts, promoting both reliability and user-friendliness in script design. Parameter sets are instrumental in maintaining clarity and flexibility in complex script scenarios, empowering script authors to cater to diverse requirements effectively and elegantly.

6.5 Returning Values from Functions

When developing PowerShell functions, it is a common requirement to return values from these functions. PowerShell, with its flexibility, supports several methods to return values, enabling developers to adopt the approach that best suits their needs. Understanding the various ways to return values from functions is fundamental to writing effective and reusable scripts.

Write-Output is the standard cmdlet used for returning a value from a function. Whenever Write-Output is called within a function, the output is sent to the pipeline, which can then be captured by the calling code or redirected as needed. Here is an illustrative example of using Write-Output in a function:

```
function Get-Square {
    param (
        [int]$number
    )
    $result = $number * $number
    Write-Output $result
}

# Calling the function
$square = Get-Square -number 4
Write-Host "The square of 4 is $square"
```

Executing this code in PowerShell will yield the following result:

```
The square of 4 is 16
```

Another method of returning values from functions is through implicit output. This is achieved by simply placing variables or expressions in the script without explicitly using Write-Output. PowerShell automatically treats these as outputs to the pipeline. Here is an example:

```
function Get-Cube {
    param (
        [int]$number
    )
    $result = $number * $number * $number
    $result # Implicitly returned
}

# Calling the function
$cube = Get-Cube -number 3
Write-Host "The cube of 3 is $cube"
```

When this script runs, it produces the following output:

```
The cube of 3 is 27
```

Next, consider cases where you need to return multiple values from a function. In PowerShell, this can also be achieved effortlessly by outputting an array or a custom object. Here is an example that demonstrates how to return multiple values using an array:

```
function Get-Multiples {
    param (
        [int]$number,
        [int]$count
    )
    $multiples = @()
    for ($i = 1; $i -le $count; $i++) {
        $multiples += $number * $i
    }
    return $multiples
}

# Calling the function
$multiples = Get-Multiples -number 5 -count 4
Write-Host "Multiples of 5: $($multiples -join ', ')"
```

This function call will generate the following output:

```
Multiples of 5: 5, 10, 15, 20
```

Alternatively, you can return a custom object to provide more structured data. Create a function that outputs a PSCustomObject:

```
function Get-RectangleDimensions {
    param (
        [int]$length,
        [int]$width
    )
    $dimensions = [PSCustomObject]@{
        Length = $length
        Width = $width
        Area = $length * $width
```

```
        Perimeter = 2 * ($length + $width)
    }
    return $dimensions
}

# Calling the function
$rectangle = Get-RectangleDimensions -length 4 -width 3
Write-Host ("Length: {0}, Width: {1}, Area: {2}, Perimeter: {3}" -f `
    $rectangle.Length, $rectangle.Width, $rectangle.Area, $rectangle.Perimeter)
```

Executing the above function will display:

```
Length: 4, Width: 3, Area: 12, Perimeter: 14
```

These examples highlight PowerShell's versatility in returning various types of data from functions. Whether through Write-Output, implicit return, arrays, or custom objects, mastering these techniques enhances the utility and robustness of your PowerShell scripts.

6.6 Scope and Lifetime of Function Variables

Understanding the scope and lifetime of variables within PowerShell functions is crucial for writing robust and error-free scripts. In PowerShell, the scope of a variable determines its visibility and accessibility within different parts of a script, while the lifetime of a variable pertains to how long the variable exists in memory during the execution of the script.

Variable Scopes

PowerShell defines several distinct scopes where variables can exist:

- **Global Scope:** Variables defined in the global scope are accessible from any part of the script or from functions defined in the same script. These variables remain available throughout the entire session unless explicitly removed.

- **Local Scope:** Local variables are confined within the specific function or script block in which they are declared. They are not accessible outside of that function or script block.

- **Script Scope:** Script-scoped variables are available throughout a single script and all the functions within it. They provide a middle ground between global and local scopes.

- **Private Scope:** Private-scoped variables are similar to local variables but are further restricted to the particular function, script block, or module where they are defined. They cannot be overridden or accessed outside their defined domain, even from subfunctions.

Example of Variable Scopes

Consider the following script:

```
$global:GlobalVariable = "I am Global"
$script:ScriptVariable = "I am Script Scoped"

function Test-Scopes {
    $local:LocalVariable = "I am Local"
    $private:PrivateVariable = "I am Private"
    Write-Output "Inside function:"
    Write-Output "`tGlobal: $global:GlobalVariable"
    Write-Output "`tScript: $script:ScriptVariable"
    Write-Output "`tLocal: $local:LocalVariable"
    Write-Output "`tPrivate: $private:PrivateVariable"
}

Test-Scopes

Write-Output "Outside function:"
Write-Output "`tGlobal: $global:GlobalVariable"
Write-Output "`tScript: $script:ScriptVariable"
Write-Output "`tLocal: ${local:LocalVariable}"
Write-Output "`tPrivate: ${private:PrivateVariable}"
```

The output upon running the above script would be:

```
Inside function:
    Global: I am Global
    Script: I am Script Scoped
    Local: I am Local
    Private: I am Private
Outside function:
    Global: I am Global
    Script: I am Script Scoped
    Local:
    Private:
```

This example illustrates the isolation of local and private variables outside the function scope. The $global:GlobalVariable and $script:ScriptVariable remain accessible both inside and outside the function, whereas $local:LocalVariable and $private:PrivateVariable are not accessible once the execution of Test-Scopes is complete.

Variable Lifetime

The lifetime of a variable is inherently connected to its scope. Global variables persist for the entire session or until explicitly removed. Script-scoped variables exist for the duration of the script execution. Local and private variables, on the other hand, only exist for the lifetime of the function or script block where they are defined. The values stored in these variables are purged from memory once the function completes execution.

Managing Variable Scope and Lifetime

Efficient management of variable scope and lifetime ensures that memory is used optimally and reduces the risk of variable conflicts or unwanted side effects. It is best practice to use the most restrictive scope that meets your needs:

- Use private scope for variables local to a module or function to prevent any accidental modifications from outside.
- Use local scope for temporary data used only within a function.
- Avoid unnecessary global and script-scoped variables unless they must be shared across multiple functions or scripts.

Example of Scope Management in a Function

The example below demonstrates efficient scope management within a PowerShell script:

```
function Process-Data {
    param(
        [string]$input
    )

    $private:result = $null # Private variable for internal use

    # Simulated data processing
    if ($input -eq "Critical") {
        $private:status = "Error"
    }
    else {
        $private:status = "Success"
    }

    # Return the status
    return $private:status
}

# Test the function
$status = Process-Data -input "Critical"
Write-Output "Processing Status: $status"
```

In this example, the function Process-Data uses $private:result and $private:status variables, which are confined to the function's internal logic.

By limiting the scope to private, these variables are prevented from causing unintended side effects elsewhere in the script.

A meticulous approach to managing scope and lifetime not only leads to cleaner, more maintainable code but also ensures that scripts perform efficiently and predictably.

6.7 Introduction to Scripts

In PowerShell, scripts are fundamental components utilized to automate tasks and execute complex sequences of commands. Unlike functions, which are generally designed for reuse and can be called within other scripts or directly from the command line, scripts typically encapsulate a specific series of operations to be executed sequentially.

Scripts in PowerShell are files with the .ps1 extension, containing a list of commands and logic structures that the PowerShell runtime executes in order. This allows for the encapsulation of repetitive tasks, the automation of administrative processes, and the centralization of elaborate command sequences.

Creating a Script

To create a PowerShell script, one simply needs to create a new text file with a .ps1 extension and populate it with the desired PowerShell commands. Using any text editor such as Notepad, Visual Studio Code, or the PowerShell Integrated Scripting Environment (ISE) can facilitate this process. For instance, consider the following simple script:

```
# SampleScript.ps1
Write-Host "Hello, World!"
```

This script contains a single command, Write-Host, which outputs a string to the console.

Running a Script

After writing a script, it must be executed within a PowerShell session. This can be done by navigating to the directory containing the script and calling it by its name preceded by a dot-slash (.
) to indicate its location. For example:

```
.\SampleScript.ps1
```

This command executes SampleScript.ps1, resulting in the output:

```
Hello, World!
```

However, executing scripts may not always be straightforward due to PowerShell's execution policy, which restricts script execution by default to prevent unauthorized and potentially harmful scripts from running.

Execution Policy

PowerShell's execution policy determines the conditions under which scripts are allowed to run. Several different execution policies exist:

- Restricted: No scripts can be run. PowerShell is limited to interactive commands only.
- AllSigned: Only scripts signed by a trusted publisher can be run.
- RemoteSigned: Downloaded scripts must be signed by a trusted publisher before they can be run.
- Unrestricted: Unsigned scripts can run, but prompts appear before running scripts downloaded from the internet.

To view the current execution policy, use the command:

```
Get-ExecutionPolicy
```

The execution policy can be modified using the Set-ExecutionPolicy cmdlet. For example, to allow running of all scripts, one might set the policy to Unrestricted:

```
Set-ExecutionPolicy Unrestricted
```

Administrator privileges are required to change the execution policy. The policy should be set responsibly, considering the balance between script execution needs and system security.

Script Structure

Scripts can include various elements such as commands, variables, expressions, control structures, functions, and comments. It's essential to write scripts that are not only functional but also maintainable and readable. For example, consider a more complex script that retrieves and displays system information:

```
# Get-SystemInfo.ps1
param (
    [string]$ComputerName = "localhost"
```

```
)
$os = Get-WmiObject -Class Win32_OperatingSystem -ComputerName
    $ComputerName
$cpu = Get-WmiObject -Class Win32_Processor -ComputerName $ComputerName

Write-Host "Computer: $($os.PSComputerName)"
Write-Host "OS: $($os.Caption) $($os.Version)"
Write-Host "CPU: $($cpu.Name)"
```

This script employs the param keyword to define a parameter, ComputerName, with a default value of localhost. It uses Get-WmiObject to gather operating system and processor information from the specified computer. This data is then printed to the console using Write-Host.

To execute the script and gather information from a remote computer named Server01, one would use:

```
.\Get-SystemInfo.ps1 -ComputerName Server01
```

Handling Errors

Proper error handling within scripts is crucial for ensuring that unforeseen issues do not cause scripts to fail unexpectedly. PowerShell provides robust error handling features through the use of try, catch, and finally blocks. Here is an example demonstrating error handling:

```
# ErrorHandlingExample.ps1
try {
    $fileContent = Get-Content -Path "C:\NonExistentFile.txt"
    Write-Host $fileContent
} catch {
    Write-Host "An error occurred: $($_.Exception.Message)"
} finally {
    Write-Host "Script execution completed."
}
```

In this script, Get-Content attempts to read a file that does not exist. The catch block captures the error and prints a descriptive message to the console. The finally block executes regardless of whether an error occurred, ensuring certain operations (e.g., cleanup actions) are always performed.

By understanding these concepts and practices, users can develop efficient and reliable PowerShell scripts that automate tasks and streamline operations.

6.8 Writing and Running PowerShell Scripts

In PowerShell, scripts serve as reusable blocks of code encapsulated in files with the .ps1 extension. These scripts facilitate automation, enable complex workflows, and streamline task management, making them indispensable for administrators and developers. Understanding how to write and run PowerShell scripts is essential for leveraging the full potential of PowerShell.

Creating a PowerShell Script

To create a PowerShell script, an editor such as Visual Studio Code, Notepad, or the PowerShell ISE can be used. The steps to create a script are as follows:

1. Open your preferred text editor.
2. Write the desired PowerShell commands, functions, or expressions.
3. Save the file with a .ps1 extension, for example, ExampleScript.ps1.

For instance, consider the following simple script that outputs a greeting message to the console:

```
# ExampleScript.ps1
Write-Output "Hello, PowerShell Scripting!"
```

Running a PowerShell Script

To execute a PowerShell script, you must have the correct execution policy set, and the script must be invoked properly from the PowerShell console or a script editor with execution capabilities.

1. Open the PowerShell console (Windows PowerShell or PowerShell Core).
2. Navigate to the script's directory using the cd command.
3. Execute the script using one of the following methods:
    - Using the relative path:

      .\ExampleScript.ps1

    - Using the full path:

```
C:\Path\To\Your\Script\ExampleScript.ps1
```

When the script is executed, the output will be displayed in the console:

```
Hello, PowerShell Scripting!
```

Execution Policies

PowerShell execution policies determine the conditions under which PowerShell loads configuration files and runs scripts. There are several execution policies available:

- Restricted: No scripts are allowed to run.
- AllSigned: Only scripts signed by a trusted publisher can run.
- RemoteSigned: Downloaded scripts must be signed by a trusted publisher.
- Unrestricted: All scripts can run.

To set an execution policy, use the Set-ExecutionPolicy cmdlet. For example, to set the policy to RemoteSigned, run the following command:

```
Set-ExecutionPolicy RemoteSigned
```

You can check the current execution policy by executing:

```
Get-ExecutionPolicy
```

Handling Script Parameters

Scripts can accept parameters, allowing them to be more dynamic and versatile. Parameters are defined using the param keyword at the beginning of the script. For example:

```
# ExampleScriptWithParams.ps1
param (
    [string]$Name,
    [int]$Age
)

Write-Output "Name: $Name"
Write-Output "Age: $Age"
```

To run this script with parameters, use the following syntax:

```
.\ExampleScriptWithParams.ps1 -Name "Alice" -Age 30
```

The output will be:

```
Name: Alice
Age: 30
```

Commenting and Documentation

Effective commenting and documentation within scripts are crucial for maintainability and collaboration. Comments in PowerShell are denoted with the # symbol. Block comments can be written using <# ... #> syntax. For example:

```
<#
This is a block comment.
It can span multiple lines.
#>

# This is a single-line comment
Write-Output "Hello, comments!"
```

Providing a description and usage details at the top of the script helps future users understand its purpose and how to execute it.

Error Handling

Proper error handling ensures scripts run smoothly and provide meaningful error messages when issues arise. PowerShell provides Try and Catch blocks for this purpose:

```
try {
    # Code that might generate an error
    Get-Item "C:\\NonExistentFile.txt"
} catch {
    # Code to handle the error
    Write-Output "An error occurred: $_"
}
```

In this example, if the file C:
NonExistentFile.txt does not exist, the catch block will handle the error, and a message will be displayed.

Best Practices

Adhering to best practices in script development ensures readability, reliability, and scalability. Key practices include:

- Consistent naming conventions for variables, functions, and files.
- Modularizing code into functions for reusability.
- Including comments and documentation.

- Using error handling to manage exceptions robustly.
- Testing scripts thoroughly in different environments.

By following these practices, scripts remain maintainable and adaptable to changing requirements.

6.9 Script Parameters and Arguments

When writing and executing PowerShell scripts, the ability to accept and utilize parameters and arguments significantly enhances the script's flexibility and applicability. Parameters and arguments allow scripts to be more dynamic by acting upon different inputs without modifying the script's internal code. This section explores defining, accessing, and utilizing parameters within PowerShell scripts, and demonstrates the different types of parameters and argument behaviors.

To define parameters in a PowerShell script, use the param keyword at the beginning of the script. The param statement is followed by a comma-separated list of parameters enclosed in parentheses. Parameters can be declared with or without types. Including type specifications helps in validating the input before the script's logic is executed.

```
param(
    [string]$name,
    [int]$age,
    [string]$city
)

Write-Output "Name: $name"
Write-Output "Age: $age"
Write-Output "City: $city"
```

Executing the above script requires passing the appropriate arguments for each defined parameter. Parameters can be provided by position, by name, or a combination of both.

```
PS C:\> .\script.ps1 -name "John Doe" -age 30 -city "New York"
Name: John Doe
Age: 30
City: New York

PS C:\> .\script.ps1 "Jane Doe" 25 "Los Angeles"
Name: Jane Doe
Age: 25
City: Los Angeles
```

Named Parameters: Using named parameters is straightforward; each parameter is prefixed with the hyphen (-) character followed by the parameter name and its corresponding value. Named parameters enhance the clarity of the script invocation and ensure that arguments are correctly mapped to parameters, regardless of their order.

Positional Parameters: Parameters can also be specified by their position in the script, relying on the order they are defined within the param block. Using positional parameters is concise but less explicit, which may lead to errors if arguments are not provided in the expected sequence.

Combining Named and Positional Parameters: PowerShell scripts allow combining named and positional parameters, but it's essential to follow positional arguments with their named counterparts to avoid confusion.

```
.\script.ps1 "Alice" -city "Seattle"
```

Default Parameter Values: Parameters can be assigned default values within the param block. Default values are utilized when no corresponding arguments are supplied during script execution.

```
param(
    [string]$name = "Default Name",
    [int]$age = 18,
    [string]$city = "Unknown"
)

Write-Output "Name: $name"
Write-Output "Age: $age"
Write-Output "City: $city"
```

Executing this script without providing any arguments will output the default values:

```
PS C:\> .\script.ps1
Name: Default Name
Age: 18
City: Unknown
```

Mandatory Parameters: It is sometimes necessary to ensure that certain parameters are provided with valid arguments whenever the script is executed. This can be achieved using the Mandatory attribute. If a mandatory parameter is not supplied, PowerShell prompts the user to provide the missing argument.

```
param(
    [Parameter(Mandatory=$true)]
    [string]$name,

    [Parameter(Mandatory=$true)]
    [int]$age
)
```

```
Write-Output "Name: $name"
Write-Output "Age: $age"
```

Running this script without arguments will prompt:

```
PS C:\> .\script.ps1
cmdlet script.ps1 at command pipeline position 1
Supply values for the following parameters:
name:
age:
```

Switch Parameters: Switch parameters are special Boolean parameters that enable or disable script behavior without requiring a corresponding argument value. Switch parameters are declared using the [switch] type.

```
param(
    [string]$filename,
    [switch]$verbose
)

if ($verbose) {
    Write-Output "Verbose mode is enabled."
}

Write-Output "Processing file: $filename"
```

Executing the script with or without the -verbose switch:

```
PS C:\> .\script.ps1 -filename "data.txt"
Processing file: data.txt

PS C:\> .\script.ps1 -filename "data.txt" -verbose
Verbose mode is enabled.
Processing file: data.txt
```

Understanding and effectively using parameters and arguments in PowerShell scripts allows for greater script flexibility and robustness, enabling script developers to create more adaptable and reusable scripts across diverse scenarios.

6.10 Signing Scripts and Execution Policies

PowerShell scripts, like other types of scripts and executable code, can be potentially harmful if run without proper validation. To mitigate risks and ensure security, PowerShell provides mechanisms to sign scripts and control their execution through execution policies.

Script Signing involves adding a digital signature to your scripts. This signature verifies that the script has not been altered since it was signed. It also confirms the identity of the script's author. To sign a script, you need a code signing certificate, which may be obtained from a trusted certificate authority or generated internally within an organization.

To sign a script, use the Set-AuthenticodeSignature cmdlet. The cmdlet requires the path to the script file and the certificate. Here is an example of signing a script named example.ps1:

```
$cert = Get-ChildItem -Path Cert:\CurrentUser\My -CodeSigningCert
Set-AuthenticodeSignature -FilePath "C:\path\to\example.ps1" -Certificate $cert
```

In this code, Get-ChildItem retrieves the code signing certificate from the certificate store. The Set-AuthenticodeSignature cmdlet then applies this certificate to the specified script file.

After signing a script, you can examine its digital signature using the Get-AuthenticodeSignature cmdlet:

```
Get-AuthenticodeSignature -FilePath "C:\path\to\example.ps1"
```

This command returns information about the script's signature, including the status, signer certificate, and timestamp.

Execution Policies in PowerShell define the conditions under which scripts are allowed to run. The purpose is to prevent the accidental execution of malicious scripts. PowerShell's execution policies are categorized as follows:

- Restricted: No scripts are allowed to run. Only individual commands are permitted.
- AllSigned: Requires all scripts and configuration files to be signed by a trusted publisher.
- RemoteSigned: Requires scripts emanating from the internet to be signed by a trusted publisher before they can be run.
- Unrestricted: Allows all scripts to run, but warns the user before executing scripts not originating from the local machine.
- Bypass: No restrictions; all scripts run without warning or prompt.
- Undefined: Removes the currently assigned execution policy from the current scope.

To view the current execution policy, use the Get-ExecutionPolicy cmdlet:

```
Restricted
```

To set a new execution policy, use the Set-ExecutionPolicy cmdlet. For example, to set the policy to RemoteSigned, execute:

```
Set-ExecutionPolicy -ExecutionPolicy RemoteSigned
```

This command adjusts the execution policy for the entire system. You may also modify the policy for the current user or the current PowerShell session by using the -Scope parameter:

```
Set-ExecutionPolicy -ExecutionPolicy RemoteSigned -Scope CurrentUser
```

```
Set-ExecutionPolicy -ExecutionPolicy RemoteSigned -Scope Process
```

For enhanced security in organizational environments, it is prudent to set the policy to AllSigned. This ensures that only scripts with a valid, trusted signature are executed.

Keep in mind the need to maintain a balance between security and flexibility. While strict policies prevent unauthorized script execution, they may also introduce challenges in environments requiring frequent script modifications and deployments.

Chapter 7

Working with Objects and the Pipeline

This chapter delves into working with objects and utilizing the pipeline in PowerShell. It explains the nature of objects, their properties, and methods, and illustrates how objects can be passed through the pipeline. Techniques for filtering, sorting, and selecting objects are discussed, alongside the usage of cmdlets like 'ForEach-Object', 'Group-Object', and 'Measure-Object'. The chapter also covers exporting and importing objects, and presents advanced pipeline techniques to enhance data manipulation and processing capabilities within PowerShell scripts.

7.1 Understanding Objects in PowerShell

PowerShell is built upon the .NET framework, and one of its core strengths lies in its object-oriented nature. In PowerShell, almost everything you work with is an object, including the data you manipulate and the tools you use for manipulation. Understanding objects is crucial to mastering PowerShell scripting.

Representation of Objects

In PowerShell, objects encapsulate both data (properties) and actions (methods). An object is an instance of a class, where a class can be thought of as a blueprint defining the structure and capabilities of its instances. Each object can have multiple properties and methods. For instance, a file object might have properties such as Name, Length, and CreationTime, and methods like CopyTo() and Delete().

To inspect an object's properties and methods, use the Get-Member cmdlet.

```
$file = Get-Item "C:\path\to\your\file.txt"
$file | Get-Member
```

This command will output detailed information about the object's members:

```
  TypeName: System.IO.FileInfo

Name          MemberType Definition
----          ---------- ----------
AppendText    Method     System.IO.StreamWriter AppendText()
...
FullName      Property   string FullName {get;}
...
```

Properties of Objects

Properties are attributes that describe the state of an object. PowerShell cmdlets return objects with properties that you can access and manipulate. For example,

```
$file.Name
$file.Length
$file.CreationTime
```

Each line accesses a specific property of the $file object. This will output:

```
file.txt
1024
01/01/2020 12:00:00
```

Not all properties are mandatory. Classes can define optional properties that might not be present in every instance of that class. If you try to access a non-existent property, PowerShell handles it gracefully by returning $null.

Methods of Objects

Methods are actions that objects can perform. These are functions defined within the object's class and can alter the object or retrieve information. For example, using the CopyTo() method:

```
$file.CopyTo("C:\path\to\new\location\file.txt")
```

This will copy the file to the specified location. Methods can have parameters to customize their actions, and they can return values that reflect the results of their execution.

Creating Custom Objects

PowerShell allows for the creation of custom objects using the New-Object cmdlet or PSCustomObject. Custom objects are particularly useful when you need to structure and manipulate data that doesn't naturally fit into existing classes. For example,

```
$customObject = New-Object PSObject -Property @{
    Name = "John Doe"
    Age = 30
    Occupation = "Developer"
}
```

Alternatively, you can use the #Create a custom object using the [PSCustomObject] technique:

```
$customObject = [PSCustomObject]@{
    Name = "Jane Doe"
    Age = 25
    Occupation = "Analyst"
}
```

Both methods yield an object with the specified properties, which can be accessed and manipulated like any other object.

Types of Objects

PowerShell objects include a wide range of types, often derived from .NET classes. Some common ones include:

- String - Represents text data.
- Int32 - Represents a 32-bit integer.
- Array - Represents a collection of items.
- Hashtable - Represents key-value pairs.
- Custom - User-defined objects.

Each type has its own set of properties and methods, reflecting its intended use. It is essential to understand how to work with various types for effective scripting.

Type Conversion

Type conversion in PowerShell allows the transformation of one object type to another. This is particularly useful when a cmdlet expects a specific type. PowerShell performs implicit conversions in some cases, but explicit conversions can be enforced using casting. For example,

```
$ageString = "30"
$ageInt = [int]$ageString
$ageInt.GetType()
```

This script converts a string containing a number into an integer. The GetType() method confirms the new type of the variable. The output would be:

```
IsPublic IsSerial Name   BaseType
-------- -------- ----   --------
True     True     Int32  System.ValueType
```

Understanding how PowerShell handles objects, including properties, methods, custom objects, types, and conversions, is fundamental. This knowledge forms the foundation for more advanced scripting techniques and effective use of the pipeline. Exploring objects and manipulating them precisely enables powerful automation scripts.

7.2 Properties and Methods of Objects

In PowerShell, objects serve as the fundamental units carrying data, along with the behaviors and functionalities defined through their properties and methods. The understanding of these components is critical for proficient PowerShell scripting and data manipulation.

Properties are attributes that hold data related to the object, whereas methods are actions or functions that an object can execute. Consider an object as an instance of a class, which is a blueprint defining the structure and behavior of objects in object-oriented programming.

Accessing Properties

Properties of an object can be accessed using the dot notation. Given an object $obj, a property Property1 can be accessed as $obj.Property1. This straightforward access method aids in both retrieving and modifying property values.

For instance, consider a simple example using a 'DateTime' object:

```
# Create a DateTime object
$date = Get-Date
```

```
# Access the Year property
$year = $date.Year
Write-Output "Year: $year"

# Access the Month property
$month = $date.Month
Write-Output "Month: $month"

# Modify the Date property
$date = $date.AddDays(5)
Write-Output "Modified Date: $date"
```

```
Year: 2023
Month: 10
Modified Date: 10/26/2023 12:34:56
```

Listing Properties

To enumerate all the properties associated with an object, the 'Get-Member' cmdlet is utilized. This cmdlet reveals both properties and methods of the object:

```
# Create a DateTime object
$date = Get-Date

# List all properties and methods of the DateTime object
$date | Get-Member
```

This command provides detailed information about the type, properties, and methods available on the object. This information is fundamental when navigating unfamiliar objects.

```
   TypeName: System.DateTime

Name         MemberType    Definition
----         ----------    ----------
Add          Method        datetime Add(timespan value)
AddDays      Method        datetime AddDays(double value)
...
Day          Property      int Day {get;}
DayOfWeek    Property      System.DayOfWeek DayOfWeek {get;}
DayOfYear    Property      int DayOfYear {get;}
...
```

Manipulating Properties

Direct manipulation of properties can be performed if the property is not read-only. Assigning new values to properties can be done using similar dot notation. For example, suppose you have an object representing a hypothetical 'Person' class:

```
# Assume $person is an object of class Person
$person = [PSCustomObject]@{
    FirstName = "John"
    LastName = "Doe"
```

```
    Age = 30
}

# Accessing properties
Write-Output "First Name: $person.FirstName"
Write-Output "Last Name: $person.LastName"

# Modifying properties
$person.Age = 31
Write-Output "New Age: $person.Age"
```

```
First Name: John
Last Name: Doe
New Age: 31
```

Invoking Methods

Methods are invoked using parentheses, potentially with arguments. When a method is called, it executes the predefined set of operations encapsulated within it. For a 'DateTime' object, invoking the 'AddDays' method is demonstrated as follows:

```
# Create a DateTime object
$date = Get-Date

# Invoke the AddDays method
$newDate = $date.AddDays(5)
Write-Output "New Date: $newDate"
```

```
New Date: 10/26/2023 12:34:56
```

Exploring Methods

Similarly, the 'Get-Member' cmdlet can be employed to explore the methods of an object. By filtering for the 'Method' 'MemberType', one can isolate and inspect these actionable components:

```
# Create a DateTime object
$date = Get-Date

# List only methods of the DateTime object
$date | Get-Member -MemberType Method
```

```
   TypeName: System.DateTime

Name          MemberType Definition
----          ---------- ----------
Add           Method     datetime Add(timespan value)
AddDays       Method     datetime AddDays(double value)
AddHours      Method     datetime AddHours(double value)
...
```

This provides an invaluable tool for discovering the functionalities available through an object's methods, enhancing the script's capabilities.

Practical Application

The practical application of these principles is pivotal as real-world PowerShell scripts often involve working with numerous object properties and methods—especially in administering and automating system tasks. Consider a scenario where you need to manage files, requiring both properties (e.g., filename, size) and methods (e.g., copy, move).

```
# Retrieve FileInfo object
$file = Get-Item "C:\path\to\file.txt"

# Access properties
Write-Output "File Name: $file.Name"
Write-Output "File Length: $file.Length"

# Invoke methods
$file.CopyTo("C:\path\to\newfile.txt")
Write-Output "File copied to new path"
```

```
File Name: file.txt
File Length: 1024
File copied to new path
```

Understanding the distinction and usage of properties and methods allows for more effective and versatile scripting, leveraging the full power of object-oriented principles within PowerShell.

7.3 Introduction to the Pipeline

The pipeline in PowerShell is a powerful mechanism that allows the transfer of objects from one command to another. This efficient way of processing data leverages the capability of PowerShell to handle objects, making it far more versatile and robust compared to traditional shell environments which primarily deal with text streams.

At a fundamental level, the pipeline takes the output of one cmdlet and uses it as the input to another cmdlet. This chaining of cmdlets enables a streamlined and modular approach to scripting. The symbol | (pipe) is used to denote the pipeline operator.

```
Get-Process | Sort-Object CPU
```

In this example, the Get-Process cmdlet retrieves all the running processes on a system. The resulting list of process objects is then piped into the Sort-Object cmdlet, which sorts these objects based on the CPU property.

Each cmdlet in the pipeline processes the incoming objects one at a time and passes them to the next cmdlet. This approach, termed as process by process, ensures that PowerShell scripts are memory-efficient, particularly when dealing with large datasets.

Pipeline Processing

Understanding the pipeline architecture is pivotal for maximizing its utility. Cmdlets can process pipeline input in three primary ways:

- ByValue: The cmdlet takes an entire object from the pipeline and processes it. It directly matches the accepted .NET object type.
- ByPropertyName: The cmdlet retrieves properties from the pipeline input that match the parameter names. They do not necessarily have to share the same object type, as long as the property names align.
- ByPosition: Though rarely used in the context of the pipeline, cmdlets can also accept parameters based on their position within the pipeline command structure.

Pipeline Parameter Binding

The behavior of the pipeline is governed by a binding system where parameters accept input from the pipeline (pipeline input parameters). Two principal ways define the binding:

```
function Process-Data {
    [CmdletBinding()]
    param (
        [Parameter(ValueFromPipeline=$true)]
        [string]$InputObject
    )
    process {
        $InputObject
    }
}
```

Here, the Process-Data function explicitly declares its param block, indicating ValueFromPipeline=$true for the InputObject parameter. This explicit declaration tells PowerShell to expect input from the pipeline, binding objects to $InputObject.

ValueFromPipelineByPropertyName binds pipeline objects by property names, allowing for more flexible input handling.

```
function Process-DataByProperty {
    [CmdletBinding()]
    param (
        [Parameter(ValueFromPipelineByPropertyName=$true)]
```

```
        [string]$Name
    )
    process {
        $Name
    }
}
```

In this example, if the pipeline objects have a property Name, it binds to the $Name parameter within Process-DataByProperty. This type of binding is particularly advantageous when working with custom objects or when another cmdlet's output matches the expected properties.

Pipeline Operations

Performing operations in the pipeline vertically (one object at a time) rather than horizontally (one cmdlet at a time) allows for continuous, real-time processing. PowerShell employs the Begin, Process, and End blocks to manage this:

```
function Example-Pipeline {
    [CmdletBinding()]
    param (
        [Parameter(ValueFromPipeline=$true)]
        [string]$Item
    )
    begin {
        # One-time setup
        Write-Output "Begin block"
    }
    process {
        # Processing each pipeline object
        Write-Output "Processing $Item"
    }
    end {
        # Cleanup operations
        Write-Output "End block"
    }
}
```

The begin block runs once before any pipeline objects are processed, the process block runs once per pipeline object, and the end block runs once all pipeline objects have been processed. These blocks allow for efficient resource management and maintain operational context across multiple stages.

When constructing PowerShell scripts, leveraging the pipeline correctly can simplify data manipulation and enhance the performance of script execution. This modular nature of the pipeline aligns with PowerShell's object-oriented framework, ensuring predictable and manageable data flows.

Understanding the principles of pipeline processing, parameter binding, and the efficient use of Begin, Process, and End blocks enables the creation of sophisticated and optimized scripts capable of handling complex automation tasks. Effective use of these techniques ensures robust, maintainable, and scalable PowerShell solutions.

7.4 Passing Objects Through the Pipeline

In PowerShell, the pipeline (|) is a fundamental feature that facilitates the streamlined processing and manipulation of objects. By understanding how objects are passed through the pipeline, you will be able to construct efficient and readable scripts that perform complex data transformations.

When you pass objects through the pipeline, you direct the output of one cmdlet as the input to another cmdlet. This mechanism enables the chaining of cmdlets, allowing for the sequential execution of operations on objects without the need for intermediate storage of data.

Consider the following simple example:

```
Get-Process | Where-Object { $_.CPU -gt 100 }
```

Here, Get-Process retrieves a collection of process objects. The pipeline operator (|) passes each process object to the Where-Object cmdlet, which filters the processes based on the condition that the CPU property is greater than 100.

To delve deeper, when objects are passed from one cmdlet to the next, the pipeline performs type-checking to ensure compatible input types. If the cmdlet expects a certain type of object and receives an incompatible type, PowerShell will raise an error. Understanding this behavior is crucial for designing robust scripts.

Objects can be passed in two ways:

- By value (directly using the object instance).
- By property name (using a common property to match incoming objects).

Passing Objects by Value:

Cmdlets often accept objects by value, meaning the actual object instance is passed down the pipeline. For instance, in the above example, each process object retrieved by Get-Process is directly passed to Where-Object.

```
Get-Service | Stop-Service
```

Here, Get-Service retrieves service objects which are directly passed by value to Stop-Service, causing each service to be stopped.

Passing Objects by Property Name:

Some cmdlets can accept objects by matching property names, providing more flexibility. When a property name matches the expected parameter name of the receiving cmdlet, the property's value is passed.

```
$services = Get-Service
$services | Select-Object Name, Status | Export-Csv -Path "services.csv"
```

In this example, Select-Object is used to create a custom object with just Name and Status properties from the service objects. These custom objects are then passed to the Export-Csv cmdlet, creating a CSV file with only the specified properties.

Pipeline Input Bound Parameter Types:

Cmdlet parameters that can accept pipeline input are tagged by PowerShell to indicate if they accept input by value or by property name. This is declared in the cmdlet's parameter attributes. To examine which parameters a cmdlet can accept via the pipeline, use:

```
Get-Help <Cmdlet-Name> -Parameter *
```

Pipeline binding types can be verified for a specific cmdlet, as demonstrated below:

```
Get-Help Stop-Service -Parameter *
```

Among the output, parameters (like -InputObject) will indicate both their pipeline input capability and the type of object expected.

Example: Combining Multiple Cmdlets in a Pipeline:

Building complex operations by chaining cmdlets enhances script functionality. The following sequence illustrates filtering, sorting, and selecting specific properties of processes:

```
Get-Process | Where-Object { $_.CPU -gt 100 } | Sort-Object -Property CPU -
    Descending | Select-Object -First 5 -Property Name, CPU
```

```
Name          CPU
----          ---
ProcessName1  250.34
ProcessName2  230.12
ProcessName3  210.45
ProcessName4  150.67
ProcessName5  120.55
```

1. Get-Process retrieves all processes. 2. Where-Object filters the process objects to include only those with CPU utilization greater than 100. 3. Sort-Object sorts the filtered processes by CPU in descending order. 4. Select-Object selects the top 5 processes, displaying only Name and CPU properties.

By harnessing the power of the pipeline, scripts become powerful, concise, and maintainable, allowing for efficient data manipulation and transformation.

7.5 Filtering Objects in the Pipeline

In PowerShell, filtering objects within the pipeline is a fundamental skill that greatly enhances script efficiency and readability. Through precise filtering, the number of unnecessary items processed by subsequent commands is minimized. We will explore techniques for filtering objects using the cmdlets Where-Object, Select-Object, and Out-GridView.

Where-Object Cmdlet

The Where-Object cmdlet allows you to filter objects based on their properties. This cmdlet evaluates a script block for each object passed through the pipeline, returning only those objects for which the script block evaluates to true. The basic syntax for Where-Object is:

```
Where-Object -Property <property_name> -Operator <comparison_operator> -Value
    <value>
```

For example, suppose you want to filter processes using the 'Process' object. To display only processes consuming more than 100MB of memory, you can execute:

```
Get-Process | Where-Object -Property WorkingSet -GT -Value 100MB
```

Within the Where-Object cmdlet, operators such as -eq (equal), -ne (not equal), -gt (greater than), -ge (greater than or equal to), -lt (less than), and -le (less than or equal to) are utilized to perform comparisons. It's also possible to directly define script blocks, which offer greater flexibility in filtering criteria. For instance:

```
Get-Process | Where-Object { $_.WorkingSet -gt 100MB }
```

In the script block, '$_' represents the current object in the pipeline. The script block syntax allows for more complex expressions and conditions, enabling intricate filtering logic.

Select-Object Cmdlet

Although primarily used to select specific properties of an object, Select-Object can also serve as a filtering tool by limiting the number of objects that pass through the pipeline. The Select-Object cmdlet features the -First and -Last parameters that permit the selection of a specified number of objects from the start or end of the result set, respectively. For instance:

```
Get-Process | Select-Object -First 10
```

This command picks the first ten processes retrieved by Get-Process. Similarly, for selecting a fixed number of objects from the end:

```
Get-Process | Select-Object -Last 10
```

Out-GridView Cmdlet

While not a traditional filtering cmdlet, Out-GridView offers an interactive way to filter objects. This cmdlet presents objects in a sortable, filterable table format. Users can select the required rows from this grid and pass them further down the pipeline. To use Out-GridView for filtering, the -PassThru parameter is critical. For example:

```
Get-Process | Out-GridView -PassThru | Where-Object { $_.CPU -gt 100 }
```

This example first displays all processes in a grid view. The user can manually select processes in the grid, which then filters out those where the CPU usage exceeds 100.

PowerShell also permits combining multiple filtering techniques to refine the object set progressively. For example, one may begin with Select-Object -First 20 to deal with a manageable subset of a large dataset, and then refine further using Where-Object.

Advanced Filtering

Combining Where-Object and script blocks Unlocks powerful filtering capabilities. For instance, to retrieve services starting with the letter "A" and are currently running, you can use:

```
Get-Service | Where-Object { $_.Status -eq 'Running' -and $_.Name -like 'A*' }
```

This illustrates the conjunction of multiple conditions within the Where-Object script block. Logical operators -and, -or, and -not help construct comprehensive queries.

To summarize the importance of mastering filtering in PowerShell pipelines, we refer to practical scenarios such as monitoring systems, diagnosing issues, and configuring environments. Most PowerShell scripts involve manipulating collections of objects, and efficient filtering ensures resource optimization and targeted results. Whether using simple comparisons or complex script blocks, the ability to filter objects accurately is indispensable for effective PowerShell scripting.

7.6 Sorting and Selecting Objects

In PowerShell, sorting and selecting objects are crucial techniques for data manipulation and retrieval. These operations enhance the effectiveness of scripts by allowing for the organization and refinement of datasets, making the information more meaningful and easier to process.

Sorting Objects

Sorting objects in PowerShell can be achieved using the Sort-Object cmdlet. This cmdlet arranges objects in ascending or descending order based on their properties. The basic syntax for Sort-Object is as follows:

```
Sort-Object [-Property] <String[]> [-Descending] [-Unique]
```

Where:

- -Property specifies the property name to sort by.
- -Descending indicates that the sorting should be in descending order.
- -Unique ensures that the sorted output contains unique values.

Consider an example where we have a list of processes and want to sort them by their CPU usage:

```
Get-Process | Sort-Object -Property CPU
```

By default, Sort-Object sorts in ascending order. To sort in descending order, use the -Descending switch:

```
Get-Process | Sort-Object -Property CPU -Descending
```

In cases where multiple properties are used for sorting, Sort-Object can handle composite keys. For example, to sort the processes first by their CPU usage and then by their memory usage, the following command can be used:

```
Get-Process | Sort-Object -Property CPU, WorkingSet
```

Selecting Objects

Selecting specific objects or properties from a collection is facilitated by the Select-Object cmdlet. This cmdlet can pick a subset of properties from objects or a subset of objects from a collection. The basic syntax for Select-Object is:

```
Select-Object [-Property] <Object[]> [-First <Int32>] [-Last <Int32>]
```

Where:

- -Property specifies the properties to select.
- -First selects the first <Int32> number of objects.
- -Last selects the last <Int32> number of objects.

For instance, to select the first 5 processes sorted by CPU usage, you can use:

```
Get-Process | Sort-Object -Property CPU | Select-Object -First 5
```

Similarly, to obtain the last 5 processes:

```
Get-Process | Sort-Object -Property CPU | Select-Object -Last 5
```

To choose specific properties from objects, such as the process name and CPU usage, the following command can be utilized:

```
Get-Process | Select-Object -Property Name, CPU
```

Working with Calculated Properties

Calculated properties enable the creation of custom properties in the output of Select-Object using expressions. This feature is essential when the exact property or transformation needed does not exist. The syntax for a calculated property is:

```
@{Name="PropertyName"; Expression={ScriptBlock}}
```

For example, if we want to display the process name along with its memory usage in megabytes, we can create a calculated property like this:

```
Get-Process | Select-Object -Property Name,
    @{Name="MemoryUsageMB"; Expression={ [math]::round($_.WorkingSet / 1MB,
        2) }}
```

Use Case Example

Combining both sorting and selecting operations can yield highly refined results. Suppose we need to identify the top 10 processes consuming the most memory and display their names, memory usage, and ID. The command could be structured as follows:

```
Get-Process | Sort-Object -Property WorkingSet -Descending |
    Select-Object -First 10 -Property Name,
    @{Name="MemoryUsageMB"; Expression={ [math]::round($_.WorkingSet / 1MB,
        2) }}, ID
```

Executing the above command would result in an output similar to:

```
Name           MemoryUsageMB  ID
----           -------------  --
process1              120.46  2340
process2              150.34  1184
...
process10              98.76  8970
```

This output identifies the top ten memory-consuming processes along with their IDs and the memory usage in megabytes, ensuring that the data is both sorted and filtered precisely.

Mastering the use of Sort-Object and Select-Object cmdlets is indispensable for effective data sorting and selection in PowerShell scripting, enhancing the adeptness and specificity of information retrieval and presentation.

7.7 Using the ForEach-Object Cmdlet

The ForEach-Object cmdlet in PowerShell plays a crucial role in processing each item passed through the pipeline, enabling iterative operations on objects. It permits the invocation of script blocks on every object sequentially, making it an indispensable tool in data manipulation and workflow automation.

The ForEach-Object cmdlet is designed for scenarios where operations need to be performed repeatedly for each object received from the pipeline. It functions by accepting a pipeline input, executing a script block for each object, and emitting the results back to the pipeline. Here is the basic syntax:

```
Get-Process | ForEach-Object { <scriptblock> }
```

Each object emitted from Get-Process in this example is passed into the script block enclosed in curly braces {}. Within the script block, $_ represents the current object being processed.

Consider the following illustrative usage of ForEach-Object:

```
Get-Process | ForEach-Object { "Process Name: " + $_.Name }
```

The script block concatenates the string "Process Name: " with the Name property of each process object. The output is a string for each process, displaying its name prefixed with "Process Name: ".

```
Process Name: chrome
Process Name: explorer
Process Name: powershell
...
```

More complex operations can be performed within the script block. For example, you can stop a set of processes whose memory usage exceeds a certain threshold:

```
Get-Process | Where-Object { $_.WorkingSet -gt 100MB } | ForEach-Object { Stop-
    Process -Id $_.Id }
```

In this scenario, Where-Object filters processes occupying more than 100MB of memory. These filtered processes are then passed to ForEach-Object, where Stop-Process terminates them using their process ID.

ForEach-Object also supports different script blocks for -Begin, -Process, and -End parameters, allowing more granular control over the operation stages.

```
Get-Process | ForEach-Object -Begin {
    $totalMemory = 0
} -Process {
    $totalMemory += $_.WorkingSet
} -End {
    "Total memory used: " + [math]::round($totalMemory / 1MB, 2) + " MB"
}
```

In this example, the -Begin script block initializes a $totalMemory variable. The -Process script block adds the WorkingSet of each process to $totalMemory, and the -End block outputs the total memory usage in megabytes, formatted to two decimal places.

ForEach-Object can be leveraged to modify properties of objects as well. Suppose you need to increment a numeric property for objects passed through the pipeline:

```
$array = @(
    [PSCustomObject]@{ Name = "Object1"; Value = 10 },
    [PSCustomObject]@{ Name = "Object2"; Value = 20 },
    [PSCustomObject]@{ Name = "Object3"; Value = 30 }
)

$array | ForEach-Object { $_.Value += 5; $_ }
```

This code snippet processes an array of custom objects, increasing the Value property by 5 for each object and returns the modified array.

```
Name    Value
----    -----
Object1 15
Object2 25
Object3 35
```

Utilizing ForEach-Object in conjunction with other cmdlets like Measure-Object, Sort-Object, or Select-Object amplifies the flexibility and capability of PowerShell scripts, making it a fundamental component for effective automation and data processing pipelines.

7.8 Group-Object and Measure-Object Cmdlets

In this section, we will explore two important cmdlets in PowerShell: Group-Object and Measure-Object. These cmdlets enable users to perform aggregation and statistical analysis on objects in the pipeline, providing crucial tools for summarizing and grouping data efficiently.

Group-Object is used to group objects based on the values of one or more properties. By grouping objects, you can easily find counts of objects sharing the same property values and summarize the data in meaningful ways.

```
$processes = Get-Process
$groupedProcesses = $processes | Group-Object -Property Company
$groupedProcesses
```

In the above example, we retrieve a list of all running processes using Get-Process. Then, we group the processes by the Company property using the Group-Object cmdlet. The result, stored in the $groupedProcesses variable, contains the processes grouped by their company property. Each group includes a Name (the value of the grouping property), a Count (the number of objects in that group), and a Group (the collection of objects in that group).

The output of Group-Object appears as follows:

```
Count Name                      Group
----- ----                      -----
   28 Microsoft Corporation     {System.Diagnostics.Process (wuauserv), ...
    5 Google LLC                {System.Diagnostics.Process (chrome), ...
    2 Apple Inc.                {System.Diagnostics.Process (mDNSResponder), ...
```

This output indicates that there are 28 processes associated with Microsoft Corporation, 5 processes with Google LLC, and 2 processes with Apple Inc.

To group objects by multiple properties, use a comma-separated list of property names in the -Property parameter:

```
$groupedMultiple = $processes | Group-Object -Property Company, ProcessName
$groupedMultiple
```

This command groups the processes firstly by Company and then by ProcessName, providing a more granular grouping of objects.

Measure-Object calculates various statistics such as count, sum, average, minimum, and maximum of the numeric properties of objects in the pipeline. This cmdlet is useful when detailed quantitative analysis is required on the objects' properties.

```
$processes | Measure-Object
```

The output of this command provides a basic count of the number of process objects passed through the pipeline:

```
Count    : 112
Average  :
Sum      :
Maximum  :
Minimum  :
Property :
```

To perform more advanced statistical calculations, specify the property on which to perform the measurements:

```
$processMetric = $processes | Measure-Object -Property CPU -Sum -Maximum -
    Minimum -Average
$processMetric
```

This command calculates the sum, maximum, minimum, and average CPU usage across all processes and outputs:

```
Count    : 112
Average  : 5.1682813049994
Sum      : 578.655478159928
Maximum  : 46.578679
Minimum  : 0
Property : CPU
```

This output shows that among 112 processes, the average CPU usage is approximately 5.17, the sum of CPU usages is 578.66, the maximum CPU usage is 46.58, and the minimum is 0.

Measure-Object can also be used with numerical properties for additional flexibility:

```
$memUsage = $processes | Measure-Object -Property WorkingSet -Sum -Maximum -
    Minimum -Average
$memUsage
```

The output of this command computes the sum, maximum, minimum, and average working set size (physical memory usage) of all processes.

```
Count    : 112
Average  : 68290559.0736607
Sum      : 7648539296
Maximum  : 387145728
Minimum  : 65536
Property : WorkingSet
```

This result shows that the average working set size is approximately 68,290,559 bytes, with a total sum of 7,648,539,296 bytes, maximum of 387,145,728 bytes, and minimum of 65,536 bytes across 112 processes.

Throughout these practices, the effective combination of Group-Object and Measure-Object cmdlets empowers users to efficiently categorize and statistically analyze data in PowerShell, facilitating advanced data manipulation and insightful reporting.

7.9 Exporting and Importing Objects

PowerShell provides robust cmdlets for exporting and importing data, enabling users to persist objects across sessions and share them with other scripts or users. This capability is crucial for data management and automation, as it allows for seamless data transfer and storage.

Exporting Objects to Various Formats

PowerShell supports exporting objects to multiple formats including CSV (Comma-Separated Values), JSON (JavaScript Object Notation), and XML (eXtensible Markup Language). Each format serves different purposes and use cases.

Exporting to CSV

The Export-Csv cmdlet allows for exporting objects to a CSV file. This is particularly useful for tabular data and can be easily ingested by various data processing tools. Below is an example of exporting a list of processes to a CSV file:

```
Get-Process | Export-Csv -Path "processes.csv" -NoTypeInformation
```

The -NoTypeInformation parameter excludes the type information from the CSV file to simplify the file contents.

Exporting to JSON

The ConvertTo-Json cmdlet is used to convert objects to the JSON format. JSON is widely used for data exchange in web applications. The following example demonstrates exporting object properties to a JSON file:

```
Get-Process | ConvertTo-Json | Set-Content -Path "processes.json"
```

Set-Content is employed to write the JSON string to a file.

Exporting to XML

The Export-Clixml cmdlet can be utilized to export objects to XML, which is suitable for complex data structures. Here is an example of exporting objects to an XML file:

```
Get-Process | Export-Clixml -Path "processes.xml"
```

XML provides a more detailed representation of the objects, capturing additional metadata.

Importing Objects from Various Formats

PowerShell also supports importing data from CSV, JSON, and XML formats, allowing for seamless integration of external data into scripts and workflows.

Importing from CSV

The Import-Csv cmdlet reads data from a CSV file and converts it back into objects. This is useful for applications that produce CSV output or for data imported from spreadsheets. Consider the following example of importing process data from a CSV file:

```
$processes = Import-Csv -Path "processes.csv"
```

```
$processes | ForEach-Object { $_.Name }
```

Import-Csv creates objects with properties based on the CSV headers. ForEach-Object processes each imported object.

Importing from JSON

Using ConvertFrom-Json, objects can be reconstructed from JSON data. The following example reads process data from a JSON file:

```
$jsonContent = Get-Content -Path "processes.json"
$processes = $jsonContent | ConvertFrom-Json
$processes | ForEach-Object { $_.Name }
```

Get-Content reads the JSON file, and ConvertFrom-Json converts the JSON string into PowerShell objects.

Importing from XML

The Import-Clixml cmdlet imports objects from an XML file. XML is advantageous for transporting serialized object state across different environments. Here is an example:

```
$processes = Import-Clixml -Path "processes.xml"
$processes | ForEach-Object { $_.Name }
```

Import-Clixml perfectly reconstructs the original objects with their types and properties.

Practical Considerations

When exporting data, considerations should include the format that best suits the intended use case, the complexity of the data, and any interoperability requirements. CSV is typically suitable for simpler tabular data, JSON for lightweight data interchange, and XML for detailed object representation.

During import, it is essential to validate the correctness and structure of the data to ensure compatibility with the script's logic. This can involve inspecting object properties, handling potential discrepancies, and debugging complex structures.

Additionally, be mindful of character encoding, especially when dealing with files containing special characters. PowerShell's cmdlets provide options to specify encoding to ensure accurate data representation.

—

The ability to export and import objects in PowerShell, thus supports not only seamless data handling but also extensive workflow automation, enabling efficient scripting and improved data accessibility across different systems and environments.

7.10 Advanced Pipeline Techniques

In PowerShell, mastering the use of the pipeline is pivotal for efficient data manipulation and processing. Advanced pipeline techniques allow for sophisticated handling of objects, enabling scripts to perform complex tasks with enhanced control and precision.

Using the Where-Object Cmdlet with Advanced Filtering The Where-Object cmdlet is essential for filtering objects passed through the pipeline. Beyond simple filters, Where-Object supports script blocks, enabling advanced filtering logic.

```
# Syntax for complex filtering with Where-Object
Get-Process | Where-Object { $_.CPU -gt 100 -and $_.WorkingSet -lt 500MB }
```

This example filters processes based on CPU usage greater than 100 and Working Set size less than 500 MB. The script block inside Where-Object allows the use of intricate conditions, combining multiple object properties.

Using Calculated Properties with Select-Object Select-Object can create calculated properties, providing a powerful way to transform and select object data. Calculated properties use a hash table to define a new property name and an expression to compute its value.

```
# Syntax for creating calculated properties with Select-Object
Get-Process | Select-Object Name, @{Name='MemoryUsageMB'; Expression={ $_.
    WorkingSet / 1MB }}
```

Here, a calculated property named MemoryUsageMB is created by dividing the WorkingSet of each process by 1MB, converting the memory usage from bytes to megabytes.

Using the ForEach-Object Cmdlet for Inline Processing ForEach-Object is versatile for executing script blocks on each object in the pipeline. This cmdlet supports multiple script blocks: -Begin, -Process, and -End, providing extensive control over pipeline object processing.

```
# Syntax for using ForEach-Object for inline processing
```

```
Get-Process | ForEach-Object -Begin { $totalCPU = 0 } -Process { $totalCPU += $_.
    CPU } -End { $totalCPU }
```

This example initializes a variable, $totalCPU, in the -Begin block, accumulates process CPU usage in the -Process block, and outputs the total CPU usage in the -End block.

Pipeline Variable: $PSItem PowerShell 5.0 introduced the $PSItem automatic variable, an alias for $_, representing the current pipeline object. This can be particularly useful for readability and consistency across scripts.

```
# Using $PSItem in place of $_ for better readability
Get-Process | Where-Object { $PSItem.CPU -gt 100 } | ForEach-Object { $PSItem.
    Name }
```

Employing $PSItem enhances script clarity by explicitly indicating that it refers to the pipeline object, making the code more understandable and maintainable.

Understanding and Using Foreach Loops in the Pipeline While ForEach-Object processes each pipeline object, PowerShell also supports the foreach statement for looping through collections. Although they have similar names, their usage contexts differ.

```
# Using foreach loop with pipeline-collected data
$processes = Get-Process
foreach ($process in $processes) {
    if ($process.CPU -gt 100) {
        $process.Name
    }
}
```

By storing pipeline output in a variable, foreach can iterate over the collection, offering an approach akin to traditional programming loops, providing flexibility outside the immediate pipeline processing.

Combining Pipelines with Subexpressions Pipelines can be embedded within expressions using subexpressions, denoted by $(). This allows for the integration of pipeline results into larger expressions or commands.

```
# Combining pipelines with subexpressions
$processCount = $(Get-Process).Count
"Total number of processes: $processCount"
```

Here, $(Get-Process) executes the cmdlet and evaluates to the collection of process objects, allowing its Count property to determine the total number of processes.

Splatting in the Pipeline Splatting simplifies command invocation with multiple parameters by using a hash table or array to pass parameters. This technique reduces syntax complexity and improves readability.

```
# Using splatting to pass parameters in the pipeline
$parameters = @{
    Name = "example.com"
    Port = 80
    Protocol = "TCP"
}

Test-NetConnection @parameters
```

In this example, the $parameters hash table contains the parameters for Test-NetConnection, demonstrating how splatting can streamline command invocation.

These advanced pipeline techniques empower PowerShell users to efficiently manipulate and process data, enabling the creation of more powerful and comprehensible scripts. Understanding these methods enhances one's ability to exploit PowerShell's capabilities for robust scripting and automation.

Chapter 8

Error Handling and Debugging

This chapter focuses on the mechanisms for error handling and debugging in PowerShell. It differentiates between terminating and non-terminating errors and explains the use of 'try', 'catch', and 'finally' blocks. Topics include working with error variables, throwing exceptions, and using the 'ErrorAction' parameter to control error responses. An introduction to debugging covers setting breakpoints, using the debugger, and common debugging techniques, providing readers with the tools to write robust scripts and troubleshoot effectively.

8.1 Introduction to Error Handling

In PowerShell, error handling is a crucial aspect of writing robust scripts. Proper error handling ensures that your scripts can gracefully handle errors and exceptions, allowing for cleaner and more predictable script behavior. Errors in PowerShell can be broadly categorized into terminating and non-terminating errors. Understanding these types of errors is essential for implementing effective error handling in your scripts.

Terminating errors are those that stop the execution of a command or script. These errors can be caused by severe issues such as syntax errors, critical resource unavailability, or other conditions that make it impossible for the command to proceed. In contrast, non-terminating errors do not stop the script execution but rather log an error and continue processing. These might occur in scenarios where certain operations on some elements of a collection fail but should not prevent an overall process from continuing.

To illustrate these concepts, consider the following examples:

```
# Attempting to call a non-existent command
NonExistent-Command
```

The above command will result in a terminating error because NonExistent-Command is not recognized by PowerShell, and the script will be stopped.

```
# Attempting to read a file that does not exist
Get-Content -Path "C:\nonexistentfile.txt"
Write-Output "This message will still be printed."
```

In this example, Get-Content generates a non-terminating error because the file does not exist. However, the script continues execution, and the message "This message will still be printed." is displayed.

PowerShell provides several mechanisms to handle these errors gracefully. The primary constructs for structured error handling in PowerShell are the try, catch, and finally blocks. These constructs enable scriptwriters to attempt a set of operations (try), catch and handle exceptions if they occur (catch), and execute cleanup or finalization code irrespective of whether an error occurred (finally).

The syntax for implementing these blocks is as follows:

```
try {
    # Code that might cause an error
}
catch {
    # Code to handle the error
}
finally {
    # Code that runs regardless of whether an error occurred
}
```

Each block has its specific role in ensuring that errors are appropriately managed. The try block encapsulates the code that might produce an exception. If an exception occurs, the execution immediately transfers to the first catch block that matches the type of exception. If no exception occurs, the catch blocks are skipped. The finally block, if present, is always executed after the try block and any catch blocks, regardless of whether an exception was thrown.

Understanding when and how to use these constructs is key for effective error handling. For instance, incorporating error handling in scripts that interact with external systems, such as file operations or network communications, is critical for creating resilient and robust scripts.

Consider the following example that demonstrates the use of try, catch, and finally blocks:

```
try {
    # Trying to open a non-existent file
    $fileContent = Get-Content -Path "C:\nonexistentfile.txt"
}
catch {
    Write-Output "An error occurred: $_"
}
finally {
    Write-Output "Execution of the try-catch block is complete."
}
```

In this example: - The try block attempts to read a file that does not exist. - The catch block captures the error and outputs a message. - The finally block outputs a completion message, ensuring that a specific action is taken regardless of whether the error occurred.

Effective error handling requires a deep understanding of potential failure points in your scripts and an ability to anticipate and manage those failures gracefully. Appropriate use of try, catch, and finally blocks, along with a clear distinction between terminating and non-terminating errors, forms the foundation of writing robust PowerShell scripts.

8.2 Types of Errors: Terminating and Non-Terminating

Errors in PowerShell are categorized into two primary types: terminating and non-terminating. Understanding the distinctions between these types is crucial for implementing effective error handling mechanisms within your scripts.

A **terminating error** is a serious error that stops the execution of a command or script altogether. Such errors are analogous to exceptions in other programming languages, where an exception must be caught or the program will halt execution. For example, syntax errors or missing mandatory parameters generally result in terminating errors.

Conversely, a **non-terminating error** allows the PowerShell script to continue running even though an error has occurred. These errors are less severe and typically deal with individual issues that do not necessitate halting the entire script. For instance, attempting to read a file that does not exist might trigger a non-terminating error, given that other parts of the script can still execute.

Terminating Errors

Terminating errors forcefully stop the command execution and, if not handled, will cause the script to terminate. To illustrate a terminating error, consider the following example:

```
# Intentional division by zero error that will terminate the script
$a = 10
$b = 0
$c = $a / $b
```

Executing the script above will result in the following error message:

```
Attempted to divide by zero.
At line:1 char:1
+ $c = $a / $b
+ ~~~~~~~~~~~~
    + CategoryInfo          : NotSpecified: (:) [], RuntimeException
    + FullyQualifiedErrorId : RuntimeException
```

This error is terminating because it stops the execution of the script at the point where the division by zero occurs. The error is not recoverable unless explicitly caught and handled using try and catch blocks.

Non-Terminating Errors

Non-terminating errors allow the script to continue running. These errors often arise from issues that do not critically affect the entire script. An example is provided below:

```
# Example of a non-terminating error
Get-ChildItem -Path "C:\NonExistentFolder"
Write-Output "This message will still be output."
```

The command attempts to list the items in a folder that does not exist. However, the script will proceed to execute the Write-Output command despite the error. The execution of the above script will reveal:

```
Get-ChildItem : Cannot find path 'C:\NonExistentFolder' because it does not exist.
At line:1 char:1
+ Get-ChildItem -Path "C:\NonExistentFolder"
+ ~~~~~~~~~~~~~~~~~~~~~~~~~~~~~~~~~~~~~~~~~
    + CategoryInfo          : ObjectNotFound: (C:\NonExistentFolder:String) [Get-ChildItem], ItemNotFoundException
    + FullyQualifiedErrorId : PathNotFound,Microsoft.PowerShell.Commands.GetChildItemCommand

This message will still be output.
```

As demonstrated, the error does not halt the script, and it proceeds to output the subsequent message.

To handle these errors explicitly, PowerShell provides a variety of constructs such as try, catch, and finally blocks, as well as the ErrorAction parameter. These tools are integral to writing scripts that effectively and gracefully manage both terminating and non-terminating errors.

By distinguishing between terminating and non-terminating errors and understanding their behaviors, you can design more resilient scripts. This foundational understanding lays the groundwork for more advanced error handling techniques discussed in subsequent sections.

8.3 Using Try, Catch, and Finally

PowerShell provides robust mechanisms for error handling through the use of the try, catch, and finally blocks. These constructs enable developers to manage and handle errors in a controlled way, ensuring scripts behave predictably even in the face of unexpected issues.

The try block encloses the code segment where errors might occur. When an error happens within this block, the control is transferred to the subsequent catch block, where the error can be addressed. Regardless of whether an error occurs, the finally block will always execute, typically used for cleanup tasks.

```
try {
    # Code that might produce an error
    $result = 1 / 0
}
catch {
    # Code that runs if an error occurs in the try block
    Write-Host "An error occurred: $_"
}
finally {
    # Code that runs regardless of whether an error occurred
    Write-Host "This block always runs."
}
```

In the example above, the try block attempts to divide by zero, which will cause a terminating error. The catch block catches this error, and the error message is displayed using Write-Host. The $_ variable within the catch block contains the error message. The finally block executes regardless of whether an error occurred, writing a message to the host.

It is important to differentiate between terminating and non-terminating errors. Only terminating errors trigger the catch block within a try statement. Non-terminating errors can be converted to terminating errors using the -ErrorAction Stop parameter.

```
try {
    # Code that might produce a non-terminating error
    Get-ChildItem -Path "nonexistentPath" -ErrorAction Stop
}
catch {
    Write-Host "Caught an error: $($_.Exception.Message)"
}
finally {
    Write-Host "Cleanup tasks can be performed here."
}
```

In this script, the Get-ChildItem cmdlet tries to list items in "nonexistentPath". By using -ErrorAction Stop, a non-terminating error is transformed into a terminating error, thereby invoking the catch block.

Multiple catch blocks can be used to handle different error types effectively. Each catch block checks the error type using specified type constraints. This allows for specialized handling for different error conditions.

```
try {
    # Simulated code that could raise multiple exceptions
    throw [System.IO.IOException] "IO error"
    throw [System.Management.Automation.MethodInvocationException] "Method
        error"
}
catch [System.IO.IOException] {
    Write-Host "Caught an IO error: $($_.Exception.Message)"
}
catch [System.Management.Automation.MethodInvocationException] {
    Write-Host "Caught a method invocation error: $($_.Exception.Message)"
}
finally {
    Write-Host "Executing cleanup code."
}
```

By differentiating catch blocks using type constraints, the appropriate error handling is enacted depending on whether an IOException or a MethodInvocationException is thrown.

Within the catch block, extensive information about the error can be accessed. Properties such as CategoryInfo, ErrorDetails, Exception, and InvocationInfo provide detailed insight into the nature of the error. This allows for more granular error handling and logging.

```
try {
    # Simulated error
    throw "An error occurred"
}
catch {
    Write-Host "Error Message: $($_.Exception.Message)"
    Write-Host "Error Category: $($_.CategoryInfo.Category)"
    Write-Host "Error Target: $($_.InvocationInfo.Line)"
}
finally {
```

```
    Write-Host "Final task always executed."
}
```

In practice, combining try, catch, and finally blocks strengthens script resilience. Careful placement of these constructs ensures that scripts can recover gracefully from errors, maintain stability, and execute necessary post-error tasks reliably.

8.4 Working with Error Variables

In PowerShell scripting, effective error handling necessitates a solid grasp on working with error variables. These variables provide details about errors that have occurred, allowing scripts to respond appropriately. The primary error variable, $Error, is an automatic variable that stores a collection of error objects in the current session, with the latest error being the first item in the array.

Each entry in the $Error array is an ErrorRecord object, which contains detailed information about an error. This information is crucial for diagnosing issues and making informed decisions within scripts.

```
$Error[0]
```

Executing the command above will display the most recent error object. We can explore the properties of the ErrorRecord object to gain more insights about the error. Key properties include:

- Exception: The exception that was thrown.
- InvocationInfo: Information about the command that caused the error.
- CategoryInfo: Classification of the error.
- TargetObject: The object that the error occurred on.

For example, to retrieve detailed information about the latest error, you can run:

```
$errorRecord = $Error[0]
$errorRecord.Exception
$errorRecord.InvocationInfo
$errorRecord.CategoryInfo
$errorRecord.TargetObject
```

Clearing the $Error array can be essential to ensure that prior errors do not interfere with subsequent error handling operations:

```
$Error.Clear()
```

To demonstrate working with error variables and understanding the information they provide, consider the following example where an attempt is made to divide by zero:

```
try {
    $result = 1 / 0
} catch {
    Write-Output "Exception Type: $($_.Exception.GetType().FullName)"
    Write-Output "Message: $($_.Exception.Message)"
    Write-Output "Target Site: $($_.Exception.TargetSite)"
}
```

When this script is executed, it catches the exception resulting from division by zero and accesses the error details from the caught exception object. Here, $_ refers to the current object in the pipeline, which in this case, is the error object in the catch block.

The output can be observed as follows:

```
Exception Type: System.Management.Automation.RuntimeException
Message: Attempted to divide by zero.
Target Site: System.Object Invoke(System.Object, System.Object[])
```

In PowerShell, local scopes for error handling can be created using $PSCmdlet. The $PSCmdlet variable facilitates accessing detailed error information. Although primarily used in advanced scripting scenarios and within functions, $PSCmdlet empowers developers with further control over error handling processes. Example:

```
function Test-ErrorHandling {
    [CmdletBinding()]
    param ()
    process {
        try {
            Write-Output "Starting division..."
            $a = 0 / 0
        } catch {
            Write-Output "Error detected..."
            $error = $PSCmdlet.GetVariableValue('error')
            Write-Output "Error Count: $($error.Count)"
            Write-Output "Most Recent Error: $($error[0].Exception.Message)"
        }
    }
}

Test-ErrorHandling
```

Executing this function will capture the divide by zero error and the function will output the error count and the most recent error message.

Another important aspect of working with error variables is managing error preference. The $ErrorActionPreference variable explicitly dictates how PowerShell should respond to non-terminating errors globally. This variable can be adjusted within scripts to ensure consistent and predictable error handling behavior. Valid values for $ErrorActionPreference are:

- Continue: Displays the error message and continues execution (default).
- Stop: Converts the error into a terminating error, triggering any surrounding catch blocks.
- SilentlyContinue: Suppresses the error message and continues execution.
- Inquire: Prompts the user for input on whether to proceed with the script.
- Ignore: Suppresses the error message and continues without impacting the $Error variable.

For example, to ensure that non-terminating errors halt script execution, set the $ErrorActionPreference to Stop:

```
$ErrorActionPreference = "Stop"
```

This line makes sure that any non-terminating error within the script will be treated as a terminating error, enforcing strict error handling policies. Balancing the use of $ErrorActionPreference appropriately within scripts can greatly contribute to writing resilient and maintainable PowerShell scripts.

Working with error variables in PowerShell is essential for robust error handling, allowing scripts to efficiently respond to and manage errors. By leveraging automatic variables such as $Error, $_, and $ErrorActionPreference, one can ensure that scripts execute smoothly and provide comprehensive diagnostic information when errors occur.

8.5 Throwing Exceptions

In PowerShell, explicitly throwing exceptions and defining custom error messages can significantly increase the robustness and clarity of your scripts. This section delves into the mechanisms of throwing exceptions, examining the throw keyword, creating custom exceptions, and manipulating exception properties.

The throw keyword is a powerful tool for generating exceptions. It is primarily used to signal a terminating error intentionally. When you use throw, the script halts execution at the point where the exception is thrown, unless it is trapped by a try block. Here is the basic syntax to throw an exception:

```
throw "An error occurred."
```

This simple usage of throw generates a generic System.Management.Automation.RuntimeException with the message "An error occurred.". However, for more sophisticated error handling, specifying the type of exception can be very beneficial. PowerShell allows you to throw objects of any type derived from the .NET System.Exception class.

To illustrate, the following example demonstrates how to throw a specific type of exception, namely System.ArgumentException:

```
$param = $null
if ($param -eq $null) {
    throw [System.ArgumentException]::new("Parameter cannot be null.")
}
```

In this example, an System.ArgumentException is thrown if the parameter $param is null, providing a clear and concise error message.

Custom exceptions can also be created to provide more specific error details tailored to the needs of your script. Custom exceptions inherit from the System.Exception class or any subclass thereof. Here's an example of defining and using a custom exception in PowerShell:

```
class MyCustomException : System.Exception {
    MyCustomException([string]$message) : base($message) {}
}

function Demo-CustomException {
    [CmdletBinding()]
    param (
        [Parameter(Mandatory=$true)]
        [int]$number
    )

    if ($number -lt 0) {
        throw [MyCustomException]::new("Negative numbers are not allowed: $number"
            )
    }

    return "Input number: $number is valid."
```

```
}

try {
    Demo-CustomException -number -1
} catch [MyCustomException] {
    Write-Error $_.Exception.Message
}
```

In the above script, MyCustomException is defined with a constructor that passes a custom error message to the base System.Exception constructor. The Demo-CustomException function checks if the input number is negative, and if so, throws a MyCustomException with a tailored message.

The catch block specifies the type of exception to catch, enabling customized responses to different error conditions. This level of detailed exception handling enhances both the readability and maintainability of your scripts.

Additionally, exception objects in PowerShell have properties that provide detailed information about the error. Key properties include Message, Source, StackTrace, and InnerException. These properties can be accessed within the catch block for logging or further diagnostic purposes:

```
try {
    throw [System.InvalidOperationException]::new("Invalid operation error")
} catch {
    $exception = $_.Exception
    Write-Host "Error Message: $($exception.Message)"
    Write-Host "Source: $($exception.Source)"
    Write-Host "Stack Trace: $($exception.StackTrace)"
    if ($exception.InnerException) {
        Write-Host "Inner Exception: $($exception.InnerException.Message)"
    }
}
```

This script throws a System.InvalidOperationException and then catches it, displaying detailed information about the exception properties. Accessing InnerException is particularly useful when dealing with nested exceptions, as it allows for deeper inspection of the root cause.

Collectively, these techniques for throwing and handling exceptions empower script authors to create robust, self-explanatory, and maintainable scripts, facilitating clearer communication of error conditions and streamlining troubleshooting processes.

8.6 Using the ErrorAction Parameter

The ErrorAction parameter is a fundamental component for error handling in PowerShell scripts. This parameter allows you to control the behavior of cmdlets and advanced functions when errors occur, providing flexibility and precision in how scripts handle unexpected conditions. The focus of this section is to explain the various settings available for the ErrorAction parameter, demonstrate their use in practical examples, and highlight the scenarios where each setting is most appropriate.

PowerShell offers several ErrorAction settings:

- Stop
- Continue
- SilentlyContinue
- Inquire
- Ignore
- Suspend

Stop: The Stop setting converts non-terminating errors into terminating errors. This causes the script to halt execution at the point of error, which can then be handled using a try...catch block. This setting is crucial when a particular error must immediately cease script execution to prevent further issues.

```
try {
    Get-Item -Path "Z:\nonexistentfile.txt" -ErrorAction Stop
}
catch {
    Write-Host "An error occurred: $_"
}
```

In the example above, the command Get-Item attempts to access a nonexistent file. Without the ErrorAction parameter set to Stop, this would result in a non-terminating error, and the script would continue execution. By specifying Stop, the error becomes terminating, allowing the catch block to handle it.

Continue: The default setting, Continue, allows the script to proceed after encountering a non-terminating error. The error is reported, but execution is not interrupted. This is useful when you need to log errors but do not want them to stop the script.

```
Get-Item -Path "Z:\nonexistentfile.txt" -ErrorAction Continue
Write-Host "Continuing script execution..."
```

In this case, the error is logged, and the script proceeds to the next line.

SilentlyContinue: When set to SilentlyContinue, cmdlet errors are neither reported nor do they stop the execution. This can be useful for scenarios where you want to suppress errors while ensuring script progress.

```
Get-Item -Path "Z:\nonexistentfile.txt" -ErrorAction SilentlyContinue
Write-Host "Execution continues without error reporting."
```

This suppresses the error message and continues execution as if no error had occurred.

Inquire: The Inquire setting prompts the user for input when an error occurs, asking whether to continue, stop, suspend, or ignore. This is effective in interactive sessions where user intervention is acceptable.

```
Get-Item -Path "Z:\nonexistentfile.txt" -ErrorAction Inquire
Write-Host "Check user input before continuing or stopping."
```

When the error occurs, a prompt is displayed for the user to decide the next action.

Ignore: Similar to SilentlyContinue, the Ignore setting suppresses the error output, but it does not add any errors to the automatic variables like $Error.

```
Get-Item -Path "Z:\nonexistentfile.txt" -ErrorAction Ignore
Write-Host "Error is ignored without logging to \$Error."
```

This ensures that no error messages or logs are created, which can be beneficial in highly controlled environments.

Suspend: The Suspend action is specifically for workflows, pausing the execution at the point of error and marking the job state as suspended. This allows for the resumption of the workflow post-error handling.

Each ErrorAction setting serves a unique purpose and is selected based on specific requirements. Utilizing these settings allows for granular control over error management strategies, ensuring that scripts perform reliably under various scenarios.

In practical application, it is crucial to understand the implications of each setting choice and to test robustly across different conditions. This approach significantly enhances script reliability and maintainability.

8.7 Writing Robust Scripts with Error Handling

Robust scripts are critical for ensuring reliability and predictability in PowerShell execution. Effective error handling not only helps to gracefully manage and remediate errors that occur during the execution of a script, but also enables detailed logging and diagnostics, which are invaluable for troubleshooting and maintenance. This section discusses advanced strategies for error handling that can be integrated into PowerShell scripts to enhance their robustness.

Integrating robust error handling starts with understanding and utilizing the try, catch, and finally blocks effectively. These constructs allow a script to handle terminating errors and execute cleanup code irrespective of an error. Below is an example demonstrating their usage:

```
try {
    # Attempt to perform an operation that might fail
    $result = Get-Content -Path "C:\NonexistentFile.txt"
    Write-Output "File content: $result"
} catch [System.IO.FileNotFoundException] {
    Write-Error "File not found. Please check the file path and try again."
} catch {
    Write-Error "An unexpected error occurred: $_"
} finally {
    Write-Output "Execution finished."
}
```

In the example, Get-Content attempts to read a file that does not exist. The catch block for System.IO.FileNotFoundException handles the specific error when the file is not found, providing a meaningful error message. The broader catch block handles any other unexpected errors, outputting the error object represented by $_. The finally block runs regardless of whether an error occurred, ensuring that any necessary cleanup or final statements are executed.

Using error variables like $Error and $? can also enhance error handling in scripts. $Error is an array that stores the error objects from the current session, with the most recent error at index zero. $? indicates the success status of the last operation, returning True if the operation succeeded and False otherwise.

Example:

```
# Attempt to remove a file
Remove-Item -Path "C:\ProtectedFile.txt"

# Check if the operation succeeded
if ($?) {
```

```
    Write-Output "File removed successfully."
} else {
    Write-Error "Failed to remove file. Error details: $($Error[0])"
}
```

In the above example, $? is used to check the success of the Remove-Item operation. If it fails, the error details are retrieved from $Error and displayed.

For more control over script execution and error handling, the ErrorAction parameter can be particularly useful. This parameter determines how PowerShell responds to a non-terminating error. The possible values for ErrorAction are:

- Continue - Displays the error message and continues execution (default).
- SilentlyContinue - Suppresses the error message and continues execution.
- Stop - Converts the error to a terminating error, which can be caught by a catch block.
- Inquire - Pauses execution and asks the user what to do.
- Ignore - Ignores the error and continues without displaying the error message; can only be used in scripts.

Example with ErrorAction:

```
try {
    # Attempt to remove a file, treating any error as terminating
    Remove-Item -Path "C:\ImportantFile.txt" -ErrorAction Stop
} catch {
    Write-Error "Error removing file: $_"
} finally {
    Write-Output "Cleanup process complete."
}
```

By setting ErrorAction to Stop, the script ensures that any error during the Remove-Item operation will be treated as terminating, triggering the catch block when an error occurs.

To further strengthen scripts, leveraging custom error handling functions is a robust approach. These functions can provide consistent error logging, notification, and recovery mechanisms throughout the script. Below is an example of a custom error handling function:

```
function Handle-Error {
    param (
        [Parameter(Mandatory = $true)]
        [string]$ErrorMessage,
        [Parameter(Mandatory = $true)]
        [Exception]$Exception
    )
    # Log the error information
    Write-Error "ERROR: $ErrorMessage"
    Write-Error "Exception: $($Exception.Message)"
    # Additional error handling actions can be added here
}

try {
    # Sample operation that may cause an error
    $result = Get-Content -Path "C:\AnotherNonexistentFile.txt"
} catch {
    Handle-Error -ErrorMessage "Failed to read file content." -Exception $_
} finally {
    Write-Output "Execution complete."
}
```

In this example, Handle-Error serves as a centralized function for error handling, detailing error messages and capturing exception information systematically.

Implementing these advanced error handling techniques significantly enhances the robustness of PowerShell scripts. By effectively managing errors, utilizing error variables, setting appropriate ErrorAction parameters, and centralizing error handling with custom functions, scripts become more resilient, maintainable, and easier to troubleshoot.

8.8 Introduction to Debugging

Effective debugging is pivotal in ensuring that PowerShell scripts run as intended. Debugging entails identifying, analyzing, and resolving errors or issues within a script. PowerShell provides several tools and techniques to facilitate this process, thus enabling developers to troubleshoot problems efficiently.

One of the primary tools for debugging in PowerShell is the integrated debugger, which allows for the examination of scripts during execution. The debugger can pause execution at specific points, known as breakpoints, allowing the user to inspect variables, execute commands, and analyze the script's behavior in a controlled environment.

Breakpoints can be set on specific lines, commands, or even based on conditions. This flexibility is advantageous for isolating and understanding issues that might not be immediately obvious. The following example sets a breakpoint on line 5 of a script:

```
Set-PSBreakpoint -Line 5 -Script "C:\Scripts\TestScript.ps1"
```

Upon execution, the script will pause at line 5, allowing for interactive examination. The Get-PSBreakpoint cmdlet lists all active breakpoints, and Remove-PSBreakpoint can be used to clear them.

```
Get-PSBreakpoint
Remove-PSBreakpoint -Id 1
```

When the script execution halts at a breakpoint, the prompt changes to indicate debug mode. In this state, standard PowerShell commands can be used to inspect the environment. For example, examining the value of a variable:

```
PS C:\Scripts\TestScript.ps1:5> $variableName
```

The 'Step Into', 'Step Over', and 'Step Out' commands control how the script progresses during debugging. Step Into executes the next command and, if it is a function, steps into that function. Step Over executes the next command but does not enter functions, while Step Out continues script execution until the end of the current function.

```
Debug> s # Step Into
Debug> v # Step Over
Debug> o # Step Out
```

Conditional breakpoints provide advanced control over the debugging process. These breakpoints trigger when a specified condition is met, allowing developers to focus on problematic scenarios. A conditional breakpoint can be set as follows:

```
Set-PSBreakpoint -Line 10 -Script "C:\Scripts\TestScript.ps1" -Condition '$i -eq 10'
```

The -Action parameter specifies a script block to execute when the breakpoint is hit, often used for logging or performing specific checks.

```
Set-PSBreakpoint -Line 20 -Script "C:\Scripts\TestScript.ps1" -Action { Write-Host "
    Breakpoint hit at line 20" }
```

Moreover, PowerShell provides the Set-PSDebug cmdlet, which enables script tracing. Tracing outputs each line of script as it is executed, thereby providing insight into the script's flow. Enabling tracing can be done as follows:

```
Set-PSDebug -Trace 1
```

In trace mode, each command executed is printed to the console, aiding in the identification of unexpected behaviors.

Deactivating script tracing is straightforward:

```
Set-PSDebug -Off
```

Another crucial debugging aid is the Write-Debug cmdlet, which outputs debug messages when debugging is enabled. This can be particularly useful for logging purposes without cluttering the console output during normal operations.

```
Write-Debug -Message "Debug message for variable value: $variableName"
```

To enable the display of debug messages, set the preference variable $DebugPreference to Continue or Inquire. Setting it to Continue will show debug messages without interruption.

```
$DebugPreference = 'Continue'
```

Contrarily, setting $DebugPreference to Inquire prompts the user to decide whether to continue executing the script after showing each debug message.

```
$DebugPreference = 'Inquire'
```

Leveraging these tools and techniques collectively enhances the debugging experience, allowing for methodical and efficient resolution of issues within PowerShell scripts. By stepping through code, examining variable states, and utilizing conditional logic for breakpoints, developers can isolate problems precisely and validate the correct behavior of their scripts.

8.9 Using Breakpoints and the Debugger

A critical aspect of developing robust and error-free PowerShell scripts involves utilizing the built-in debugging tools effectively. Understanding how to set and use breakpoints and the debugger allows you to inspect script execution at specific points, facilitating the identification and resolution of errors.

Breakpoints in PowerShell can be set using the Set-PSBreakpoint cmdlet. Breakpoints can be applied at a script line, variable, or command and provide a powerful mechanism to halt script execution, enabling real-time inspection and interaction. There are three primary types of breakpoints: line breakpoints, variable breakpoints, and command breakpoints.

To set a simple line breakpoint at a specific line within a script, you use the following syntax in PowerShell:

```
Set-PSBreakpoint -Script "C:\\Scripts\\MyScript.ps1" -Line 10
```

This command sets a breakpoint at line 10 in the script located at C:
Scripts
MyScript.ps1. When execution reaches this line, the script will pause, allowing you to inspect the current state.

Variable breakpoints allow you to pause execution when a specified variable's value changes. This is particularly useful when tracking down issues caused by unexpected modifications to a variable. To set a variable breakpoint, use the following syntax:

```
Set-PSBreakpoint -Variable "myVar" -Mode Write
```

This command sets a breakpoint that triggers whenever the variable myVar is modified. The -Mode parameter can be either Read, Write, or ReadWrite, depending on whether you want to break on read access, write access, or both.

Command breakpoints are used to halt execution when a specific cmdlet or function is invoked. For instance, to break when the Get-Process cmdlet is called, you would use:

```
Set-PSBreakpoint -Command "Get-Process"
```

Upon encountering the specified cmdlet, the execution will pause, allowing you to examine the environment.

Once breakpoints are set, you can view all defined breakpoints using the Get-PSBreakpoint cmdlet:

```
Get-PSBreakpoint
```

To remove a breakpoint, utilize the Remove-PSBreakpoint cmdlet with the breakpoint ID, obtained from Get-PSBreakpoint:

```
Remove-PSBreakpoint -Id 1
```

The PowerShell debugger provides a rich set of commands that enable detailed control over script execution. Once execution pauses at a breakpoint, the following debugger commands can be utilized:

- list: Displays the code around the current execution point.
- k or Get-PSCallStack: Displays the call stack.
- v or Get-PSBreakpoint: Lists all breakpoints.
- c or Continue: Resumes execution until the next breakpoint or the end of the script.
- s or StepInto: Executes the next statement, stepping into functions and scripts.
- o or StepOut: Steps out of the current function to the calling context.
- q or Quit: Exits the debugger and terminates script execution.

An example debugging session might look like this:

```
PS C:\> Set-PSBreakpoint -Script "C:\\Scripts\\MyScript.ps1" -Line 3
PS C:\> .\MyScript.ps1
Breakpoint hit: Line 3 in C:\Scripts\MyScript.ps1

At C:\Scripts\MyScript.ps1:3 char:1
+ $result = 1 + 1
+ ~~~~~~~~~~~~~~~
[DBG]: PS C:\> list
    1 # My PowerShell script
    2
    3* $result = 1 + 1
    4 Write-Output $result
[DBG]: PS C:\> k
 # Func Line Command
-- ---- ---- -------
 0 MyScript.ps1 3 $result = 1 + 1
[DBG]: PS C:\> c
2
```

In this session, a line breakpoint at line 3 of C:
Scripts
MyScript.ps1 was set. When the script execution reaches line 3, it pauses. The list command shows nearby lines of code, and k displays the call stack. Finally, c resumes execution, which outputs the result of the script.

Effectively using breakpoints and the debugger in PowerShell allows for precise control over scripts and aids significantly in troubleshooting and refining code. This contributes to writing concise, effective, and maintainable scripts.

8.10 Common Debugging Techniques

Debugging in PowerShell is as crucial as writing the actual scripts because it helps in identifying, analyzing, and resolving issues that may not be obvious at first glance. This section delves into common debugging techniques that can be employed within the PowerShell environment to ensure your scripts run efficiently and error-free.

One of the foundational methods for debugging in PowerShell is through the effective use of Write-Debug and Write-Verbose cmdlets. These cmdlets provide insight into the script's execution flow and values of variables at various stages.

```
function Test-Debugging {
    [CmdletBinding()]
    param (
        [int]$value1,
        [int]$value2
    )
    Write-Debug "Function Test-Debugging started with parameters: value1=$value1,
        value2=$value2"
    $result = $value1 + $value2
    Write-Debug "Calculated result: $result"
    return $result
}

# Enable debugging output
$DebugPreference = 'Continue'
Test-Debugging -value1 10 -value2 20
```

In this example, Write-Debug statements are added to a function to output debugging information. These statements are only displayed if $DebugPreference is set to Continue. This technique helps track the flow of data through the function.

Similarly, the Write-Verbose cmdlet can be used for more detailed output messages. This is beneficial for providing users or developers with more context while executing scripts.

```
function Test-Verbose {
    [CmdletBinding()]
    param (
        [int]$value1,
        [int]$value2
    )
    Write-Verbose "Starting calculation with value1=$value1 and value2=$value2"
    $result = $value1 * $value2
    Write-Verbose "Result of multiplication: $result"
    return $result
}

# Enable verbose output
$VerbosePreference = 'Continue'
Test-Verbose -value1 10 -value2 20
```

PowerShell's built-in debugger is another powerful tool. The debugger allows setting breakpoints, stepping through the code line-by-line, and inspecting the state of variables at different points in the script.

Breakpoints can be set using the Set-PSBreakpoint cmdlet. These can be set on specific lines, functions, or even commands. Below is an example of setting a line breakpoint:

```
Set-PSBreakpoint -Script "C:\Scripts\Example.ps1" -Line 3

# Start debug session
$DebugPreference = 'Continue'
Enter-Debugger
```

In this case, a breakpoint is set on line 3 of the script Example.ps1. The Enter-Debugger command initiates the debugging session where you can use commands like s (step into), v (step over), and o (step out) to navigate through the script.

Inspecting variable states at breakpoints is crucial. The Get-Variable cmdlet can be used to view the values of variables at any point in the debug session.

```
PS C:\> Enter-Debugger
[DBG]: PS C:\Scripts\File.ps1:5> get-variable myVariable
```

Conditional breakpoints provide the capability to pause execution when a certain condition is met, using the Condition parameter in Set-PSBreakpoint.

```
Set-PSBreakpoint -Script "C:\Scripts\Example.ps1" -Line 5 -Condition '$value1 -eq 10'
```

This command sets a breakpoint at line 5 that will only trigger if the variable $value1 equals 10.

Using the Trace-Command cmdlet can provide deep insights into how commands are processed. Trace-Command allows tracing of command execution, module loads, and parameter binding.

```
Trace-Command -Name ParameterBinding -Expression { Test-Verbose -value1 10 -
    value2 20 } -PSHost
```

This example traces the parameter binding process of the Test-Verbose function, outputting detailed information to the host.

Debugging can also benefit significantly from logging best practices. Incorporating meaningful and descriptive logging via Write-Output, Write-Information, and other cmdlets can create a robust mechanism for understanding script behavior over time.

These techniques, when applied diligently, equip developers to identify root causes of issues swiftly and improve script reliability. Such practices, amalgamated with structured error handling, form the cornerstone of robust PowerShell script development.

Chapter 9

File Operations and Manipulation

This chapter examines file operations and manipulation tasks in PowerShell. It covers reading from and writing to files, copying, moving, and deleting files, as well as working with file paths. Additionally, it discusses creating and managing directories, handling file permissions, and employs cmdlets like 'Get-Content' and 'Set-Content'. Special focus is given to working with CSV files using 'Import-Csv' and 'Export-Csv', as well as handling binary files, offering a comprehensive overview of file management techniques in PowerShell.

9.1 Introduction to File Operations

File operations are fundamental in any scripting or programming environment, and PowerShell provides robust capabilities for managing and manipulating files. This section will discuss the various types of file operations available in PowerShell, such as reading from, writing to, copying, moving, and deleting files. We will also explore how to handle file paths, manage directories, and set file permissions.

PowerShell cmdlets enable efficient and straightforward file manipulation. This section introduces some of the essential cmdlets that will be explored in-depth in subsequent sections.

To begin with, understanding and working with basic file and directory commands is crucial. The following scripts demonstrate simple yet powerful file operations in PowerShell.

1. Reading the content of a file:

The Get-Content cmdlet in PowerShell is utilized to read the contents of a file. It can handle various file types, providing a flexible mechanism to retrieve data from text files, log files, and more.

```
# Specify the file path
$filePath = "C:\example\sample.txt"

# Read the content of the file
$content = Get-Content -Path $filePath

# Display the content
$content
```

This script assigns the file path to the variable $filePath and uses Get-Content to read and display the file's content.

2. Writing to a file:

The Set-Content cmdlet is used for writing data to a file. This cmdlet can replace the existing contents of a file with new data.

```
# Specify the file path
$filePath = "C:\example\sample.txt"

# Define the content to be written
$newContent = "This is a new line of text."

# Write the content to the file
Set-Content -Path $filePath -Value $newContent
```

In this example, the script writes the string "This is a new line of text." to the file located at C:\example\sample.txt.

3. Copying a file:

The Copy-Item cmdlet is used to copy files and directories. Here is a simple script to copy a file:

```
# Specify the source and destination file paths
$sourceFilePath = "C:\example\sample.txt"
$destinationFilePath = "C:\backup\sample.txt"

# Copy the file
Copy-Item -Path $sourceFilePath -Destination $destinationFilePath
```

The Copy-Item cmdlet copies sample.txt from the example directory to the backup directory.

4. Moving a file:

To move a file, you can use the Move-Item cmdlet. It functions similarly to Copy-Item but removes the source file after it has been copied to the destination.

```
# Specify the source and destination file paths
$sourceFilePath = "C:\example\sample.txt"
$destinationFilePath = "C:\archive\sample.txt"

# Move the file
Move-Item -Path $sourceFilePath -Destination $destinationFilePath
```

This script moves sample.txt from the example directory to the archive directory.

5. Deleting a file:

The Remove-Item cmdlet is used to delete files and directories. The following script demonstrates how to delete a file:

```
# Specify the file path
$filePath = "C:\example\sample.txt"

# Delete the file
Remove-Item -Path $filePath
```

This script deletes the file sample.txt from the example directory.

6. Working with file paths:

Correctly handling file paths is critical in file operations to avoid errors. PowerShell offers several cmdlets for working with file paths, such as Join-Path and Split-Path.

```
# Define the components of the path
$path1 = "C:\example"
$path2 = "sample.txt"

# Join the components to form a full path
$fullPath = Join-Path -Path $path1 -ChildPath $path2

# Display the full path
$fullPath
```

In this example, Join-Path combines C:\example and sample.txt into a single path C:\example\sample.txt.

7. Creating and managing directories:

The New-Item cmdlet is used to create new files and directories. You can specify the item type as a directory to create new directories.

```
# Specify the directory path
$directoryPath = "C:\example\new_directory"

# Create the directory
New-Item -Path $directoryPath -ItemType Directory
```

This script creates a new directory named new_directory inside the example directory.

Understanding these basic file operations is essential before moving on to more complex tasks such as handling file permissions, reading and writing to CSV files, or dealing with binary files. As we delve further into this chapter, we will build upon these foundational operations to work with more sophisticated file manipulation techniques in PowerShell.

9.2 Reading from Files

Reading from files in PowerShell is an essential skill that allows scripts to process and utilize data stored on disk. This section covers the methods and cmdlets available for reading file content effectively. We will discuss the Get-Content cmdlet primarily, but also explore other techniques suitable for different scenarios.

The Get-Content cmdlet is the primary cmdlet used for reading from files. It reads the content of a file line by line and returns a collection of strings, each representing a line in the file. Here is a basic example:

```
# Load the file content into a variable
$fileContent = Get-Content -Path "C:\example.txt"

# Display the file content on the console
$fileContent
```

If C:\example.txt contains the following lines:

```
Line 1
Line 2
Line 3
```

Executing the above script will display:

```
Line 1
```

```
Line 2
Line 3
```

Get-Content can be used with several parameters to tailor its behavior. The -Path parameter specifies the path to the file to read. If the file path contains spaces, it should be enclosed in quotes.

For large files, reading all lines into memory might not be efficient. PowerShell provides the -TotalCount parameter to limit the number of lines read:

```
# Read the first 2 lines of the file
$fileContent = Get-Content -Path "C:\example.txt" -TotalCount 2

# Display the file content on the console
$fileContent
```

This script will output:

```
Line 1
Line 2
```

If there is a need to read a specific line number, using the Select-Object cmdlet in conjunction with Get-Content can achieve this:

```
# Read the third line of the file
$thirdLine = Get-Content -Path "C:\example.txt" | Select-Object -Index 2

# Display the third line
$thirdLine
```

This will output:

```
Line 3
```

By default, Get-Content reads files as text. For files with special encoding (e.g., UTF-8, ASCII), the -Encoding parameter is useful:

```
# Read file content with UTF-8 encoding
$fileContent = Get-Content -Path "C:\example_utf8.txt" -Encoding UTF8

# Display the file content
$fileContent
```

Reading from binary files requires different handling, as binary data is not typically processed line by line. The [System.IO.File]::ReadAllBytes() method reads the contents of a file into a byte array:

```
# Read binary file content into a byte array
```

```
$binaryContent = [System.IO.File]::ReadAllBytes("C:\binaryfile.bin")

# Display the byte array
$binaryContent
```

Several advanced scenarios might involve processing files line by line in a pipeline. For example, consider the scenario where specific lines matching a pattern need to be extracted:

```
# Get all lines containing the word 'important'
$importantLines = Get-Content -Path "C:\example.txt" | Where-Object { $_ -like "*
    important*" }

# Display the important lines
$importantLines
```

This script extracts lines containing the word important and stores them in $importantLines.

For exceptionally large files, using the System.IO.StreamReader class can be more efficient since it reads files incrementally. An example of this approach:

```
# Create a StreamReader object
$streamReader = [System.IO.StreamReader]::new("C:\largefile.txt")

# Read each line incrementally
try {
    while ($null -ne ($line = $streamReader.ReadLine())) {
        # Process each line
        Write-Output $line
    }
}
finally {
    # Close the StreamReader to release resources
    $streamReader.Close()
}
```

This method ensures that the file is read line by line, minimizing memory usage. The [System.IO.StreamReader] class provides greater control, making it apt for scenarios demanding efficient memory management.

Employing these methods and cmdlets for reading files in PowerShell allows handling various data extraction scenarios effectively, catering to both simple and complex requirements. Mastery of these techniques is essential for developers and system administrators aiming to proficiently manage file-based operations within scripts.

9.3 Writing to Files

Writing to files is a fundamental operation in PowerShell, enabling the storage of data persistently. This section covers different techniques and cmdlets for writing data to text files, emphasizing practical examples and command structures.

The primary cmdlet for writing to files in PowerShell is Set-Content. This cmdlet is designed for overwriting files with specified content. Another cmdlet, Add-Content, appends data to existing files without overwriting their content.

```
# Write a single line of text to a file
Set-Content -Path "example.txt" -Value "Hello, World!"

# Write multiple lines of text to a file
$lines = @(
    "Line 1: PowerShell is powerful.",
    "Line 2: Mastering file operations.",
    "Line 3: Writing to files is essential."
)
Set-Content -Path "example.txt" -Value $lines
```

In the example above, the first Set-Content command writes a single line of text, "Hello, World!", to example.txt. When specifying multiple lines to be written, an array is used as shown in the second example where three lines of text are written to example.txt.

Using Add-Content follows a similar pattern but appends data rather than overwriting it.

```
# Append a single line of text to a file
Add-Content -Path "example.txt" -Value "This line is appended."

# Append multiple lines of text to a file
$additionalLines = @(
    "Appended Line 1: Continuing from last content.",
    "Appended Line 2: Adding more data.",
    "Appended Line 3: Appending operations."
)
Add-Content -Path "example.txt" -Value $additionalLines
```

This snippet demonstrates how Add-Content appends a single line and multiple lines to example.txt. This cmdlet ensures existing data in the file is preserved while adding new content.

Both Set-Content and Add-Content have versatile parameters, such as -Encoding, which specifies the file encoding. The -NoNewline switch controls whether a newline character is added after the content written.

```
# Write a line with UTF8 encoding
```

```
Set-Content -Path "encodedExample.txt" -Value "This is UTF8 encoded text." -
    Encoding UTF8

# Append without newline
Add-Content -Path "example.txt" -Value "No newline after this text." -NoNewline
```

The above commands demonstrate writing a file with UTF8 encoding and appending text without a newline character at the end. This flexibility is advantageous in scenarios where precise control over the output format is necessary.

For more advanced writing operations, such as creating CSV files, the Export-Csv cmdlet is highly useful. This cmdlet automatically converts objects to a CSV format.

```
# Create an array of objects representing data
$data = @(
    [PSCustomObject]@{ Name = "Alice"; Age = 30; Occupation = "Engineer" },
    [PSCustomObject]@{ Name = "Bob"; Age = 25; Occupation = "Analyst" },
    [PSCustomObject]@{ Name = "Charlie"; Age = 35; Occupation = "Manager" }
)

# Export to a CSV file
$data | Export-Csv -Path "employees.csv" -NoTypeInformation
```

The script creates a collection of custom objects representing employee data, which is then exported to employees.csv using Export-Csv. The -NoTypeInformation parameter omits the type information header, resulting in a cleaner CSV file.

For binary file operations, the .NET System.IO.File class offers methods such as WriteAllBytes.

```
# Define binary data
$binaryData = [System.Text.Encoding]::UTF8.GetBytes("This is binary data.")

# Write to a file
[System.IO.File]::WriteAllBytes("binaryData.bin", $binaryData)
```

In this code, the UTF8 encoded binary data is written to binaryData.bin using WriteAllBytes method from the .NET System.IO.File class.

PowerShell provides comprehensive capabilities for writing data to files, covering text, CSV, and binary formats. Each cmdlet or method discussed provides essential options for encoding, appending, and formatting to meet various requirements. It is critical to understand and leverage these capabilities to efficiently manage file output operations in PowerShell scripts.

9.4 Copying, Moving, and Deleting Files

In PowerShell, file manipulation capabilities are extensive and designed to streamline the processes of copying, moving, and deleting files. The cmdlets Copy-Item, Move-Item, and Remove-Item are essential tools for performing these operations. In this section, we will delve into these cmdlets, exploring their syntax, options, and practical applications.

Copying Files with Copy-Item

The Copy-Item cmdlet is used to copy files and directories. Its basic syntax is as follows:

```
Copy-Item -Path <source> -Destination <destination> [-Force] [-Recurse] [-Container] [-Credential <credential>] [-Filter <filter>] [-Include <string[]>] [-Exclude <string[]>] [-PassThru] [-Verbose] [-WhatIf] [-Confirm]
```

The Path parameter specifies the source file or directory, while the Destination parameter defines the target location. The -Force parameter can be used to overwrite existing files without prompting.

Example of copying a file from one location to another:

```
Copy-Item -Path C:\Source\File.txt -Destination C:\Destination\
```

To recursively copy all contents within a directory, including subdirectories, the -Recurse parameter is utilized:

```
Copy-Item -Path C:\Source\ -Destination C:\Destination\ -Recurse
```

Moving Files with Move-Item

The Move-Item cmdlet moves files or directories from one location to another. It is functionally similar to Copy-Item, but instead of copying, it removes the source item after transferring it to the destination. The basic syntax is:

```
Move-Item -Path <source> -Destination <destination> [-Force] [-Credential <credential>] [-Filter <filter>] [-Include <string[]>] [-Exclude <string[]>] [-PassThru] [-Verbose] [-WhatIf] [-Confirm]
```

For example, moving a file to a new directory:

```
Move-Item -Path C:\Source\File.txt -Destination C:\Destination\
```

When dealing with potential file overwrites, the -Force parameter ensures the move is completed without error:

```
Move-Item -Path C:\Source\File.txt -Destination C:\Destination\ -Force
```

Deleting Files with Remove-Item

The Remove-Item cmdlet deletes files, directories, and their contents. The basic syntax includes:

```
Remove-Item -Path <path> [-Force] [-Recurse] [-Credential <credential>] [-Filter <
    filter>] [-Include <string[]>] [-Exclude <string[]>] [-PassThru] [-Verbose] [-
    WhatIf] [-Confirm]
```

To delete a single file:

```
Remove-Item -Path C:\Destination\File.txt
```

Deleting an entire directory along with its contents requires the -Recurse parameter:

```
Remove-Item -Path C:\Destination\ -Recurse
```

Forcing the deletion of read-only files or directories is possible with the -Force parameter:

```
Remove-Item -Path C:\Destination\ -Force
```

Practice Application: Cleaning Up Old Files

One practical use case of these cmdlets is cleaning up old files that exceed a certain age. The following script identifies and removes files older than 30 days from a specified directory:

```
$targetFolder = "C:\Destination\"
$days = 30

Get-ChildItem -Path $targetFolder -File | Where-Object { $_.LastWriteTime -lt (Get-
    Date).AddDays(-$days) } | Remove-Item -Force
```

This script leverages Get-ChildItem to list files, filters them based on their modification date using Where-Object, and then removes the filtered files with Remove-Item.

Error Handling with Copy, Move, and Remove Operations

Proper error handling is essential when performing file manipulations to ensure reliable script execution. Using Try-Catch blocks in PowerShell can effectively manage errors:

```
try {
    Move-Item -Path C:\Source\File.txt -Destination C:\Destination\ -ErrorAction
        Stop
} catch {
    Write-Host "An error occurred: $($_.Exception.Message)"
```

```
}
```

In the example above, any errors thrown by the Move-Item cmdlet will be caught, and a descriptive message will be displayed, enhancing script robustness and user feedback.

The integration of these techniques provides a solid foundation for file operations, integrating seamlessly into automation scripts or interactive sessions for effective file management.

9.5 Working with File Paths

Handling file paths effectively is integral to performing file operations in PowerShell. This section delves into building, parsing, and manipulating file paths using PowerShell functions and automatic variables. It is essential to understand these concepts to manage file systems efficiently.

PowerShell provides several built-in automatic variables and cmdlets that facilitate working with file paths, including:

- $PSScriptRoot
- $PSCommandPath
- Join-Path
- Split-Path
- Resolve-Path

$PSScriptRoot contains the directory from which the current script is being executed. For instance, if you have a script located at C:\Scripts\Example.ps1, running $PSScriptRoot within that script would return C:\Scripts. This variable is useful when referencing other files relative to the script's location.

$PSCommandPath holds the full path to the executing script, including the script name. For example, executing a script located at C:\Scripts\Example.ps1 would set $PSCommandPath to C:\Scripts\Example.ps1.

The Join-Path cmdlet allows for the construction of file paths by combining multiple path elements. This cmdlet ensures directory separators are correctly handled:

```
$folder = "C:\Scripts"
$file = "Example.txt"
$fullPath = Join-Path -Path $folder -ChildPath $file
Write-Output $fullPath # Output: C:\Scripts\Example.txt
```

The Split-Path cmdlet is useful for extracting specific components of a path. By default, it returns the parent directory:

```
$path = "C:\Scripts\Example.txt"
$parentDir = Split-Path -Path $path
Write-Output $parentDir # Output: C:\Scripts
```

To extract the leaf element (e.g., the file name) from a path, use the -Leaf parameter:

```
$fileName = Split-Path -Path $path -Leaf
Write-Output $fileName # Output: Example.txt
```

Resolve-Path resolves a given path to its absolute form, navigating through any symbolic links:

```
$relativePath = ".\Example.txt"
$absolutePath = Resolve-Path -Path $relativePath
Write-Output $absolutePath # Output: C:\CurrentDirectory\Example.txt
```

PowerShell also supports the use of wildcards in path operations. For example, Get-ChildItem can be used to list files in a directory that match a given pattern:

```
$directory = "C:\Scripts"
$pattern = "*.ps1"
$scripts = Get-ChildItem -Path $directory -Filter $pattern
foreach ($script in $scripts) {
    Write-Output $script.FullName
}
```

Additionally, understanding how to encapsulate special characters in file paths is important. For instance, spaces and special characters in file names should be handled appropriately by enclosing paths in quotes:

```
$pathWithSpaces = 'C:\Path With Spaces\File.txt'
Write-Output $pathWithSpaces # Output: C:\Path With Spaces\File.txt
```

Remember that certain characters, such as $, #, and %, may need to be escaped using the backtick (̀) character:

```
$pathWithSpecialChar = "C:\PathWith`$Dollar`#Hash`%Percent\File.txt"
Write-Output $pathWithSpecialChar # Output: C:\PathWith$Dollar#Hash%Percent\
    File.txt
```

Effective manipulation of file paths ensures robust script execution and file management, minimizing potential errors from incorrect path handling.

9.6 Creating and Managing Directories

Creating and managing directories in PowerShell is essential for organizing files and maintaining a structured file system. This section discusses commands and techniques for creating, renaming, and removing directories. Additionally, handling directory attributes and permissions is examined.

To create a new directory in PowerShell, use the New-Item cmdlet. By specifying the -ItemType parameter as directory, you can ensure that a directory is created rather than a file.

```
New-Item -Path "C:\ExamplePath\NewDirectory" -ItemType "directory"
```

Alternatively, the mkdir (or md) command can be used since it is an alias for New-Item -ItemType Directory:

```
mkdir "C:\ExamplePath\NewDirectory"
```

To rename a directory, the Rename-Item cmdlet is used. This cmdlet requires specifying the current directory name and the new directory name:

```
Rename-Item -Path "C:\ExamplePath\OldDirectoryName" -NewName "
    NewDirectoryName"
```

To remove a directory, use the Remove-Item cmdlet. The -Recurse parameter is essential when removing directories that contain files and subdirectories. Without -Recurse, an error will occur if the directory is not empty:

```
Remove-Item -Path "C:\ExamplePath\DirectoryToDelete" -Recurse
```

The Get-ChildItem cmdlet is valuable for listing directories. By specifying the -Directory parameter, only directories are displayed:

```
Get-ChildItem -Path "C:\ExamplePath" -Directory
```

Managing directory attributes involves several cmdlets, such as Get-Item, Set-ItemProperty, and Clear-ItemProperty. To inspect attributes, use the Get-Item cmdlet to retrieve the directory object and view its properties:

```
$dir = Get-Item -Path "C:\ExamplePath\Directory"
$dir.Attributes
```

To modify attributes, such as setting a directory to read-only or hidden, use the Set-ItemProperty cmdlet:

```
Set-ItemProperty -Path "C:\ExamplePath\Directory" -Name "Attributes" -Value "
    ReadOnly"
Set-ItemProperty -Path "C:\ExamplePath\Directory" -Name "Attributes" -Value "
    Hidden"
```

Clearing an attribute can be performed with the Clear-ItemProperty cmdlet:

```
Clear-ItemProperty -Path "C:\ExamplePath\Directory" -Name "Attributes"
```

Handling directory permissions in PowerShell is done using the Get-Acl and Set-Acl cmdlets. To view the Access Control List (ACL) for a directory, use Get-Acl:

```
$acl = Get-Acl -Path "C:\ExamplePath\Directory"
$acl
```

Modifying ACLs involves creating a new access rule and applying it to the directory. Here is an example of adding full control for a user:

```
$acl = Get-Acl -Path "C:\ExamplePath\Directory"
$rule = New-Object System.Security.AccessControl.FileSystemAccessRule("UserName",
    "FullControl", "Allow")
$acl.SetAccessRule($rule)
Set-Acl -Path "C:\ExamplePath\Directory" -AclObject $acl
```

Copying directory structure without the contained files can be done with robocopy, a robust file and directory copy command-line utility:

```
robocopy "C:\SourceDirectory" "C:\DestinationDirectory" /E /XF *
```

The /E switch ensures all subdirectories, including empty ones, are copied, while /XF * excludes files.

Creating and managing directories in PowerShell is both versatile and powerful, providing a comprehensive toolkit for file system organization and maintenance. By leveraging these cmdlets and techniques, users can efficiently handle a wide variety of directory-related tasks in their PowerShell scripts.

9.7 Handling File Permissions

File permissions are a critical aspect of file management, ensuring that only authorized users can access or modify files. In PowerShell, managing file permissions involves using cmdlets that interact with the Windows security subsystem. This section will delve into the mechanisms by which file permissions can be viewed and altered, focusing on practical applications through PowerShell scripting.

To handle file permissions, we primarily use the Get-Acl and Set-Acl cmdlets, which get and set the access control list (ACL) of a file or directory. An ACL is a list of access control entries (ACEs) that define the permissions for users and groups.

Viewing File Permissions with Get-Acl

The Get-Acl cmdlet retrieves the ACL of a specified file or directory, allowing you to view its current permissions. Consider the following example:

```
$acl = Get-Acl -Path "C:\\Example\\File.txt"
$acl
```

The above script stores the ACL of File.txt located in C:\Example into the $acl variable and then outputs it. The output, encapsulated within the $acl object, provides detailed information about the file's permissions, including the owner, group, and various ACEs.

To format the output for readability, use the Format-List cmdlet:

```
$acl | Format-List
```

The Format-List cmdlet displays the ACL properties in a list format, making it easier to interpret.

Altering File Permissions with Set-Acl

Modifying file permissions requires creating or modifying ACEs within the ACL and then applying this updated ACL back to the file using Set-Acl. Below is a step-by-step guide:

- Retrieve the existing ACL.
- Create a new ACE or modify an existing one.
- Apply the updated ACL to the file.

```
$acl = Get-Acl -Path "C:\\Example\\File.txt"

$permission = "DOMAIN\\User","FullControl","Allow"
$ace = New-Object System.Security.AccessControl.FileSystemAccessRule $permission

$acl.SetAccessRule($ace)

Set-Acl -Path "C:\\Example\\File.txt" -AclObject $acl
```

In this script:

- The original ACL of File.txt is retrieved.
- A new ACE is created with New-Object, granting FullControl to DOMAIN\User.
- The new ACE is added to the ACL.
- The modified ACL is applied back to File.txt using Set-Acl.

Removing File Permissions

To remove an ACE from an ACL, use the RemoveAccessRule method. The process is similar to adding permissions but with a focus on removing specific rules.

```
$acl = Get-Acl -Path "C:\\Example\\File.txt"

$permission = "DOMAIN\\User","FullControl","Allow"
$ace = New-Object System.Security.AccessControl.FileSystemAccessRule $permission

$acl.RemoveAccessRule($ace)

Set-Acl -Path "C:\\Example\\File.txt" -AclObject $acl
```

In this script, the RemoveAccessRule method is used to remove the ACE that grants FullControl to DOMAIN\User.

Changing Ownership of Files

Changing the owner of a file involves modifying the owner property of the ACL. This is done using the following sequence:

- Retrieve the existing ACL.
- Modify the owner.
- Apply the updated ACL to the file.

```
$acl = Get-Acl -Path "C:\\Example\\File.txt"
$acl.SetOwner([System.Security.Principal.NTAccount]"DOMAIN\\NewOwner")
Set-Acl -Path "C:\\Example\\File.txt" -AclObject $acl
```

Here, the owner is set to DOMAIN\NewOwner, and the updated ACL is applied to File.txt.

Script Execution Permissions

It is important to note that modifying file permissions programmatically requires appropriate script execution permissions. Running these scripts usually necessitates administrative privileges to alter ACLs successfully. To run PowerShell with elevated privileges, right-click on the PowerShell application and select Run as administrator.

Understanding and managing file permissions using PowerShell is fundamental for secure and efficient file operations. Applying the concepts discussed in this section will enable precise control over file access, enhancing both security and functionality in file management tasks.

9.8 Using Get-Content and Set-Content

PowerShell provides powerful cmdlets for handling file content: Get-Content and Set-Content. These cmdlets allow you to read from and write to files, respectively, and they are fundamental tools in file manipulation.

The Get-Content cmdlet reads the content of a file line by line and returns it as an array of strings, where each string represents one line of the file. By default, Get-Content reads text files, but it can also handle other file types when used with appropriate parameters.

```
# Reading the content of a text file
$file_content = Get-Content -Path "C:\example\file.txt"
```

In the above example, the content of "C:\example\file.txt" is read and stored in the variable $file_content. If the file consists of multiple lines, $file_content will be an array where each element corresponds to a line in the file.

To read only a specific number of lines from the beginning or end of the file, you can use the -TotalCount and -Tail parameters respectively.

```
# Reading the first 10 lines of a file
$first_ten_lines = Get-Content -Path "C:\example\file.txt" -TotalCount 10
```

```
# Reading the last 5 lines of a file
$last_five_lines = Get-Content -Path "C:\example\file.txt" -Tail 5
```

When working with large files, it's often useful to filter content as it's being read. This can be achieved using the Select-String cmdlet in combination with Get-Content. This approach is efficient when searching for specific patterns within a file.

```
# Searching for lines containing the word "error"
$errors = Get-Content -Path "C:\example\log.txt" | Select-String -Pattern "error"
```

The Set-Content cmdlet writes content to a file. It replaces the entire content of the target file with the specified string or array of strings. If you provide multiple strings, each string will be written as a separate line in the file.

```
# Writing content to a file
Set-Content -Path "C:\example\output.txt" -Value "This is a new file."

# Writing multiple lines to a file
$lines = @("First line", "Second line", "Third line")
Set-Content -Path "C:\example\output.txt" -Value $lines
```

When using Set-Content, the output file is overwritten if it already exists. To append content to an existing file without overwriting it, you can use the Add-Content cmdlet.

```
# Appending a new line to an existing file
Add-Content -Path "C:\example\output.txt" -Value "This line is appended."
```

To modify specific lines of a file, you can first read the file content into a variable, make the necessary changes, and then write the modified content back to the file using Set-Content.

```
# Reading file content
$file_content = Get-Content -Path "C:\example\file.txt"

# Modifying a specific line (e.g., changing the third line)
$file_content[2] = "This is the new third line."

# Writing the modified content back to the file
Set-Content -Path "C:\example\file.txt" -Value $file_content
```

Both Get-Content and Set-Content have extended functionalities that cater to more complex file operations. For instance, you can use the -Encoding parameter to specify different character encodings when reading from and writing to files.

```
# Reading a file with UTF-8 encoding
$file_content = Get-Content -Path "C:\example\file_utf8.txt" -Encoding UTF8
```

```
# Writing to a file with ASCII encoding
Set-Content -Path "C:\example\output.txt" -Value $lines -Encoding ASCII
```

For binary files or files with newlines encoded in a particular format, these encoding options are indispensable to ensure the integrity of data during file operations.

```
# Reading a binary file as bytes
$file_bytes = [System.IO.File]::ReadAllBytes("C:\example\binaryfile.bin")

# Writing bytes back to a binary file
[System.IO.File]::WriteAllBytes("C:\example\output.bin", $file_bytes)
```

Additionally, the -ReadCount parameter in Get-Content can be used to specify the number of lines read at a time, which can help optimize memory usage when processing large files.

```
# Reading file content in chunks of 100 lines
Get-Content -Path "C:\example\bigfile.txt" -ReadCount 100 | ForEach-Object {
    # Process each chunk of 100 lines
    $_
}
```

Monitoring file changes in real-time is another powerful use case of Get-Content. The -Wait parameter allows you to watch a file for new content as it gets added.

```
# Monitoring a log file for new entries
Get-Content -Path "C:\example\logfile.txt" -Wait
```

The ability to read and write files efficiently and flexibly using Get-Content and Set-Content empowers scripts to handle various file operations seamlessly, ensuring PowerShell's robustness in administrative and automation tasks.

9.9 Using Import-Csv and Export-Csv

The Import-Csv and Export-Csv cmdlets are essential tools in PowerShell for working with CSV (Comma-Separated Values) files. These cmdlets enable efficient import and export operations, allowing users to read from and write to CSV files seamlessly. CSV files are widely used due to their simplicity and compatibility with various data-processing applications.

Import-Csv reads a CSV file and converts each row into a PowerShell object, where each column becomes a property of that object. Conversely, Export-Csv takes objects and writes them to a CSV file, creating a row for each object and a column for each property.

Syntax of Import-Csv:

```
Import-Csv -Path <string> [-Delimiter <char>] [-Header <string[]>] [-QuoteChar <
    char>]
```

Syntax of Export-Csv:

```
Export-Csv -Path <string> -InputObject <psobject> [-Delimiter <char>] [-Force] [-
    Append]
```

To illustrate the usage of these cmdlets, consider a CSV file named employees.csv. This CSV file contains the following data:

```
Name,Department,Title
Alice,HR,Manager
Bob,IT,Developer
Charlie,Finance,Analyst
```

Using Import-Csv: The following PowerShell command imports the data from employees.csv and stores it in the variable $employees:

```
$employees = Import-Csv -Path "C:\Data\employees.csv"
```

This command reads the CSV file and converts each row into a PowerShell object. As a result, $employees contains the following objects:

```
Name    Department  Title
----    ----------  -----
Alice   HR          Manager
Bob     IT          Developer
Charlie Finance     Analyst
```

To access the properties of these objects, use standard object notation:

```
foreach ($employee in $employees) {
    Write-Output "Name: $($employee.Name), Department: $($employee.Department),
        Title: $($employee.Title)"
}
```

This loop outputs:

```
Name: Alice, Department: HR, Title: Manager
Name: Bob, Department: IT, Title: Developer
Name: Charlie, Department: Finance, Title: Analyst
```

Using Export-Csv: After modifying or creating new object data, you might need to write this information back to a CSV file. The Export-Csv cmdlet accomplishes this. Consider the following example where we add a new employee to the list and export it:

```
$employees += [PSCustomObject]@{ Name="David"; Department="Marketing"; Title
    ="Coordinator" }
$employees | Export-Csv -Path "C:\Data\employees_updated.csv" -
```

```
NoTypeInformation
```

The $employees array includes the new David object, and the Export-Csv cmdlet writes the entire array to employees_updated.csv.

Custom Delimiters and Headers: By default, Import-Csv and Export-Csv use a comma (',') as the delimiter. However, other delimiters can be specified using the -Delimiter parameter. For example, to import a pipe-delimited file:

```
$employees = Import-Csv -Path "C:\Data\employees_pipe.csv" -Delimiter '|'
```

For files that lack a header row, use the -Header parameter to specify column names directly:

```
$employees = Import-Csv -Path "C:\Data\employees_noheader.csv" -Header "Name",
    "Department", "Title"
```

Appending Data: To append data to an existing CSV file rather than overwriting it, use the -Append parameter with Export-Csv:

```
$newEmployee = [PSCustomObject]@{ Name="Eve"; Department="Legal"; Title="
    Advisor" }
$newEmployee | Export-Csv -Path "C:\Data\employees_updated.csv" -Append -
    NoTypeInformation
```

This command ensures that Eve's information is added to the existing employees_updated.csv without deleting the previous content.

Excluding Type Information: The -NoTypeInformation parameter is used with Export-Csv to exclude the type information header that is added by default. This is particularly useful for creating files intended for use by other applications, avoiding compatibility issues.

Practical Example: Exporting System Data: Consider a scenario where you need to export a list of running processes to a CSV file. This can be done as follows:

```
$processes = Get-Process
$processes | Select-Object -Property Name, Id, CPU | Export-Csv -Path "C:\Data\
    processes.csv" -NoTypeInformation
```

This script gets the current running processes, selects specific properties (Name, Id, and CPU), and exports this data to processes.csv.

Handling Large Files: When dealing with large CSV files, performance optimizations might be necessary. One approach is to process the file line-by-line using Get-Content to read the file and Add-Content to write to a new file, avoiding the memory overhead associated with loading the entire file at once into memory.

In summary, Import-Csv and Export-Csv provide robust capabilities for CSV file manipulation, allowing seamless import and export of tabular data in PowerShell. Through careful use of their parameters, such as specifying delimiters, custom headers, and appending data, these cmdlets offer extensive flexibility for handling CSV files in various scenarios.

9.10 Handling Binary Files

Handling binary files is a critical aspect of file manipulation, especially when dealing with non-text data such as images, executables, and other complex file types. PowerShell provides powerful tools and cmdlets to read, write, and manipulate binary files efficiently. This section delves into the specifics of these operations, covering reading binary data, writing binary data, and modifying binary file content.

To work with binary files in PowerShell, the 'System.IO.FileStream' class is generally employed, which offers a stream for file operations providing both synchronous and asynchronous read and write operations. Below, we explore fundamental techniques for handling binary files.

```
$filePath = "C:\path\to\binaryfile.bin"
$binaryReader = [System.IO.File]::Open($filePath, [System.IO.FileMode]::Open, [
    System.IO.FileAccess]::Read)
```

In this example, the 'Open' method from the 'System.IO.File' class is used to open an existing binary file for reading. The file is opened in 'Open' mode with read access. Once opened, a binary reader can be used to read the data.

Reading Binary Data

The 'BinaryReader' class in .NET provides methods that simplify reading binary data from a file. Here is how to utilize the 'BinaryReader' to read binary contents:

```
$binaryReader = [System.IO.BinaryReader]::new($binaryStream)
try {
    $bufferSize = 1024
    $buffer = New-Object byte[] $bufferSize
    $bytesRead = $binaryReader.Read($buffer, 0, $bufferSize)
    while ($bytesRead -gt 0) {
        # Process the buffer content
        $bytesRead = $binaryReader.Read($buffer, 0, $bufferSize)
```

```
    }
} finally {
    $binaryReader.Close()
    $binaryStream.Close()
}
```

In this snippet, a 'BinaryReader' is instantiated with a file stream, and a buffer is read in chunks of 1024 bytes. The 'Read' method fills the buffer with the binary data and returns the number of bytes read. This continues in a loop until the end of the file is reached, at which point the stream is closed.

Writing Binary Data

Writing to binary files requires the 'BinaryWriter' class, which can write various data types to a stream in their binary form. Here's an example of how to open a binary file for writing and write binary data to it:

```
$filePath = "C:\path\to\outputfile.bin"
$binaryWriter = [System.IO.BinaryWriter]::new([System.IO.File]::Open($filePath, [
    System.IO.FileMode]::Create, [System.IO.FileAccess]::Write))
try {
    $buffer = [byte[]](0x01, 0x02, 0x3F, 0x4A)
    $binaryWriter.Write($buffer)
} finally {
    $binaryWriter.Close()
}
```

In this example, a binary file is opened for writing in 'Create' mode, meaning an existing file will be overwritten, or a new file will be created if it does not exist. The 'BinaryWriter' then writes a byte array to the file, and upon completion, the writer is closed.

Modifying Binary File Content

Modifying content within a binary file often involves reading the binary data, making the necessary changes, and then writing the modified data back. Below is an example where a portion of a binary file is read, modified, and saved back.

```
$filePath = "C:\path\to\modifiablefile.bin"
$binaryStream = [System.IO.File]::Open($filePath, [System.IO.FileMode]::Open, [
    System.IO.FileAccess]::ReadWrite)
$binaryReader = [System.IO.BinaryReader]::new($binaryStream)
$binaryWriter = [System.IO.BinaryWriter]::new($binaryStream)

try {
    $binaryStream.Seek(0, [System.IO.SeekOrigin]::Begin)
    $buffer = $binaryReader.ReadBytes(1024)

    # Modification logic (example: flip all bits in the buffer)
    for ($i = 0; $i -lt $buffer.Length; $i++) {
        $buffer[$i] = -bxor $buffer[$i]
    }
```

```
    $binaryStream.Seek(0, [System.IO.SeekOrigin]::Begin)
    $binaryWriter.Write($buffer)
} finally {
    $binaryReader.Close()
    $binaryWriter.Close()
    $binaryStream.Close()
}
```

This code reads 1024 bytes from the start of the file, flips all bits in the buffer (an example modification), and writes the modified buffer back to the beginning of the file. Note the use of the 'Seek' method to reset the stream position before writing.

Mastering binary file operations allows for nuanced control over file content, beyond what is possible with text files. By leveraging the 'System.IO.FileStream', 'BinaryReader', and 'BinaryWriter' classes, robust and efficient handling of binary data in PowerShell is achievable.

Chapter 10

Advanced Scripting Techniques

This chapter explores advanced scripting techniques in PowerShell. Topics include creating and using modules, building custom cmdlets, and advanced parameter features. It also covers working with JSON and XML, leveraging PowerShell remoting, and using background jobs. Handling asynchronous operations and profile scripting are examined, alongside best practices for script optimization. These techniques provide readers with enhanced capabilities to develop sophisticated and efficient PowerShell scripts.

10.1 Introduction to Advanced Scripting

PowerShell scripting provides powerful capabilities that extend well beyond basic command execution. This section introduces advanced scripting techniques, which are essential for developing robust, efficient, and maintainable scripts. Mastering these advanced concepts enables script automation, streamlining of administrative tasks, and enhancement of overall productivity.

1. Fundamental Concepts: Advanced scripting in PowerShell builds on basic scripting knowledge. Key principles include understanding script structure, command syntax, flow control, and error handling.

These concepts serve as the foundation for more complex scripting techniques.

2. Modularization: Creating reusable, modular scripts improves code maintainability and reduces redundancy. By packaging related functions into modules, scripts become more organized and shareable across multiple projects.

```
# MyModule.psm1

function Get-HelloWorld {
    [CmdletBinding()]
    param (
        [string]$Name = "World"
    )
    Write-Output "Hello, $Name!"
}

Export-ModuleMember -Function Get-HelloWorld
```

To utilize the module, it must be imported into the PowerShell session:

```
Import-Module -Name MyModule
Get-HelloWorld -Name 'PowerShell'
```

```
Hello, PowerShell!
```

3. Custom Cmdlets: Developing custom cmdlets enhances PowerShell's native functionality. These cmdlets can incorporate complex logic, utilize .NET capabilities, and offer parameterized input, maximizing script versatility.

```
function ConvertTo-UpperCase {
    [CmdletBinding()]
    param (
        [string]$InputString
    )
    return $InputString.ToUpper()
}
```

When executed, this cmdlet converts a given string to uppercase:

```
ConvertTo-UpperCase -InputString 'hello world'
```

```
HELLO WORLD
```

4. Advanced Parameter Features: Leveraging advanced parameter attributes enhances script utility and user interaction. Parameters can be more precisely defined using attributes like ValidateSet, ValidateRange, and ValidatePattern.

```
function Set-Environment {
    [CmdletBinding()]
    param (
```

```
        [Parameter(Mandatory=$true)]
        [ValidateSet('Development', 'Testing', 'Production')]
        [string]$Environment
    )
    Write-Output "Selected Environment: $Environment"
}
```

When executed with an invalid value, this function prompts an error:

```
Set-Environment -Environment 'InvalidEnv'
```

```
Set-Environment : Cannot validate argument on parameter 'Environment'. The argument "InvalidEnv" does not belong to the set "Development,Testing,Production" specified by the ValidateSet attribute. Supply an argument that is in the set and then try the command again.
```

5. Script Optimization: Efficient script performance is crucial in advanced scripting. Techniques such as minimizing unnecessary variables, optimizing loops, and reducing pipeline usage help in refining script execution.

Consider the following suboptimal loop:

```
# Calculate the sum of the first 100000 numbers
$sum = 0
1..100000 | ForEach-Object { $sum += $_ }
Write-Output $sum
```

This can be optimized by using a direct loop:

```
# Calculate the sum of the first 100000 numbers
$sum = 0
for ($i = 1; $i -le 100000; $i++) { $sum += $i }
Write-Output $sum
```

Advanced scripting requires a deep understanding of these principles and the ability to apply them effectively. The knowledge of modularization, custom cmdlet creation, advanced parameter handling, and script optimization collectively empowers a PowerShell scripter to tackle complex automation tasks proficiently.

10.2 Creating and Using Modules

PowerShell modules encapsulate a set of related functions, cmdlets, variables, and more, which can be distributed and reused across multiple scripts and projects. Modules enable organization, code reuse, and simplified distribution of scripts. This section details the creation, usage, and benefits of modules, including best practices and examples.

Creating a Module

Creating a module starts with a directory that contains all the necessary files. The primary file of a module is a PowerShell script with a .psm1 extension. The following steps outline the process of creating a basic module:

1. Create a directory for the module named MyModule.
2. Inside MyModule, create a file named MyModule.psm1.
3. Write the functions intended for the module in the MyModule.psm1 file.

For example, consider the following functions defined in MyModule.psm1:

```
function Get-Greeting {
    param ($Name)
    return "Hello, $Name"
}

function Get-Farewell {
    param ($Name)
    return "Goodbye, $Name"
}
```

Exporting Functions

By default, all functions in a .psm1 file are available when the module is imported. However, it is a good practice to explicitly export the intended functions using the Export-ModuleMember cmdlet to avoid namespace pollution.

```
Export-ModuleMember -Function Get-Greeting, Get-Farewell
```

Manifest File

A module manifest file provides metadata, including the module version, author, compatibility with specific PowerShell versions, and more. The manifest is a .psd1 file commonly created using the New-ModuleManifest cmdlet. In the MyModule directory, create a MyModule.psd1 file:

```
New-ModuleManifest -Path ".\MyModule.psd1" `
                   -RootModule "MyModule.psm1" `
                   -ModuleVersion "1.0" `
                   -Author "Your Name" `
                   -Description "A sample module"
```

The above command generates a manifest file with the specified properties. Open the MyModule.psd1 file to examine or manually edit its contents as needed.

Importing a Module

To use a module in a PowerShell session, employ the Import-Module cmdlet. Prior to importing, ensure the module directory is placed in a path listed within the $env:PSModulePath environment variable, or provide the full path when importing.

```
Import-Module -Name ".\MyModule"
```

Once imported, the functions defined in MyModule.psm1 are readily available:

```
Get-Greeting -Name "Alice"
Get-Farewell -Name "Bob"
```

```
Hello, Alice
Goodbye, Bob
```

Module Versioning

To manage different versions of a module, specify the ModuleVersion in the manifest file and update it upon any significant change. Furthermore, PowerShell supports side-by-side installation of different module versions, which you specify during import:

```
Import-Module -Name MyModule -RequiredVersion 1.0
```

Dependencies and Required Modules

Modules can declare dependencies on other modules using the RequiredModules key in the manifest file. When importing the primary module, PowerShell automatically imports the required dependencies.

Edit the MyModule.psd1 manifest file to include required modules:

```
@{
    ...
    RequiredModules = @('RequiredModule1', 'RequiredModule2')
}
```

Publishing and Distributing Modules

PowerShell modules can be published to repositories such as the PowerShell Gallery or distributed as files. To publish a module, use the Publish-Module cmdlet after creating an account and obtaining an API key from the repository.

```
Publish-Module -Name MyModule -Repository PSGallery -NuGetApiKey <
    API_KEY>
```

Upon successful publishing, users can install the module directly from the repository:

```
Install-Module -Name MyModule
```

Following these practices ensures that your PowerShell modules are well-organized, easily distributed, and maintainable across projects.

10.3 Building Custom Cmdlets

In this section, we will explore the creation of custom cmdlets in PowerShell. A cmdlet (pronounced *command-let*) is a lightweight command used in the Windows PowerShell environment. Unlike scripts, cmdlets are instances of .NET classes; they derive from the Cmdlet base class. Writing custom cmdlets allows you to extend the functionality of PowerShell to meet specific administrative or operational needs.

To begin building a custom cmdlet, we need to define a class that inherits from System.Management.Automation.Cmdlet or System.Management.Automation.PSCmdlet. The class should be decorated with the Cmdlet attribute, which specifies the verb and noun pair that identifies the cmdlet.

Below is an example of a simple cmdlet that increments an integer value. This example introduces the fundamental components required for building a custom cmdlet in PowerShell.

```
using System;
using System.Management.Automation;

[Cmdlet(VerbsCommon.Add, "Number")]
public class AddNumberCmdlet : Cmdlet
{
    [Parameter(Mandatory = true, Position = 0)]
    public int Value1 { get; set; }

    [Parameter(Mandatory = true, Position = 1)]
    public int Value2 { get; set; }

    protected override void ProcessRecord()
    {
        int result = Value1 + Value2;
        WriteObject(result);
    }
}
```

In the above example:

- The class AddNumberCmdlet inherits from Cmdlet.

- The Cmdlet attribute specifies VerbsCommon.Add as the verb and Number as the noun, resulting in the cmdlet name Add-Number.
- The properties Value1 and Value2 are decorated with the Parameter attribute to define them as parameters. Mandatory = true indicates that these parameters must be provided by the user.
- The ProcessRecord method is overridden to implement the cmdlet's processing logic. The WriteObject method outputs the result to the PowerShell pipeline.

Next, we compile this code into a DLL and load it into PowerShell to use our custom cmdlet. The following commands illustrate how to compile the example using csc.exe (C# compiler) and load the generated assembly into PowerShell.

```
csc /target:library /reference:System.Management.Automation.dll /out:
    AddNumberCmdlet.dll AddNumberCmdlet.cs

Import-Module ./AddNumberCmdlet.dll
```

After loading the module, we can use the Add-Number cmdlet in PowerShell:

```
PS> Add-Number -Value1 5 -Value2 7
12
```

A robust custom cmdlet should handle errors gracefully and support features like pipeline input and output type constraints. Consider the following enhanced example that includes error handling:

```
using System;
using System.Management.Automation;

[Cmdlet(VerbsCommon.Add, "SafeNumber")]
public class AddSafeNumberCmdlet : Cmdlet
{
    [Parameter(Mandatory = true, Position = 0)]
    public int Value1 { get; set; }

    [Parameter(Mandatory = true, Position = 1)]
    public int Value2 { get; set; }

    protected override void ProcessRecord()
    {
        try
        {
            int result = Value1 + Value2;
            WriteObject(result);
        }
        catch (Exception ex)
```

```
        {
            WriteError(new ErrorRecord(ex, "AdditionFailed", ErrorCategory.
                OperationStopped, null));
        }
    }
}
```

In the enhanced example:

- A try-catch block is used in ProcessRecord to handle any unexpected errors.
- The WriteError method logs the exception as an ErrorRecord with a custom ErrorCategory.

We can further enrich our cmdlets by implementing support for pipeline input. This is achieved by decorating parameters with the ValueFromPipeline and ValueFromPipelineByPropertyName attributes. The following example demonstrates a cmdlet that supports both direct and pipeline input:

```
using System;
using System.Management.Automation;

[Cmdlet(VerbsDiagnostic.Test, "PipelineInput")]
public class TestPipelineInputCmdlet : Cmdlet
{
    [Parameter(Mandatory = true, ValueFromPipeline = true,
        ValueFromPipelineByPropertyName = true)]
    public string InputString { get; set; }

    protected override void ProcessRecord()
    {
        WriteObject($"Received: {InputString}");
    }
}
```

In this example:

- The InputString parameter supports input directly from the pipeline (ValueFromPipeline = true) and by property name mapping from pipeline objects (ValueFromPipelineByPropertyName = true).

These techniques elevate the flexibility and power of custom cmdlets, allowing the seamless integration of custom logic into PowerShell workflows. Continued exploration of cmdlet parameter attributes, input handling, and error management will provide a stronger foundation for developing advanced cmdlets tailored to specific requirements.

10.4 Advanced Parameter Features

PowerShell provides a rich set of features for defining and managing parameters in scripts and functions. Understanding these advanced parameter features allows script authors to create more versatile and user-friendly scripts. This section delves into key advanced parameter features, including parameter attributes, validation, and parameter sets.

Parameter Attributes

PowerShell allows the inclusion of various attributes to parameters, enhancing their functionality and user interaction. Common attributes include Mandatory, Position, ParameterSetName, and ValueFromPipeline. These attributes are specified within square brackets preceding the parameter declaration.

Consider the following example of defining a parameter with multiple attributes:

```
function Get-FileInfo {
    param (
        [Parameter(Mandatory=$true, Position=0, ValueFromPipeline=$true)]
        [string]$FilePath,

        [Parameter(Position=1)]
        [switch]$Verbose
    )
    # Function body
}
```

In this script: - FilePath is a mandatory positional parameter that can accept input from the pipeline. - Verbose is an optional switch parameter.

Parameter Validation

PowerShell supports several parameter validation attributes that help ensure parameters meet specified criteria before the function or script executes. These include:

- ValidateNotNull
- ValidateNotNullOrEmpty
- ValidateRange(min, max)
- ValidateLength(minLength, maxLength)
- ValidatePattern(regex)

An example demonstrating parameter validation is shown below:

```
function Set-Age {
    param (
        [Parameter(Mandatory=$true)]
        [ValidateRange(18, 65)]
        [int]$Age
    )
    Write-Output "Age is within range: $Age"
}
```

Here, the Age parameter must be an integer between 18 and 65. If the user inputs a value outside this range, an error is raised automatically.

Parameter Sets

Parameter sets are used to create mutually exclusive groups of parameters. This feature is beneficial for functions that support different modes of operation with distinct sets of parameters. A parameter can be part of one or more parameter sets, and PowerShell ensures that only parameters from the same set are used together in a single command invocation.

The following example illustrates how to define parameter sets:

```
function Invoke-Operation {
    param (
        [Parameter(Mandatory=$true, ParameterSetName="ByName")]
        [string]$Name,

        [Parameter(Mandatory=$true, ParameterSetName="ById")]
        [int]$Id
    )
    switch ($PSCmdlet.ParameterSetName) {
        "ByName" { Write-Output "Operating by Name: $Name" }
        "ById" { Write-Output "Operating by Id: $Id" }
    }
}
```

In this script: - Name belongs to the "ByName" parameter set. - Id belongs to the "ById" parameter set.

The switch statement then determines the active parameter set and executes the corresponding block of code.

Dynamic Parameters

Dynamic parameters are parameters added at runtime based on certain conditions. These are more advanced and rarely used but can be powerful in complex scenarios. Defining dynamic parameters requires implementing the IDynamicParameters interface.

Below is an example illustrating the use of dynamic parameters:

```
function Get-DynamicParam {
    [CmdletBinding()]
    param ()

    dynamicparam {
        $RuntimeParamDictionary = New-Object System.Management.Automation.
            RuntimeDefinedParameterDictionary

        $AttributeCollection = New-Object System.Collections.ObjectModel.Collection[
            System.Attribute]
        $AttributeCollection.Add((New-Object System.Management.Automation.
            ParameterAttribute))

        $RuntimeParam = New-Object System.Management.Automation.
            RuntimeDefinedParameter('DynamicParam', [string], $AttributeCollection)
        $RuntimeParamDictionary.Add('DynamicParam', $RuntimeParam)

        return $RuntimeParamDictionary
    }

    process {
        $DynamicParamValue = $PSBoundParameters['DynamicParam']
        Write-Output "Dynamic parameter value: $DynamicParamValue"
    }
}
```

Here: - A dynamic parameter named DynamicParam is defined during execution. - The process block uses this parameter and outputs its value.

These advanced features of PowerShell parameters empower script authors to create robust, flexible, and user-friendly scripts. Combining these features appropriately can lead to significant improvements in script maintainability and usability.

10.5 Working with JSON and XML

JSON (JavaScript Object Notation) and XML (eXtensible Markup Language) are widely-used formats for data interchange. Understanding how to effectively manipulate and utilize these formats is crucial for advanced PowerShell scripting.

PowerShell offers robust cmdlets to handle both JSON and XML data. These cmdlets facilitate the conversion of data between these formats and PowerShell objects, allowing seamless data processing and automation tasks.

JSON Handling in PowerShell

To work with JSON in PowerShell, the primary cmdlets used are ConvertTo-Json and ConvertFrom-Json.

Consider a scenario where you have a PowerShell object and need to convert it to JSON format:

```
$person = @{
    FirstName = "John"
    LastName = "Doe"
    Age = 30
    Address = @{
        Street = "123 Elm St"
        City = "Somewhere"
        State = "NY"
        Zip = "10001"
    }
}

$json = $person | ConvertTo-Json
Write-Output $json
```

The above PowerShell script creates a hashtable representing a person, converts it to JSON using ConvertTo-Json, and outputs the JSON string.

The output will be:

```
{
    "FirstName": "John",
    "LastName": "Doe",
    "Age": 30,
    "Address": {
                "Street": "123 Elm St",
                "City": "Somewhere",
                "State": "NY",
                "Zip": "10001"
            }
}
```

To convert JSON data back into a PowerShell object, use the ConvertFrom-Json cmdlet:

```
$json = '{
    "FirstName": "John",
    "LastName": "Doe",
    "Age": 30,
    "Address": {
                "Street": "123 Elm St",
                "City": "Somewhere",
                "State": "NY",
                "Zip": "10001"
            }
}'

$personObject = $json | ConvertFrom-Json

Write-Output $personObject.FirstName
Write-Output $personObject.Address.City
```

The ConvertFrom-Json cmdlet processes the JSON string and converts it into a corresponding PowerShell object.

XML Handling in PowerShell

PowerShell provides robust support for XML processing through the use of the XML type accelerator [xml]. This powerful feature allows easy manipulation, query, and traversal of XML documents.

Consider an XML document stored in a string:

```
$xmlString = @"
<person>
    <firstname>John</firstname>
    <lastname>Doe</lastname>
    <age>30</age>
    <address>
        <street>123 Elm St</street>
        <city>Somewhere</city>
        <state>NY</state>
        <zip>10001</zip>
    </address>
</person>
"@

[xml]$xmlDoc = $xmlString
```

The script uses the [xml] type accelerator to convert the string into an XML document, accessible through the $xmlDoc variable.

To navigate the XML document and extract specific data, use dot notation:

```
$firstName = $xmlDoc.person.firstname
$city = $xmlDoc.person.address.city

Write-Output $firstName
Write-Output $city
```

This extracts the firstname and city nodes' text and displays them.

Adding elements to the XML document involves creating new XML nodes and appending them to existing nodes:

```
$newElement = $xmlDoc.CreateElement("phone")
$newElement.InnerText = "555-1234"

$xmlDoc.person.AppendChild($newElement)

Write-Output $xmlDoc.OuterXml
```

The new phone element is added to the person node, and the updated XML document is output.

Manipulating XML attributes uses similar techniques. When creating or modifying attributes, use the SetAttribute method:

```
$xmlDoc.person.SetAttribute("id", "12345")

Write-Output $xmlDoc.OuterXml
```

Using this method, the id attribute is added to the person element.

Integrating JSON and XML handling with PowerShell scripts enriches the ability to automate tasks within diverse IT environments. These techniques provide flexibility in processing configuration files, data interchange, and APIs, improving the overall efficiency of automation workflows.

10.6 Leveraging PowerShell Remoting

PowerShell Remoting is a powerful feature that allows administrators to manage and automate tasks across multiple remote machines. This capability is especially valuable in environments with numerous servers or workstations. Remoting in PowerShell can be performed using different methodologies, each appropriate for specific scenarios. This section will delve into these methodologies and their applications.

To enable PowerShell Remoting, the Enable-PSRemoting cmdlet is used. This cmdlet configures the computer to receive remote commands and creates the necessary firewall rules. Examples provided in this section assume PowerShell Remoting is enabled on the target machines.

```
Enable-PSRemoting -Force
```

It is crucial to understand the two primary types of remoting available in PowerShell: session-based remoting and one-to-one interactive remoting.

1. Session-Based Remoting

Session-based remoting allows for executing a series of commands in the same session on a remote computer, which is essential for maintaining state information between commands. The New-PSSession cmdlet is used to create a new session on a remote computer.

```
$session = New-PSSession -ComputerName "RemoteServer" -Credential (Get-
    Credential)
```

Once a session is established, the Invoke-Command cmdlet can be used to run commands within the context of that session.

```
Invoke-Command -Session $session -ScriptBlock {
    Get-Process
}
```

You can also copy files to and from a remote session using the Copy-Item cmdlet in conjunction with session objects.

```
Copy-Item -Path "C:\LocalFile.txt" -Destination "C:\RemoteFile.txt" -ToSession
    $session
```

When finished with the session, it is prudent to remove it to free up resources.

```
Remove-PSSession -Session $session
```

2. One-to-One Interactive Remoting

One-to-one interactive remoting involves establishing an interactive session with a remote computer, similar to SSH or Telnet sessions. This method is appropriate for real-time administration where continuous interaction is required. The Enter-PSSession cmdlet enables this form of remoting.

```
Enter-PSSession -ComputerName "RemoteServer" -Credential (Get-Credential)
```

In this session, all PowerShell commands executed interact directly with the remote computer. Use Exit-PSSession to terminate the interactive session.

```
Exit-PSSession
```

3. Configuring Trusted Hosts and Authentication Methods

For environments without an active directory or where Kerberos is not feasible, configuring the TrustedHosts list is necessary. This configuration allows connections to and from specified remote computers using less secure authentication methods, such as Basic or NTLM.

```
Set-Item WSMan:\localhost\Client\TrustedHosts -Value "RemoteServer"
```

It is also important to consider the various authentication methods which can be specified in the New-PSSession, Enter-PSSession, and Invoke-Command cmdlets. These include:

- Basic
- Default

- Negotiate
- CredSSP

The appropriate authentication method depends on the security requirements and network configuration.

```
$session = New-PSSession -ComputerName "RemoteServer" -Credential (Get-
    Credential) -Authentication Basic
```

4. Remoting over HTTPS

To secure remote operations over the internet or untrusted networks, PowerShell remoting can be configured to use the HTTPS protocol instead of HTTP. This configuration requires installing and binding an SSL certificate to the WSMan listener on the remote machine.

Generate or obtain an SSL certificate and then bind it with the following PowerShell command:

```
New-Item -Path WSMan:\localhost\Service\CertificateThumbprint -Value '
    CERTIFICATE_THUMBPRINT'
Set-WSManInstance -ResourceURI winrm/config/Listener -SelectorSet @{Address="*";
    Transport="HTTPS"} -ValueSet @{Port="5986"; CertificateThumbprint="
    CERTIFICATE_THUMBPRINT"}
```

After configuring the HTTPS listener, connect to the remote server using the HTTPS protocol:

```
$session = New-PSSession -ComputerName "RemoteServer" -UseSSL -Credential (Get-
    Credential)
```

Understanding these advanced techniques for PowerShell remoting allows for efficient management and automation of tasks across a network of computers. By leveraging these capabilities, administrators can streamline processes, enhance security, and maintain control over distributed environments.

10.7 Using Background Jobs

Background jobs in PowerShell allow scripts to perform tasks asynchronously, facilitating the execution of other commands or scripts without waiting for the initial tasks to complete. This section provides a detailed examination of the mechanisms, methods, and practices for creating, managing, and utilizing background jobs effectively.

A background job runs in a separate process on the local or remote computer, enabling long-running tasks to be offloaded and managed independently. The primary cmdlets used for managing background jobs are: Start-Job, Get-Job, Receive-Job, Stop-Job, and Remove-Job.

To initiate a background job, the Start-Job cmdlet is utilized. This cmdlet requires a script block { } to execute the command asynchronously. For instance:

```
Start-Job -ScriptBlock { Get-Process }
```

The above command starts a job that retrieves the processes running on the system. The job runs in the background, freeing the terminal for immediate other uses.

To query the status of the job, Get-Job retrieves information about all background jobs in the current session:

```
Get-Job
```

The output displays the job ID, name, state, and the command associated with each job. To examine a specific job, utilize the job ID or name:

```
Get-Job -Id <JobId>
```

or

```
Get-Job -Name <JobName>
```

Once a job completes, its output is retrieved using Receive-Job:

```
Receive-Job -Id <JobId>
```

The Receive-Job cmdlet captures the result of the job. If the job is still running, this cmdlet will return no data unless specified otherwise with the -Wait parameter, which holds the command open until the job completes.

To halt an ongoing background job, Stop-Job is employed:

```
Stop-Job -Id <JobId>
```

Upon concluding the job's relevance, removing it from the session is advisable to maintain an uncluttered workspace. The Remove-Job cmdlet achieves this:

```
Remove-Job -Id <JobId>
```

For a practical scenario, consider monitoring disk space asynchronously while continuing other operations. An exemplary script:

```
$job = Start-Job -ScriptBlock {
    while ($true) {
        Get-PSDrive
        Start-Sleep -Seconds 60
    }
}
```

This job continues to retrieve the disk space usage every 60 seconds. To monitor job output intermittently without halting execution:

```
Receive-Job -Id $job.Id
```

PowerShell enables background jobs not only on local systems but also remotely, provided the appropriate remoting configurations are in place. Using the -AsJob parameter with cmdlets like Invoke-Command can start a background job on remote systems.

For example:

```
Invoke-Command -ComputerName Server01 -ScriptBlock {
    Get-EventLog -LogName Application
} -AsJob
```

The output can be retrieved in a similar fashion using Receive-Job.

Error handling in background jobs ensures robust script execution. To capture errors during the execution of the script block, use the -ErrorVariable parameter:

```
$job = Start-Job -ScriptBlock {
    Get-Process -Name 'NonExistentProcess'
} -ErrorVariable jobError

$jobError
```

This captures any errors generated within the script block into the jobError variable for subsequent review.

The lifecycle of background jobs—starting, querying, retrieving results, and cleanup—is crucial for efficient scripting. Leveraging these capabilities enhances script responsiveness and resource management.

Efficient job management often involves combining essential cmdlets with iteration constructs. For example, to handle multiple jobs and retrieve their results efficiently:

```
$jobs = @()
1..5 | ForEach-Object {
```

```
    $jobs += Start-Job -ScriptBlock { Start-Sleep -Seconds 10 }
}

$jobs | ForEach-Object {
    $job = $_
    $jobResult = Receive-Job -Id $job.Id -Wait
    Remove-Job -Id $job.Id
}
```

This ensures all background jobs are managed and their outputs collected systematically.

Integrating background jobs enhances script functionality, providing the flexibility and control necessary for complex automation tasks in PowerShell. Effective utilization can lead to significant improvements in the performance and maintainability of scripts, particularly when working with long-running operations or tasks requiring parallel execution.

10.8 Handling Asynchronous Operations

PowerShell supports asynchronous operations, which enable scripts to perform tasks without blocking the execution flow. This capability is crucial when dealing with long-running tasks or operations that can be executed independently, optimizing overall script efficiency and performance. Asynchronous operations can be managed using background jobs, runspaces, and the Start-Job cmdlet.

Asynchronous operations allow scripts to continue running while waiting for other tasks to complete. This is especially useful for scripts that interact with external systems or perform extensive computations. By leveraging asynchronous operations, scripts can handle multiple tasks concurrently, providing a responsive and efficient scripting environment.

Background Jobs

Background jobs are a fundamental feature in PowerShell for running commands or scripts in the background. This allows the main script to continue executing while the background job completes its task. The Start-Job cmdlet is used to initiate background jobs.

```
# Example of starting a background job
$job = Start-Job -ScriptBlock {
    # Long-running task
    Start-Sleep -Seconds 10
    "Job completed"
}
```

```
# Monitor job status
while ($job.State -eq 'Running') {
    Write-Host "Job is still running..."
    Start-Sleep -Seconds 1
}

# Retrieve job result
$result = Receive-Job -Job $job
Write-Host "Job result: $result"

# Clean up job
Remove-Job -Job $job
```

In this example, a background job is started with the Start-Job cmdlet, executing a script block that simulates a long-running task. The script then monitors the job's state and waits for it to complete. Once finished, the result is retrieved using the Receive-Job cmdlet, and the job is removed from the job queue with Remove-Job.

Runspaces

Runspaces provide a more advanced method for achieving asynchronous operations in PowerShell. A runspace is essentially an isolated environment where PowerShell commands can be executed independently of the main execution thread. Multiple runspaces can be run concurrently, allowing for greater control over asynchronous execution.

```
# Example of creating and using a runspace
$runspace = [powershell]::Create().AddScript({
    # Long-running task
    Start-Sleep -Seconds 10
    "Runspace completed"
})

# Start the runspace asynchronously
$runspace.BeginInvoke()

# Monitor runspace status
while (!$runspace.EndInvoke.IsCompleted) {
    Write-Host "Runspace is still running..."
    Start-Sleep -Seconds 1
}

# Retrieve runspace result
$result = $runspace.EndInvoke()
Write-Host "Runspace result: $result"

# Dispose of the runspace
$runspace.Dispose()
```

This example demonstrates the creation and use of a runspace. A runspace is created and started asynchronously using BeginInvoke(). The script then monitors the runspace's status, waits for it to complete, retrieves the result with EndInvoke(), and finally disposes of the runspace to release resources.

Best Practices for Using Asynchronous Operations

When implementing asynchronous operations in PowerShell, consider the following best practices:

- **Resource Management:** Ensure that resources such as runspaces and jobs are properly disposed of after use to prevent resource leakage.
- **Error Handling:** Implement robust error handling to manage exceptions that may occur during asynchronous execution.
- **State Monitoring:** Monitor the state of asynchronous tasks and jobs to handle their completion or failure appropriately.
- **Result Collection:** Collect results from background jobs or runspaces carefully, ensuring synchronization between tasks when necessary.

Example: Combining Background Jobs and Runspaces

Combining background jobs with runspaces enhances the flexibility and power of asynchronous operations in PowerShell. For example, consider a scenario where multiple long-running tasks need to be managed asynchronously:

```
# Function to create a runspace for a given script block
function Start-Runspace {
    param (
        [scriptblock]$ScriptBlock
    )
    $runspace = [powershell]::Create().AddScript($ScriptBlock)
    $runspace.BeginInvoke()
    return $runspace
}

# Start multiple runspaces
$runspaces = @(
    Start-Runspace -ScriptBlock { Start-Sleep -Seconds 5; "Task 1 completed" }
    Start-Runspace -ScriptBlock { Start-Sleep -Seconds 10; "Task 2 completed" }
    Start-Runspace -ScriptBlock { Start-Sleep -Seconds 15; "Task 3 completed" }
)

# Monitor and collect results from all runspaces
$results = @()
foreach ($runspace in $runspaces) {
    while (!$runspace.EndInvoke.IsCompleted) {
        Write-Host "Runspace is still running..."
        Start-Sleep -Seconds 1
    }
    $results += $runspace.EndInvoke()
```

```
    $runspace.Dispose()
}

# Display collected results
Write-Host "All runspaces completed:"
foreach ($result in $results) {
    Write-Host $result
}
```

This example defines a function Start-Runspace to create and start runspaces for given script blocks. Multiple runspaces are then started and their results are monitored and collected. Once all runspaces have completed, the results are displayed. This approach demonstrates the power of combining background jobs and runspaces to handle multiple complex tasks concurrently.

With these techniques and best practices, scripts can effectively handle asynchronous operations, improving efficiency and responsiveness without compromising manageability.

10.9 Profile Scripting

PowerShell provides a mechanism for users to customize their environment with profile scripts. These scripts allow users to configure their session, define aliases, functions, and set environment variables that load automatically when a PowerShell session starts. Understanding and leveraging profile scripting can significantly enhance productivity by automating routine tasks and ensuring a consistent environment setup.

PowerShell supports multiple profile scripts, each with its own scope and application. The profile paths are determined by the host application (e.g., PowerShell console, PowerShell ISE), the user, and the system. The following command displays the various profile paths available:

```
$profile | Format-List -Force
```

This command will output:

```
/Users/UserName/Documents/PowerShell/Microsoft.PowerShell_profile.ps1
/Profile.ps1
/Users/UserName/Documents/PowerShell/Microsoft.PowerShellISE_profile.ps1
/Users/UserName/Documents/PowerShell/Microsoft.VSCode_profile.ps1
/Users/UserName/Documents/PowerShell/profile.ps1
```

Each profile serves a different purpose:

- $profile.AllUsersAllHosts: This profile applies to all users and all hosts. It's useful for system-wide configurations.
- $profile.AllUsersCurrentHost: This profile applies to all users but only for the current host.
- $profile.CurrentUserAllHosts: This profile applies to the current user and all hosts. It is ideal for user-specific configurations.
- $profile.CurrentUserCurrentHost: This profile is specific to both the current user and the current host application.

To create a profile script, first check if the file exists using Test-Path, and create it if it does not.

```
if (-not (Test-Path -Path $profile)) {
    New-Item -ItemType File -Path $profile -Force
}
```

After creating the profile file, open it using a text editor such as Notepad:

```
notepad $profile
```

Within the profile script, you can define a variety of customizations. Common customizations include:

- Creating aliases for often-used commands.
- Defining custom functions or cmdlets.
- Setting environment variables.
- Importing commonly used modules.
- Customizing the prompt.

To define an alias, use the Set-Alias cmdlet:

```
Set-Alias ll Get-ChildItem
```

This creates an alias ll for the Get-ChildItem cmdlet. Custom functions can also be defined within the profile script. For instance, the following function retrieves system information:

```
function Get-SystemInfo {
    Get-ComputerInfo
}
```

Environment variables can be set using the $env provider:

```
$env:EDITOR = 'notepad'
```

To load specific modules each time a session starts, use the Import-Module cmdlet:

```
Import-Module -Name Pester
```

Customizing the PowerShell prompt often involves modifying the function Prompt:

```
function Prompt {
    "PS $($executionContext.SessionState.Path.CurrentLocation)> "
}
```

The example above sets a simple prompt displaying the current path.

Profile scripting not only standardizes the configuration across different sessions, but also enhances efficiency by automating repetitive tasks. This supports a streamlined and tailored environment, optimizing the PowerShell usage experience. This custom approach should align carefully with user preferences and organizational policies to ensure consistency and dependability across multiple installations.

10.10 Best Practices and Script Optimization

Effective PowerShell scripting demands not only functional competence but also adherence to best practices and optimization techniques. This section elucidates numerous strategies to enhance both the efficiency and readability of PowerShell scripts.

1. Commenting and Documentation

Properly documenting code is paramount. Use comments to explain the purpose and functionality of scripts, making them easier to understand and maintain.

```
# This function retrieves user information from Active Directory
function Get-UserInfo {
    param (
        [string]$Username
    )
    # Query to get user details based on username
    $user = Get-ADUser -Identity $Username -Properties DisplayName, EmailAddress
    return $user
}
```

2. Consistent Naming Conventions

Adopt consistent naming conventions for variables, functions, and script files. Use camelCase or PascalCase for variable and function names to improve readability.

```
# CamelCase for variable
$userDisplayName = $user.DisplayName

# PascalCase for function
function Expand-UserDisplayName {
    param ([string]$DisplayName)
    return "User Display Name: $DisplayName"
}
```

3. Modular Script Design

Break scripts into smaller, reusable functions and modules. This approach promotes code reuse and simplifies troubleshooting.

```
function Get-DiskInfo {
    Get-PSDrive -PSProvider FileSystem | Where-Object { $_.Used -gt 0 }
}

function Get-MemoryUsage {
    Get-WmiObject Win32_OperatingSystem | Select-Object @{Name="TotalMemory"
        ; Expression={$_.TotalVisibleMemorySize}},
                                                @{Name="FreeMemory"; Expression={$_.
                                                    FreePhysicalMemory}}
}
```

4. Error Handling

Implement robust error handling using try, catch, and finally blocks to manage and log errors effectively.

```
try {
    $user = Get-ADUser -Identity $Username -ErrorAction Stop
    Write-Output "User found: $user"
}
catch {
    Write-Output "Error: User not found in Active Directory"
}
finally {
    Write-Output "Execution completed"
}
```

5. Performance Optimization

Optimize script performance by minimizing the use of unnecessary commands, loops, and data retrieval. Employ cmdlets like Measure-Command to measure the execution time of scripts.

```
# Measure time taken to retrieve user information
Measure-Command {
    $user = Get-ADUser -Identity $Username -Properties DisplayName, EmailAddress
```

```
}
```

Utilize array processing techniques, such as the pipeline and foreach method, instead of traditional for loops when processing large datasets.

```
# Using pipeline for better performance
Get-Content 'users.txt' | ForEach-Object { Get-ADUser -Identity $_ -Properties
    DisplayName }

# Alternative foreach method
$users = Get-Content 'users.txt'
$users.ForEach({ Get-ADUser -Identity $_ -Properties DisplayName })
```

6. Script Security

Adhere to best practices in script security by avoiding hard-coded credentials and using secure methods to handle sensitive information.

```
# Prompt user for a secure password
$password = Read-Host "Enter password" -AsSecureString

# Convert the secure string to plain text only when necessary
$unsecurePassword = [System.Runtime.InteropServices.Marshal]::PtrToStringAuto([
    System.Runtime.InteropServices.Marshal]::SecureStringToBSTR($password))
```

Implement execution policy control and ensure scripts are signed to prevent unauthorized execution.

```
# Set execution policy to RemoteSigned
Set-ExecutionPolicy -ExecutionPolicy RemoteSigned

# Sign the script with a valid certificate
Set-AuthenticodeSignature -FilePath "MyScript.ps1" -Certificate $cert
```

7. Logging and Debugging

Enable comprehensive logging and debugging mechanisms to track script execution and troubleshoot issues.

```
# Enable detailed logging
Start-Transcript -Path "ScriptLog.txt"
try {
    # Script code here
}
catch {
    Write-Error "An error occurred: $_"
}
finally {
    Stop-Transcript
}
```

Use the Write-Debug cmdlet to output debug information during script execution. Set the debug preference to control the level of debug messages displayed.

```
$DebugPreference = "Continue"
Write-Debug "Debugging information: fetching user details"
$user = Get-ADUser -Identity $Username -Properties DisplayName, EmailAddress
```

8. Code Review and Testing

Conduct code reviews and thorough testing to ensure script reliability and functionality. Leverage unit testing frameworks such as Pester for testing PowerShell scripts.

```
# Pester test example
Describe "Get-UserInfo" {
    It "Should return a user object when a valid username is provided" {
        $username = "testuser"
        $result = Get-UserInfo -Username $username
        $result | Should -Not -BeNullOrEmpty
    }
}
```

Following these best practices not only simplifies the development process but also improves script performance and maintainability. Adopting these guidelines facilitates the creation of efficient and robust PowerShell scripts, enhancing overall scripting proficiency.

Made in the USA
Monee, IL
05 November 2026

67911523R00154